MARY HAYWOOD METZ

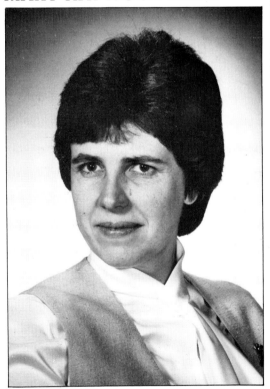

Mary Haywood Metz is Associate Professor of
Educational Policy Studies at the University of
Wisconsin-Madison. She has a PhD in sociology
from the University of California at Berkeley, and is
the author of *Classrooms and Corridors* (1978) and
several articles based on her ethnographic studies
of schools.

Different
by Design

Different by Design

The Context and Character of Three Magnet Schools

Mary Haywood Metz
Department of Educational Policy Studies
University of Wisconsin, Madison

Routledge & Kegan Paul
New York and London

For Don

First published in 1986
by Routledge & Kegan Paul Inc.

in association with Methuen Inc.

29 West 35th Street, New York, NY 10001

Published in Great Britain by
Routledge & Kegan Paul plc
11 New Fetter Lane, London EC4P 4EE

Set in Linotron Times, 10 on 12 pt
by Input Typesetting Ltd, London
and printed in Great Britain
by Billing & Sons Ltd, Worcester

Library of Congress Cataloging in Publication Data

Metz, Mary Haywood.

Different by design.
Bibliography: p.
Includes index.
1. Magnet schools   United States   Case studies.
2. School integration   United States   Case studies.
I. Title.
LB2818.M47   1986   370.19'342   85–19294

ISBN 0-7102-0071-4

Contents

Contents

Preface

Magnet schools are schools which accomplish racial desegregation on a voluntary basis; they attract volunteers by offering innovative education. This book is a study of three magnet schools and the school system, or school district, of which they were a part. It tells the story of the 'Heartland' school system and three of its magnet schools in some detail. The information on which it is based was gathered as I studied each of the three schools for a semester, and the district for over three years. I attempt to portray the life of each of the three schools as a whole, to convey the texture of the experience of adults and students in the school, and the feelings and as well as the actions of the participants. From this whole, I have attempted to identify the most important influences which shaped the schools' lives.

The major purpose of the book lies in the search for an understanding of these influences, the links among them, and their effect on the experience of the schools' participants. While the school district and the schools were each in some ways unique, they were in most ways very typical of American urban school systems and schools. Influences which were important in Heartland should be important throughout American schools and school districts.

The book is addressed to researchers and students interested in understanding schools and school districts, and to policy-makers and practitioners concerned with operating and perhaps changing them. I am a sociologist with training in the study of organizations more generally, as well as of schools; I bring a perspective from the sociology of organizations to bear upon the issues. However, as I attempted to understand the linkage between the schools and the district as a whole, it was necessary to analyze the political processes which surrounded the establishment and the mainten- ance of the magnet schools and the broader politics of race, class, and education within which the magnet schools were set. The book therefore addresses both organizational and political issues in the formation of the schools.

The title, *Different by Design*, calls attention to the fact that each magnet school was established with a well-publicized fran- chise to approach education in a distinctive way. At least in prin- ciple, each had a distinctive design or blueprint for education which it should follow. As the title states, the differences among the schools were announced as fully intentional, the result of planning, not the result of happenstance or an unplanned historical development. But, as the title implies, what is different by design may not be different in practice; though the schools were designed to be different, they were not always so in practice. The title calls attention to the question of organizational mechan- isms for creating and sustaining innovations, a vexed question in the field of education and an important one in the lives of Heart- land's magnet schools.

For a while, I considered calling the book *Different But Equal?* to call attention to the political issues which surrounded the schools' distinctiveness. This phrase underscores the school district administrators' efforts to make the magnet schools diverse, different, and so attractive, but no better than other schools. To announce that they were better schools than others would have created an overwhelming irony, since they were introduced to desegregate the district, which is to say they were part of an attempt to do away with the inequality created by racially segre- gated schools. To create difference and maintain equality is not simple, however. The phrase 'different but equal' is not a familiar one in the United States – though I am told it is often used in Britain. It parallels the phrase 'separate but equal' which has been used to summarize the U.S. Supreme Court's doctrine supporting racial segregation in *Plessy v. Ferguson* in 1896, a doctrine struck down by the Court in *Brown v. Board of Education* in 1954. This parallelism reminds us of the suspicion of inequality which has grown up in the United States around public schools which differ from others in any formal way.

Despite this suspicion, it would be wishful thinking, not practical politics, to ask parents voluntarily to send their children out of their neighborhoods on long bus rides to schools which offer no hint of superiority. It would, however, be a form of wishful thinking consistent with the proclamation of equality of opportunity through education in the rhetoric of American schooling. The Heartland school system therefore advertised the schools as merely different at the rhetorical level, but gave the magnet schools some extra, unadvertised resources. From the outset, then, the magnet school plan was caught up in the complex and contradictory themes of American schooling related to competition for advantage among races and classes.

The individual schools were affected by these issues as the district struggled to make them seem not just different, but also equal and superior at the same time. Political pressures made themselves felt in the schools' development, sometimes as vital influences, sometimes only as a vague context, within which the vivid challenges and interactions of daily life were played out. Thus, although this book remains primarily a study of the organizational life of the schools, it analyzes the intimate interrelationship of political and organizational influences in the shaping of educational experiences for children in individual schools.

There will inevitably be a few readers of this book who know, or think they know, the identity of the school district to which I have given the pseudonym 'Heartland.' To these readers, I must say that it was *not* my task to form a judgment about whether the Heartland school district and its schools performed well or poorly in creating equity and providing good education. If that had been the task, I would have asked different questions and found different answers. Rather, it was my task to understand all perspectives as empathetically as possible in order to discover the important causal influences which shaped practice in the district and the schools, and which can be expected to shape practice elsewhere.

Defenders of the school system will probably find me unduly critical, feeling that I have emphasized problems more than successes. Like other sociological accounts, this one does tend to emphasize strains, for it is where social systems encounter stress, contradiction, and failure that the influences which shape them are most clearly visible. On the other hand, detractors of the system will probably find my account unduly positive. An attempt to understand a system, especially one based on participation in it, inclines one to be sympathetic with participants as they struggle with limiting conditions and with one another.

I have had a great deal of help with this book, for which thanks here provide a meager return. I am most grateful to the men and women of the Heartland School District, who opened their district and their schools to study in the midst of the political turmoil of the desegregation process and the early years of school innovations. Many, many teachers, administrators, students, and parents allowed themselves to be observed, took time to talk with me, and, in addition, were gracious in making a stranger feel comfortable in their midst. I am truly grateful; the study would not have been possible without their openness and assistance.

The study also would not have been possible without the financial support of the National Institue of Education, which funded the research under Project No. 8–0640. The Institute also provided intellectual community by putting grantees with similar interests in touch with one another. Gail MacColl, the project officer for the study, was a wonderful source of moral support and constructive criticism during the long formative period of the fieldwork, analysis of data, and writing. The Institute and its personnel of course bear no reponsibility for, and lend no endorsement to, the content of this work.

Transformation of the final report to the National Institute of Education into a book was funded by a grant from royalty funds through the Wisconsin Center for Education Research. The Center has also provided intellectual support, as conversations with other researchers there have improved the quality of my thought about the project.

I have written papers on this research. Some short passages in the text here have appeared earlier in 'Sources of Constructive Social Relationships in an Urban Magnet School,' *American Journal of Education*, vol. 91, no. 2 (February 1983), pp. 202–45, and in 'The Life Course of Magnet Schools: Organizational and Political Influences,' *Teachers College Record*, vol. 85, no. 3 (Spring 1984), pp. 411–30. Some of the ideas in Chapter 4 appeared in an account from a different perspective, 'The Principal's Role in the Establishment of a Magnet School' in George W. Noblit and Bill Johnston, eds, *The Principal and School Deseg-*

regation: An Anthology of Interpretive Studies, Charles C. Thomas, 1982, pp. 61–95.

Although I did the fieldwork for the study alone, several graduate students at the University of Wisconsin in Madison have been assistants as I analyzed the data and wrote the book. Gregory Gossetti read interviews with students and wrote descriptions of the schools based solely upon them, which I then compared with my conclusions drawn from the whole body of data. Martha de Acosta, Leslie Rothaus, and Hazel Symmonette reviewed relevant literature and helped to organize data. Carrie Rothburd did an outstanding job of editing the last draft; she substantially improved its expression.

Several people have read and commented on papers leading up to the manuscript or on drafts. I am grateful for critical assistance to Michael Apple, Nancy Lesko, Jeffrey Leiter, Gail MacColl, Linda McNeil, Fred Newmann, Michael Olneck, Reba Page, and Francis Schrag. They have sharpened my thought and improved my prose, though they are not to be held responsible for those places where their efforts failed.

Most of the field notes and interviews for the study were recorded on audiotape. Susan Barney and Marsha Stein patiently and skillfully translated those recordings into thousands of pages of typed transcripts. I entered the world of computerized word processing halfway through composing the final manuscript; Mary Jo Gessler, Jean Kennedy, and Cheryl Roberts typed several drafts of the first half. Cheryl Roberts also edited one chapter. Michael Richards translated their last, computerized version from one computer language to another so that I could revise it conveniently. I thank them all.

Finally, I owe a great debt to my family. My sons, David and Michael, have accepted my preoccupation with good grace. They have also acted as patient and often incisive informants on life in public elementary schools. My husband and colleague, Don Metz, has shared domestic tasks, provided emotional support, and most of all helped me to keep the project in perspective and my sense of humor intact.

Chapter 1

Introduction

Magnet schools have stirred considerable interest in the United States. They are racially mixed public schools which draw students on a voluntary basis by offering educational innovations which are attractive to parents. They appeal to many educational constituencies by simultaneously creating desegregation without mandatory busing and an opportunity to blow a fresh breeze of educational innovation into city school systems.

If magnet schools can deliver a means of voluntary desegregation and a lever to introduce innovation into public schools, they will be a social invention worthy of considerable respect. Before they are hailed as the solution to two of the hardest problems in American public education, however, they need to be carefully studied as they function in practice. Since they alter the basis of recruitment to schools and the formally standardized character of public education, they attempt to change entrenched patterns in the relation of education to the politics of race and class and to uproot fixed traditions of educational practice. Such an undertaking will inevitably meet some resistance. The way in which the attempt took shape in the lives of one district and three schools forms the subject of this book.

Purpose of the book

This book presents a case study of three magnet schools and of the school system of which they were a part. The schools were middle schools, each offering a different educational approach, and each open to enrollment within racial quotas by volunteering students from throughout the large midwestern city of 'Heartland' (a pseudonym). The city used magnet schools as the centerpiece of a court-ordered desegregation plan.[1] The book shows the place of the schools within the political processes which surrounded the establishment and institutionalization of magnet schools in the district as a whole, then deals in depth with the influences which shaped the internal lives of the three individual schools.

A good deal of literature appeared before the commencement of this study which suggested that innovations which are planned at the top of a school hierarchy, even by school system administrators or by principals, are rarely implemented as they are designed (Berman and McLaughlin, 1976; Gross, Giacquinta, and Bernstein, 1971; Sarason, 1971; Sussmann, 1977; Wolcott, 1977). This pattern has been further documented in the intervening years (e.g. Deal and Nutt, 1983; Farrar, DeSanctis, and Cohen, 1980; Firestone, 1980a). Consequently, this study was not designed to find out whether the magnet schools studied implemented the innovations which were planned for them, but rather to find out what kind of experience they did in fact offer to their students. The task was to describe that experience and then to seek the influences which shaped it.

The way in which these particular schools developed the kind of life they did is described as a means to identify important influences in the shaping of magnet schools and innovative schools more broadly. Even ordinary schools develop quite distinctive and varied internal lives (Metz, 1978b; Rutter, Maughan, Mortimore, and Ouston, 1979). By studying innovative schools where pressure for change makes the influences which shape life in all schools more readily evident, it is possible to develop an analysis which will also throw light upon the sources of diversity in the life of 'traditional' schools.

Any research of this kind must investigate its subject from a certain perspective. This study is grounded in the sociological study of organizations. The major analytic categories for explaining the internal life of the schools, presented in Chapter 3, stem from organizational analysis. More specifically, this study is part of a smaller tradition interested in the life of organizations as wholes. That tradition takes an interest in the quality of life in an organization and sees events and patterns of behaviour as shaped by actors who make a host of decisions not prescribed by the formal parameters of their roles. These decisions may alter mandated practices and develop informally defined regularities. To study an organization from this perspective, it is necessary to look in detail at what happens on a daily basis and at how the actors understand their social context. Consequently the method for the research was ethnographic; data were drawn from the author's extensive participation in the schools, from open-ended interviews with participants, and from analysis of documents.

The central datum to be explained at each school is the school's 'character'. I choose this term with reference to Selznick's (1957) term 'organizational character', though I do not include Selznick's strong psychological analogy. The term is intended to suggest the distinctiveness associated with an individual's character, its emergent nature, which is more than the sum of its parts and is continuous without being fixed. Practitioners point to one aspect of organizational character when they speak of the 'atmosphere' of a school, the 'feel of the place'. This atmosphere needs more concrete referents; it has been little studied in formal research[2] despite practitioners' statements of its importance.[3] It has much to do with relationships between persons and with the feelings which give a tone to those relationships. It is expressed in many formally planned activities, but also in spontaneous but repetitive practices. It is also reflected in what participants consider salient in the setting, what they pass over briefly or fail to notice at all, and what they think and talk about at length.

This research looked at the schools from the adults' point of view, asking what experiences they offered the students and why they did so, rather than asking how these experiences were interpreted by the students. It looked at students' responses to the school primarily as one of the influences bearing upon the adults.

Though the study uses an organizational perspective as its main framework, it explores the ways in which the schools' lives were profoundly shaped by the district's political life. Both in decisions affecting the schools made at the district level and in their internal lives, the struggle of racial and class groups for competitive advantage and the impact on individuals of experiences shaped by race and class were significant issues.

3

The city of Heartland

This study is set in the city of 'Heartland,' a pseudonym for one of the thirty-five largest cities in the United States. The population of the city is over half a million, and that of the metropolitan area is well over a million. The number of children in the city's public schools is somewhat fewer than 100,000. Heartland is a midwestern city with a diversified industrial base, but one which emphasizes heavy manufacturing.[4] The city is located on a large river upon which ships transport the products of its industry and those of the surrounding agricultural area. It also is served by a commercial airport, railroads, and interstate highways.

Table 1–1 compares Heartland to the hundred largest cities in the country. The data are from the census of 1980, which was the last year of the study, just before the recession of the early 1980s. Heartland's labor force, both white and black, was more heavily blue-collar than that of the cities combined, and, within the blue-collar category, it had especially large numbers of workers in the category of 'operators, fabricators, and laborers,' reflecting its large number of heavy industries which employ relatively unskilled labor. Heartland's whites were slightly better off economically than the residents of the hundred largest cities overall, and its blacks were slightly worse off. Whites were slightly less often unemployed or in poverty, and their median income was slightly higher than the average for whites in the hundred largest cities. Blacks were slightly worse off than the average in all these respects. Because of Heartland's relatively low proportion of non-whites, the total figures for the city show its population to be considerably better off on all these indicators than that of other cities.

Fewer of both whites and blacks in Heartland had finished either high school or college than had their counterparts in cities overall, and the median years of education for the adult population was also slightly lower than elsewhere. The population's prosperity compared to that of other cities seems to have rested on its large cadre of well-paid, but often not skilled, white blue-collar workers. Even more than in other cities, compared to the white population, the black population was noticeably less educated and far less well paid. Blacks were almost three times more likely to be unemployed and more than three times as likely to be living in poverty.

4

TABLE 1-1 *Characteristic of the Heartland population*

	Heartland			100 Largest cities*		
	White	Black	Total	White	Black	Total
Percent in blue-collar occupations†	47.1	65.7	50.6	37.7	56.0	42.0
Percent operators, fabricators, and laborers	21.3	35.5	24.1	14.7	24.1	17.1
Percent unemployed	5.2	14.0	7.0	5.5	12.8	7.4
Percent below poverty level	8.1	29.9	13.8	11.0	29.6	17.1
Median family income	21,347	12,671	19,738	20,774	12,710	18,329
Percent 25 years and over who completed high school	67.0	52.8	64.2	69.6	54.5	64.9
Percent 25 years and older who completed 4 years college	13.6	6.5	12.4	20.9	8.4	17.7
Median years of school completed	12.4	12.1	12.4	12.6	12.1	12.5

*Comparison figures on occupational category and on median years of schooling are based on figures for the central cities of urbanized areas, areas with populations of 50,000 or more. Other comparison figures are based on data for the one hundred largest central cities in the nation.

†'Blue-collar occupations' include the census categories of (a) precision production, (b) operators, fabricators, and laborers, and (c) service occupations. The measure is a rough one.

Source: *U.S. Census*, 1980

Heartland was founded in the middle of the nineteenth century and settled by waves of Northern and then Eastern European immigrants. Its ethnic traditions are strong; its neighborhoods are often stable and tightly knit and many have ethnic identities.

Residents often speak of the city as having some of the qualities of a small town or a collection of neighboring small towns. Strangers are friendly in public and helpful to a person in need of direction.

The map in Figure 1–1 shows the geography of the city and its socially defined areas. The South Side (really the south-eastern part of the city) claims the pleasant waterfront east of the harbor and is convenient to the downtown area, which is just north of the River, east of a major tributary which divides the eastern and western halves of the city. It is known as the location for the elite, though some neighborhoods on the 'near South Side' have poorer, often transient families. High-ranking city officials and a few leading professionals live in the large houses near the River and give the area its reputation. There is also a branch of the state university in this neighborhood, and quite a few faculty, staff, and graduate students add to the high educational level and help to support some business establishments selling relatively exotic goods. The suburbs which extend eastward along both sides of the river are the home of old money.

The West Side of the city, across a major tributary of the River from the South Side, is the home of blue-collar factory workers, many of them of Eastern European extraction. It extends from the River to the northern edge of the city. In some of the newer neighborhoods at its northern edge, it provides a haven from the rest of the city for prosperous city employees, especially policemen and firemen, who must live within the city limits but who identify with the newer suburbs beyond them.

East of the tributary which divides the West Side from the rest of the city, and on the city's northern edge, lies the North Side, an expanding, pleasant area of modern homes populated by aspiring lower-middle to upper-middle-class families. This area is edged by the most prosperous, but newer, suburbs. Beyond these suburbs stretches a chain of small towns which are being increasingly populated by exurbanites, especially along the main highway which goes north a few hours' drive to the state capital.

Finally, the city's East Side, east of the major tributary and between the North and South Sides, is its black area. The city's black population was only 15 percent of the total in 1970, 23 percent in 1980. Economic conditions in this area, while bad, are not as desperate as in many large cities. As in many midwestern cities, most of the housing in this part of the city consists

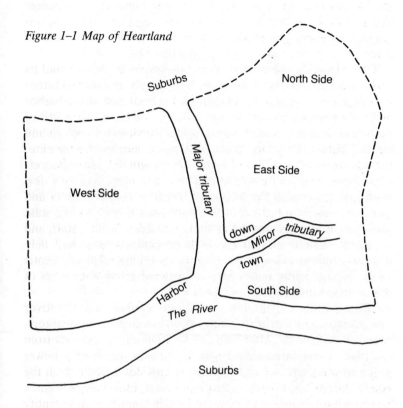

Figure 1–1 Map of Heartland

of older two- and three-storey houses which look fairly well-maintained from the outside, though inside most are split up into many units and some have inadequate cooking and sanitary facilities.

The relatively small size of the black population may help to keep tensions between the races manageable. But signs of prejudice, such as one of the highest indexes of housing segregation in the nation, along with the large disparities in employment rates and income among the employed, suggest that racial barriers are high. Indeed the very ethnic self-consciousness and neighborhood solidarity which lend color and warmth to the city for white residents may exacerbate the distance between blacks and whites. During the 1960s, there were civil rights demonstrations over schools and housing, the latter met by white violence. There was also a central city riot.

The city also has a small but rapidly growing Hispanic population. It was 2 percent of the population in 1970 and 4 percent in 1980. Hispanic residents are concentrated on the West Side just across the tributary from the downtown area near the River, in a neighborhood surrounding an industrial area. In the desegregation order they were counted as white. They have entered into the politics of desegregation mostly in their efforts to maintain a large enough concentration of their children in individual schools to secure meaningful bilingual-bicultural programs. Though their importance in school policy is bound to increase, they have not been major actors in the history of the magnet schools and they were not visible as a group in the individual schools of the study. I will say little more about them.

Heartland's school system reflects its character as a city. The central administration, until very recently, was staffed almost exclusively by white males who had extensive ties of experience and acquaintance. Blacks were not hired even as teachers in any numbers at all until the late 1960s and early 1970s. They were first promoted into principalships under heavy federal pressure in the early seventies. After that, under continuing pressure from the black community, they began to be hired for visible human relations positions and began trickling into other positions in the central office.

The school board was elected at large until the early 1980s.[5] It included representatives of very different demographic groups and different perspectives. Educated liberals from the South Side and from the Anderson Springs neighborhood (an active, intentionally integrated area between the North and East Sides near the city's center) were over-represented. There were also, however, staunchly conservative representatives of the laboring whites on the West Side and of the upwardly mobile whites on the North Side. In the years surrounding the study, the number of blacks on the board varied from one to three. All were college-educated professionals or upper white-collar workers.

While Heartland, like any city, has unique features, it can still be taken as reasonably representative of midwestern cities of the second rank in size, in fairly good economic condition, where whites are still numerically and politically dominant in the central city despite a sizable and growing number of minority residents.

8

The court order and the founding of magnet schools

In the winter of 1976, after a suit that lasted more than a dozen years, a federal judge ruled that the Heartland schools had been intentionally segregated and ordered that they be desegregated starting in September, 1976. He gave the school board time to come up with a plan for desegregation to be submitted for his approval. According to the court order, in the fall of 1976, one-third of the city's schools had to be desegregated; in 1977, two-thirds, and in 1978, all. With the black school enrollment climbing towards the 50 percent mark,[6] the acceptable percentage of black students in desegregated schools was set at 25 to 50 percent. In later years, it was modified to 25 to 60 percent.

In responding to the court order, the school board became embroiled in internal conflict; it voted to appeal the decision in a series of bitterly contested votes which consistently split eight to seven. In response to the court order, Dr Stewart, the newly arrived superintendent, and the administration decided to try to desegregate without mandatory reassignments of students. Their plan provided three vehicles for voluntary movement of students. First, it offered magnet schools, which drew volunteers from anywhere in the city, accepted within quotas for race. Second, another set of magnet schools drew children from their own neighborhood 'attendance area' and children of a different race from a larger 'zone'. Both groups of magnet schools were called 'alternative schools'; the first were called 'citywide alternative schools', the second 'attendance area alternative schools'. Third, children were invited to enroll in any school in the city where their presence would enhance racial balance.

In July and August of 1976, there was an intensive campaign by mail and in the print and electronic media to announce the opening of the new magnet schools. Each magnet school held a well-advertised open house. Principals and counselors in neighborhood schools wrote to parents and met with them encouraging them to send their children to magnet schools or to other schools where they would enhance racial balance.

There were too few magnet schools, however, for them to carry the major burden of desegregating the city alone. There had to be movement of new racial groups into traditional schools as well. To encourage this movement, most of the magnet schools were located in black neighborhoods and many black neighborhood schools were closed or reduced in enrollment. Though every house in the city had a formal attendance area school, school closings which expanded attendance areas for already crowded black neighborhood schools, together with reduced enrollment limits at most black schools, required substantial proportions of black students to choose schools elsewhere in the city. Even though no individual child was given a mandatory reassignment, many black children could not choose to go to their old neighborhood school. Black children were pushed toward empty seats in outlying white neighborhood schools as well as pulled towards those in magnet schools.

The campaign was successful. In the fall of 1976, slightly over one-third of the schools were desegregated according to the court's guidelines. In planning for the second year, more magnet schools were designed, and more black schools were slated for closing or reduction in enrollment. In the spring of 1977, in preparation for the second year, the possibility of mandatory assignment entered the scenario. Every parent of a public school child had to fill out a form listing three choices for his or her child, only one of which could be the neighborhood school. Once again the campaign was successful, and two-thirds of the schools were desegregated. The vast majority of children received their first choice school. Virtually all were assigned to one of their choices.

In the fall of 1977, before planning for the last and most difficult stage was well under way, the appeals court returned the case to the local judge, asking for review of the propriety of desegregating the whole school system. The United States Supreme Court had recently enunciated a principle that courts could only require desegregation of a total system if there were evidence that previous segregation had had systemwide effects. A new trial was held to determine whether the board's already proven intent to segregate students had affected all the schools in the city. The judge ruled that it had. But before he offered his remedy, the plaintiffs' attorneys decided to settle out of court, leaving twenty elementary schools and two middle schools predominantly black, rather than to risk an appeal to a conservative Supreme Court which might give even less relief. The settlement stated that the remedy was to extend for five years. Later decisions of the Supreme Court made it appear that the plaintiffs were overly pessimistic, but by that time, the out of court settlement was in place.

Heartland succeeded in desegregating its schools without using mandatory reassignment of students, a very unusual accomplishment for a city of its size. All the students being bused for desegregation had chosen their new schools. Both the local and national media have emphasized the role of magnet schools in creating this voluntary desegregation. But neither press accounts nor school system spokespersons have generally mentioned the fact that 90 percent of the students who ride buses to desegregated schools outside their neighborhoods are black. Nor have they mentioned that virtually all of the 10 percent of the busriders who are white are traveling to magnet schools. They are matched by another 10 percent, who are black children riding to magnet schools. The remaining 80 percent of the children riding buses to school are black children going to traditional schools in white neighborhoods.[7]

The citywide magnet schools have for the most part drawn well. Those which have not have been quietly dropped. 'Attendance area' magnet schools have been less successful; some have been turned into citywide schools and others have become essentially traditional neighborhood schools which retain only the name of a special program. Almost all the middle schools were given some special label, but after a few years of attempts to promote them on this basis, use of the labels faded away.

For 1981–2, the year following the study of the individual schools, twelve out of 115 elementary schools were citywide magnet schools and three attendance area magnet programs still existed. Among the nineteen middle schools, there were three citywide magnet schools. There were three citywide magnet high schools and a special citywide program housed in one of the other high schools. All of the other eleven high schools also included distinctive career preparation programs which did not enroll the whole student body, but which were designed to encourage students from other parts of the city to attend the school.

The schools studied

This book deals in detail with the three middle schools, established as citywide magnets, which served sixth through eighth graders. Children in these grades in the United States go to school in a great variety of situations. Some go to elementary school through

11

the eighth grade – as in one section of Heartland, the South Side. Some go to junior high schools from the seventh through ninth grade; these are what their name implies, early high schools organized as secondary schools and staffed by teachers who have been trained and certified to teach grades seven through twelve. Junior high schools were the dominant pattern in Heartland until the fall of 1980, when all such schools were converted to middle schools. The citywide schools started the middle school pattern earlier.

Middle schools are intended to be a distinctive kind of school which combines elements from elementary and secondary schooling. Since elementary teachers are usually certified to teach up to the eighth grade, and secondary teachers usually are certified to teach down to the seventh, middle schools can have teachers and principals from either tradition and often have a mixture of the two. The schools in the study differed in whether they leaned toward the elementary or the secondary side of their in-between status.

The 'distinctiveness' appropriate to magnet schools is variably understood. The definition upon which federal funds depend emphasizes distinctiveness based on offering some special content, rather than upon the mode of instruction. The magnet high schools in Heartland were defined primarily by special programs offering preparation for different kinds of careers; some of the elementary schools had substantive emphases, while others had special styles of instruction. None of the middle schools was defined by the substance of its offerings. Two were defined by the kind of instruction they offered and the third by its population.

The first of the middle schools studied was Adams Avenue Middle School which offered Individually Guided Education, known as IGE. IGE is an educational approach defined by special organization of the curriculum, of instruction, and of the roles of the school staff developed by a research center at the University of Wisconsin and systematically disseminated across the country. The second school was Jesse Owens Middle School, which offered a type of open education which the staff had worked out themselves after reading and attending workshops led by national figures in the field. The third was Horace Mann Middle School for the Gifted and Talented. It was the only one of the schools to have selective admission; it enrolled children recommended by their former teachers as gifted or talented and promised an enriched traditional curriculum.

The three schools not only had different special educational programs, but were founded at different times and so in different political contexts. Initiative for their special programs came from different quarters. Their ages, and so stages of development, were different at the time they were studied. Still, though the three faced somewhat different political problems and organizational tasks, they were all part of the same school system, all part of the effort to desegregate the city as a whole, all schools with a mandate to create a special kind of education, and all expected to be effective with a diverse student body.

To understand the nature of each school, it will be necessary to give a fairly detailed account of its historical development, and of the interdependence of that history with events in the school system as a whole. Consequently, Appendix A presents a time line of events in the district and in the three schools for the reader's reference throughout the book.

Methods of research

The purpose of this study dictated the use of qualitative methods: observation, open-ended formal and informal interviews, and analysis of documents. To describe and explain the character of the life of each school in a holistic way, the researcher needed to participate in that life, to observe and in some measure experience the life the adults and students led. Observation made it possible to note important events and patterns of interaction which participants might never mention because they took them as 'natural'. It allowed the researcher to be present when participants spontaneously and unselfconsciously discussed the issues of life in the school with one another. Observation also allowed the researcher to see and form an independent picture of events which were later interpreted by participants in interviews.

Open-ended interviews which allowed students, teachers, administrators, and parents to respond to questions in their own words and at length made it possible to explore their perspectives. They also allowed an analysis of the context in which interviewees' comments were made and of the words they chose to describe persons and events. Because interviewees could raise related topics and could answer as tersely or expansively as they liked, their answers indirectly conveyed the differential salience of various topics at the different schools.

Data from the three schools were collected by the author, working alone, between January 1979 and June 1980. Observation was conducted in classrooms, halls, cafeterias, playgrounds, and girls' bathrooms and in teachers' lounges and dining-rooms. I was present in meetings of committees, teaching teams, and whole faculties, as well as at meetings with parents at each school. I listened to school board meetings on the radio from 1977 to 1982, attended some meetings of a citywide committee of parents established to advise on desegregation, and during 1978–9 and much of 1979–80, regularly attended the smaller monthly meetings of representatives from citywide alternative schools to that committee with other parents from those schools.

At each school, formal interviews were conducted with a small sample of students, most teachers and administrators, and a few parents. Conversations with a wide variety of persons were recorded in field notes. In the spring of 1981, interviews were conducted at the central office: with supervisors of curriculum, with the administrator directly above the middle school principals, with administrators responsible for external funding of magnet schools, with persons administering special central office programs which included magnet schools, with the Deputy Superintendent, and with three members of the school board.

Documents used for analysis included student and faculty handbooks from each school, bulletins for students and faculty, announcements of meetings, and a variety of other written statements. District level planning statements and announcements to the public were also collected. Standardized test scores were obtained for tests taken in the fifth and seventh grade by the cohort in the seventh grade at the time of the study at each school.

Details concerning the patterns of observation at each school and the samples of persons interviewed are included in Appendix B. There is also some discussion of the researcher's role in the school and of the processes by which conclusions were drawn from the data.

Chapter 2

The school system's influence on the magnet schools

This chapter explores conditions and pressures at the district level which affected the lives of the three middle schools. Individual magnet schools were caught up in the politics which surrounded the instigation of desegregation in the Heartland district as a whole. Furthermore, the schools were given multiple missions which they had to pursue within constraints set at the district level: desegregation, innovation, and effective social and academic education of diverse student bodies. Not only the school board and central office, but other actors, such as the teachers' union and parents, played a part in decisions and practices at the school system level which had profound consequences for individual schools.

The political context of the magnet schools

The initial political viability of magnet schools

The magnet schools were founded primarily for the purpose of solving a pressing political problem; they were designed to prevent active, dramatic, and possibly violent resistance by some whites to the creation of the desegregated schools required by the court. Heartland started to desegregate while public memory of civic disorder in response to desegregation in Boston and of protests in Louisville was still vivid. Furthermore, Heartland had its own history of violent opposition to marches for open housing.

The plan that the Heartland administrators developed was

crafted to offer something to everyone and to ask something of every one. Black families got the chance to attend desegregated schools, a chance for which they had been fighting in court, but their children had to ride buses to other neighborhoods. White families who feared having their children reassigned to schools in black neighborhoods enjoyed the privilege of remaining in their neighborhood schools, but they had to be willing to share those schools with black children who were bused in. White families willing to forgo remaining in their neighborhood schools were rewarded with the privilege of choosing a particular kind of education at a magnet school for the inconvenience of putting their children on buses to other neighborhoods. Some black families also got the reward of magnet schools for traveling out of their neighborhoods, but most who rode buses did not go to magnet schools but to traditional schools in white neighborhoods.

The political aim of defusing resistance to desegregation was also pursued by describing the plan in a rhetoric which emphasized its educational benefits and underplayed the fact of racial mixing which was its stimulus and purpose. Administrators, especially the superintendent, introduced the plan as one which would eliminate problems of overcrowding by moving children from crowded central city schools to under-enrolled schools on the city's periphery, and as one which met the varied educational needs of children through the creation of 'alternative schools'. Further, by allowing parents the right to choose a school for their children, the rhetoric surrounding the alternative schools introduced desegregation as something which increased, rather than decreased, parents' control over their children's educational fate.

Community support for the plan was also strengthened by the establishment of a working group of 100 citizens to advise the board and central office. They were elected by a broadly representative process, in equal proportions from the schools and neighborhoods around each high school. They played a part in the development of the desegregation process for two or three years, then gradually faded from sight. None the less, in the early years, this committee provided a channel through which active parents from all over the city could become acquainted and could organize both formally and informally to let their views be heard. It also made visible to the city a group of parents elected from every region, the majority of whom favored desegregation as the morally right thing to do and a majority of whom supported the alternative schools.

The details of the plan for establishing the magnet schools were drawn up with the goal of attracting as much broad public support and parental participation as possible. The central office planners who were responsible for stimulating and winnowing ideas for magnet programs sought to develop an array of schools, each of which would appeal to both blacks and whites, and all of which, taken together, would appeal to parents from all areas of the city and all walks of life. Notices about the schools and the periods for signing up were mailed to the family of every public school child and advertised in the media. The application process was made extremely simple to make it as easy as possible for parents who were not well versed in dealing with bureaucratic procedures to enroll their children in magnet schools. Applications could be obtained and submitted at any public school; they asked for little more than the name and address of parent and child and the child's current grade and school.

The administrators responsible for the plan were aware that the magnet schools, though different from others, must appear equal with them. Making magnet schools superior could backfire by making traditional neighborhood schools appear inferior by comparison (Felix and Jacobs, 1977), and creating competition among categories of schools and conflict over the equity of superior public schools. They attempted to deal with this problem by always speaking of the magnet schools in terms of the diversity of their educational approaches, and by calling them 'alternative schools,' a more neutral term than magnet schools.

There is an inherent problem, however, in creating schools which are equal but which will induce parents to send their children a good distance from home on a voluntary basis. Though there is little experience to provide an empirical test, it is not at all clear that educational diversity alone has much drawing power.[1] The administrators of the Heartland system, apparently, did not dare to risk difference alone. They opened most of the magnet schools with amenities which made them superior in practice though not in name. Old buildings were imaginatively refurbished. Most of the magnet schools at least initially had extra staff who offered special programs and lowered ratios of students to teachers. Not only the career programs in the high schools, but the elementary schools, received new, in some cases unusual, equipment. Special activities, ranging from the use of computers for elementary school children to lunch-time programs of arts and crafts and drama and dance, were instituted.

The physical improvements made the schools visually attractive and erased the taint of their often rundown neighborhoods. The special equipment and activities and the extra staffing provided a tangible basis of distinctiveness which the school staff could point to, to show the advantages of the school. Parents were given something concrete with which to persuade themselves that their children were gaining an educational advantage in recompense for leaving the neighborhood and joining a racially diverse and unknown group of peers.[2]

Magnet schools as a violation of the politics of American schooling

The political contradiction of American schooling
To understand the consequences of the Heartland administrators' strategy in setting up magnet schools, it is necessary to consider the context of political thought about schooling in this country. Americans treat the relationship between education and social status with discomfort and avoidance. While in official social proclamations we maintain that the society offers equal opportunity to all children primarily by offering an equal education, as individuals we struggle to give our children an education that is more than equal in order to give them superior opportunities.

We smooth over the contradiction between equality of opportunity and the pursuit of educational advantage by pretending that the latter cannot exist. As John Meyer and Brian Rowan (1978) have pointed out in another context, we have developed a myth of standardization in public education; as a society we have come to believe in the existence of real, standardized entities such as 'fourth grade work' and 'sophomore geometry.' Within school districts, the common supervisory bureaucracy and the standardized district curriculum guide affirm the equivalence of similarly labeled experiences. More broadly, there is a belief that a child who finishes the fourth grade in one school system should be able to move to another anywhere in the country and be able to do the work in the fifth grade.

At the same time, it is an open secret throughout the nation that, both within and between districts, schools are anything but equivalent. They have different access to resources, not only to those which money can buy, but also to intangible resources such as high morale and a sense of academic purpose. Officially standardized neighborhood schools develop well-recognized local reputations on the basis of such resources.

The schools which develop reputations as 'good' tend to be in areas with more affluent families who have more education and more prestigious occupations, that is, where the social class of the clientele is higher. Realtors all over the country include the names of these 'good' public schools in advertisements for houses in their attendance areas. Parents who can afford it will pay more for these houses to get their children into schools with good reputations. Most often parents with higher incomes, education, and social power withdraw from the central cities to suburbs, where ordinances concerning lot size and rental policy effectively require a minimum level of affluence for residence. A paler form of the same process occurs as middle-class parents cluster in the more expensive neighborhoods of a city, where the schools with the best reputations and best test scores are most often found.

The social class composition of the student body of a school becomes a working indicator of school quality for many parents. Parents, especially middle-class and upwardly mobile parents, seek a school where their children will be with peers of the same or higher social class than they, as a sign that they will receive a superior education.

Race is relevant in the same way. One important thrust behind desegregation addresses just this issue. Desegregation gives black children access to the better educational facilities and programs that white parents use their influence to obtain for their own children. Desegregation thus changes the political balance in society as it requires children of different races to share the same schools and classrooms and so to have access to the same privileges. It seeks to make real the offically proclaimed comparability of schools and the opportunity they provide. Resistance to desegregation must be understood as being in part resistance to this equalization, not just to racial contact.

Simultaneous, if contradictory, belief in both the standardization and the differentiation of schools[3] allows communities and neighborhoods to compete for scarce resources for the education of their children, while they deny that such competition exists or that some might enter it with more advantages than others. It allows individuals to seek advantage for their children by placing them in 'good' districts or 'good' attendance area schools without admitting that they are seeking unequal opportunity at public expense.

The political meaning of Heartland's magnet school plan

Reputations tend to cling to schools even when the student body changes. With a desegregation plan, even if children ride yellow buses and have no contact with neighborhoods around schools, whites are much more reluctant to have their children attend schools in poor and black areas in the inner city than to have them attend school with the same mix of students in their home neighborhoods. Heartland's desegregation plan was designed to defuse the resistance of whites by requiring no one to transfer to a school where the education would appear to be worse than in his or her old school. Black children left the inner city schools which stand at the bottom of the informal hierarchy in cities and moved 'up' to white neighborhood schools. The children of whites who were deeply attached to their neighborhoods stayed in their old schools with old peers and teachers and only had to accept new companions. Those white families who were willing to move, moved 'up' because the magnet schools promised special educational programs at an explicit level and educational superiority at an implicit level.

The plan was very effective in avoiding resistance in the short run because no group felt they would lose as much as they feared. But while it worked well because it allowed every one to gain, or at least not to lose, it had hidden costs. It changed the rhetoric customary in schooling and in doing so violated the means by which the contradictory beliefs underlying American schooling are reconciled. The magnet schools were made *formally* different from others; they were not standardized schools. While, formally, the schools were *only* different, offering equal though differentiated education, there quickly developed a perception that they were superior. The visible amenities in physical renovation and extra staff and activities given to them in order to attract parents supported this conclusion. Further, this superiority was of a kind that could be more openly and easily discussed than that based on the social class or race of students.

Thus, while implicit superiority in the magnet schools was a strength in the short run by offering visible educational rewards to anyone who wanted to take advantage of them, in the long run it sparked controversy because it undermined the formal claim that the schools of the city were all equal. By formally casting aside the standardization of its schools, Heartland called their equality into question, and seemed to give public sanction to the formerly unspoken struggle for competitive advantage in schooling. Parents in ordinary schools could no longer persuade themselves that their children were getting the same education they would anywhere in the city, and the system could no longer argue that it was impartially offering the same education in every school.

Later political problems of the magnet schools

The formal differentiation of the magnet schools and their apparently visible superiority combined with other political problems in the desegregation plan as a whole as time passed. Several features of the total plan which had helped to avoid protest in the short run turned out to create discontent in the long run. Black community leaders increasingly questioned the fairness of the plan, noting a series of burdens it placed on black children. Black children were 90 percent of the children who left their own neighborhoods and had to ride buses. High school students had to wait on snowy corners before dawn in order to make transfers on city buses and arrive at school in outlying areas by 7:30 am. In addition, black students often were made to feel like unwelcome invaders in white neighborhood schools by white students, parents, and teachers. Because black children chose white neighborhood schools on an individual basis, there was no nucleus of black parents with community ties with one another at these schools and therefore no sense of black community participation in them. There were longer waiting lists for blacks at magnet schools than there were for whites, and in some cases blacks were on waiting lists while there were open spaces for whites. Despite these problems with desegregated schools, many black students could not attend their neighborhood schools because they had new, stringent enrollment limits. Consequently, many black families did not experience their enrollment in a desegregated school as 'voluntary.'[4]

Black community leaders began to characterize the desegregation plan as imposing a 'black burden.' Effective education and equity became their watchwords. Partly following national trends (Bell, 1980), they also began to question whether an effective education could not be as well or better offered in all-black schools. Beginning in the second year of the plan, and with increasing force and frequency, black communities began to resist the closing of their schools and the establishment of citywide magnet schools to replace black neighborhood schools.

Black leaders noted that while magnet schools might offer effective education, most black students who had to travel for desegregation could not get into their few spots. They suspected that the disproportionate attention magnets received drew attention away from the needs of the majority of students, so that magnet schools could be said actually to inhibit equity by making it politically unnecessary to develop effective education for the majority of black children in the city. Black leaders, therefore, regarded magnet schools with increasing suspicion.

Meanwhile, white parents in the neighborhoods most resistant to desegregation also were not happy with the costs and rewards they had been offered. When the desegregation suit was settled out of court, whites who had opposed desegregation ceased to fear that their children might be bused into black areas. White families to whom busing was a calamitous eventuality and the inner city a frightening place had initially been glad to let other white families willing to send their children on buses into the central city receive the rewards of special educational approaches. But as the possibility of mandatory two-way busing faded away, these families once more began to regard the ability to go to schools in their own neighborhoods as an inalienable right and began to look with a jaundiced eye at the special resources given to the magnet schools, often grossly exaggerating those resources. They pointed out that their schools were desegregated too, something they considered a significant burden. They asked why families willing to ride a bus should get more educational resources than they did. Some such parents even decided to try magnet schools, only to find that the oversubscription of whites at some of the most popular ones resulted in their children being turned away. They were then doubly angered.

In short, among the parents and teachers in the city who did not participate in them, the magnet schools began to develop a reputation as privileged enclaves for the elite. Middle-class families were more likely to choose magnet schools than were working-class families, and families from the cosmopolitan South Side were more likely to do so than were families from the stable ethnic enclaves of the West Side. Thus there were differences among whites, if not in access to the privileges of magnet schools, at least in use of those privileges. These differences occurred along lines of social class and (white) ethnicity, which paralleled differences in access to power and privilege in the city's broader life.

The middle class was especially drawn to a few schools, for example, at the elementary level, a Montessori school, a creative arts school, and a gifted and talented school (which offered the third through fifth grades), and at the middle school level, the school for the gifted and talented. Many observers thought that this was no accident; they noted that schools with names and programs most likely to attract the upper middle class had received the most attractive buildings, the most physical amenities, and the most generous staffing. It is possible that city leaders and middle-class parents simply quickly discovered the most thoroughly endowed schools. However, it was important to the success of the plan that the magnet schools be attractive to community opinion leaders who could play a key role in publicizing them and lending them an aura of acceptability.[5] Thus the central office needed to ensure that the schools most likely to appeal to these groups be sufficiently attractive as the plan was first taking hold.

Once these schools began to develop identities as middle-class schools, that identity became attractive in itself. Upper-middle-class families sought them out in large numbers, as did ambitious blue-collar families, because of the social characteristics of the students and their high test scores, published each spring. These schools then developed long waiting lists which only added to the attractiveness of their images.

Further, there was a snowballing effect in the benefits these schools accrued, as their parent bodies were relatively heavily populated with well-educated, articulate parents who had established community influence and a knowledge of political processes. The concentration of these parents was then both a direct and indirect cause of the schools' receiving more attention from the media, the board, and the public.

Recruitment for all the schools of the city became interdependent at every age level. There was a limited pool of academically able children, children of well-educated parents, and children

23

of community leaders. If a large number of children from that pool went to any one, or any few, schools, then the other schools were relatively deprived. Jealousies arose among the magnet schools,[6] as well as between them and the other schools, over the issue of recruitment of strong students and politically capable parents, as well as over the issue of financial resources and assistance from the central office. Thus the introduction of magnet schools threw all the schools of the system into an open competition for resources. Such a competition had always existed, but competition for students and parents had been rigidly constrained by rules about attendance areas, and competition for monetary resources had been less visible. Differences between schools had been informal and publicly understated in a formally standardized system; now they were formal and often overestimated in a formally diversified system.

The fact that the most successful schools in this competition were magnet schools tainted all of the magnet schools with the label of elitism. The image created was not entirely accurate, since all of the magnet schools did not attract middle-class students. Indeed, if the middle schools were at all representative, even though the middle class attended magnet schools more, the majority of students in the magnet schools were not middle-class. Heartland was, after all, a school district where half the lunches served were to students qualifying for free or reduced price meals, and a city where only 12 percent of the adult population had completed college. The elite did not supply enough students to make a great deal of impact on many schools. Two of the three study schools – that is, two of the three magnet schools available at the middle school level – had student bodies which hardly anyone would call elite. None the less, the image of elitism in the magnet schools had an effect on all of them.

The district's response to perceived privileges of the magnet schools

The school board reflected community concerns about undue privileges for the magnet schools and undue burden upon black students. Black and liberal white members were sympathetic to blacks' complaints of inequity, while conservative white board members were sympathetic to complaints from whites attached to neighborhood schools. However, these sympathies led neither group to oppose the existence of the magnet schools but only to be ambivalent about them. Both thought they were necessary to the continuance of a desegregation plan that was acceptable to both the community and the court.

One result of these feelings was extended board discussion of a great variety of concrete issues in the light of the principle of 'equity.' Three concrete results relevant to the magnet schools eventuated. First, the board did not replace shrinking federal funds for the magnet schools with local money. Most of the special funding for the magnet schools' extra staff and activities, of which other schools were jealous, came from federal funds either for magnet schools in particular or for the cushioning of the desegregation process. These funds were designed to help schools in transition and therefore were available in steadily decreasing amounts. The fact that most of the schools had succeeded in establishing racially mixed clienteles, and many had waiting lists, by the time that federal funds began to become slim, gave the board confidence in not replacing them. One conservative board member said explicitly in June 1980 that there was no reason to give magnet schools any special funds, as long as they continued to attract adequate numbers of both races.

Consequently, magnet schools which had unusually labor-intensive methods, or other reasons to need special funds, found that the rivalry among schools and the tag of elitism affected their ability to continue being distinctive in very concrete and crucial ways. At the same time, though the board was reacting to political pressure in not giving magnet schools special local funds, it was in neither their interest nor that of the magnet schools to advertise this fact, lest the magnet schools should seem less attractive to the parents of young children coming up who were needed as volunteers to keep them full. As a result, the politics of the situation led the schools gradually to lose their special financial privileges, but not their reputation for them.

The second consequence of the elitist reputation of the schools was the board's insistence that the magnet schools accept all comers without regard either to achievement or familial power. It established elementary and middle schools for the gifted and talented and a high school for the college-bound early, before much pressure over elitism had developed. The definitions of skills for admission to these were extremely broadly defined but, as the

25

years went on, still subject to constant controversy. The board consistently voted for the broadest possible interpretation of eligibility standards. Other schools were not allowed to have any admission criteria at all, except that students could not enter higher grades in Montessori and foreign language immersion elementary schools without prior experience in their special ways of instruction.

The board's third response to charges of inequity in the desegregation plan consisted of paying special attention to the needs of low-income and minority students. One important direction these efforts took involved setting up a number of mandatory practices for all schools designed to help such students. Most of these initiatives bore fruit after the study. Thus, in the fifth and sixth years of desegregation, the board required all schools to use a single set of texts in reading and in math in order to make transitions smoother for children who move frequently. They required competency tests and more detailed school-by-school reports on standardized test results. These changes had the potential to undercut the diversity for which magnet schools were established by placing pressure on their staffs to follow a narrowly specified curriculum and to teach to specified tests.

Despite these actions, which expressed the board's uneasiness over the equity of the desegregation plan as a whole, once the school system had put itself on record as finding educational value in offering parents the opportunity to choose a school with an educational approach matching their children's needs, it was difficult to withdraw that opportunity and return to mandatory assignment of students. The superintendent had opened Pandora's box; once the idea of a right to choice was loose among the populace it could not easily be withdrawn. Even the parents who objected to the amenities given the magnets often did so in terms of wanting them extended rather than withheld.

Furthermore, the board itself was reaping rewards from the magnet schools. Outside of Heartland, little was known of quarrels over the level of equity in its plan, but much was known of its success in creating a network of desegregated schools without mandatory reassignment. The magnet schools were generally given credit for the feat. Further, some of the most successful schools became the subject of national magazine articles and received visitors from school systems across the nation wanting to learn how they accomplished so much. The school board had reason to maintain them despite political pressure about their privileges.

The multiple missions of the magnet schools

Despite debate over their equity, magnet schools were established and functioned to accomplish important purposes for the district as a whole and for their own students. They were intended to further both desegregation and educational innovation. Since these two goals were not inherently related to one another, sometimes courses of action which advanced one did not advance the other. The interaction of these missions was therefore an important theme both in the relations of the schools to the larger district and in their internal lives.

Desegregation

As the district dealt with the magnets as a group, it seemed clear that they were designed primarily as a tool for desegregation in the system as a whole. They came into existence as a way of meeting the terms of a court order for desegregation; they would not have been established in such numbers without that impetus, nor would they have gained political and administrative support without it. Even though there were important actors at every level who rejoiced that desegregation had provided the leverage for educational innovations, the criterion for a school's practical success, and the necessary condition for its continued life as a magnet, was its ability to draw and retain volunteering children in acceptable racial ratios. A school which succeeded in following its educational blueprint but did not draw volunteers, or drew them from only one race, had not fulfilled its mission. A school which differed from neighborhood 'traditional' schools in little except its rhetoric, but drew students and parents in the appropriate racial ratios and kept them content enough to return had succeeded in practical terms, even though some enthusiasts for its educational specialty might grumble.

The magnet schools played a role in systemwide desegregation not only by being desegregated themselves. The magnet schools furthered desegregation when they took over the buildings of all black schools so that the students formerly assigned to those schools had to scatter to other schools. (A few would re-enroll in the citywide specialty, but they did not receive special preference even in filling the quota for their own race.) This second use of the magnets for desegregation turned out to be of special importance for the middle schools, all of which were either moved or considered for moving into formerly black schools, even after they were already operating as magnet schools.

Innovation

Educational distinctiveness was, however, also an important aspect of the magnet schools' mission in the eyes of system level administrators. Since Heartland drew significant amounts of money from federal magnet school grants, the school district had to be able to justify their continued requests for such funds on the grounds of the educational distinctiveness of each program. It was the belief of the key officers in the central administration that distinctiveness was the road to voluntary recruitment, at least initially, while the schools were building reputations. Consequently they pushed the schools to follow their diverse educational mandates conscientiously and thoroughly. Federal funds for training of teachers, for special materials and equipment, and for extra staffing for the special programs helped the schools in this quest.

Distinctiveness, however, invited public disapprobation as well as approval. If a school were to be truly different from others, especially at the elementary and middle school levels where variety was created through different educational approaches more often than through the substance of curricular offerings, it had to depart from the educationally tried and true. It thus ran the danger of appearing 'far out.'

In 1981, at the close of the fifth year of the magnet programs and after they had completed their major work in desegregation, secondary curriculum supervisors and personnel with responsibilities for magnet schools, whom I interviewed at the central office, seemed to give implicit approval or disapproval to various magnet programs in inverse relationship to the degree of distinctiveness of the program. This was particularly true of the curriculum supervisors, who had spent their careers selecting and constructing curricula which some of the schools now cast aside.

A school which could draw parents and please them, which demanded little attention, and which did not change the fundamental curriculum or style of traditional schools but simply added some special learning opportunities seemed to find the most favor with these central office personnel. As money contracted, these administrators felt justified in starting to make cautious statements about 'program quality' in the magnets. Program quality, as understood by these middle level supervisors, seemed to be associated with preparation for either academic excellence or a vocation; it seemed to include a minimum of 'frills.'[7]

Still, these persons conveyed such judgments mostly in asides and personal comments before or after the research interview rather than in their answers to formal questions. It was still very much the policy of the district to support the full range of diversity in the alternative schools, and these middle level central office employees were good subordinates who would not directly question that policy.

Persons whose responsibilities lay in line administration differed from these interviewees. They were strongly supportive of the full range of alternative schools, both as tools for desegregation and as means for providing for a variety of students' needs and families' values. They had had more experience in dealing with students and families who did not fit in traditional schools under the old system and so were more aware of problems that diversity solved.

Programs for diverse student bodies

Though the magnet schools were established for the sake of desegregation, for placing students of different races in the same school, the district as a whole did little to advertise them as *integrated* schools, as schools which furthered positive inter-racial understanding and friendship. At the system level, the magnet schools' programs were discussed as general educational innovations offered to desegregated groups, not as innovative designs for integrated education.

Whether it was formally proclaimed or not, however, the schools did have a special mission as they worked with student bodies which in most cases were diverse not only in race, but in social class and in academic achievement and skills as well. Social and academic diversity brought with it major readjustments; by default or by design, the school programs were shaped by the way the adults dealt with this diversity as much as by their announced programs. But since the task of dealing with diversity was formally unrecognized, it was up to the building staff to define the school's philosophy and practice in working with racial, social, and academic diversity.

Still, the central office did play some quiet part in this process. Administrators there were alert lest racial resegregation occur within the schools; to prevent this occurrence, they made it clear that the schools were expected to compose classes of heterogeneous academic ability. Consequently, teachers had to learn strategies of instruction which would be effective with students whose skills could vary over an extremely wide range. It was not unusual in at least two of the middle schools to have seventh graders whose reading levels varied from the third to the tenth grade in a class requiring reading skills. Though most of the students were black or white, there were a few Hispanic, Native American and Asian students present and there was a range of economic backgrounds represented. The schools had to deal with cultural diversity which went beyond black and white differences.

The central office did pass federal money from Title VII and Title VI on to the magnet schools; some of those funds were ones earmarked to ease the difficulty of dealing with academic and social diversity in newly desegregated schools. Also there was a human relations support team from the central office available to any of the desegregated schools having difficulty with social relations. The team's assistance was more needed in the neighborhood schools and I barely heard about it in the magnet schools, but its existence signaled a quiet but very real concern of the central office over diversity – its potentiality for generating active and visible conflict among students or between students and teachers.

While it was an unannounced mission, dealing with racial, academic, social, and cultural diversity was as important as desegregating the schools and developing their special programs. The schools were required to find ways to instruct children with different cultural styles and with widely differing academic skills so that all would learn effectively. To maintain a good public image, the schools also had quietly to prevent friction between different races. If the school staff were so inclined, they could seek ways to build positive relations between the races as well.

System level constraints on the design and practice of the magnet schools

The magnet schools were affected not only by the politics of the district and by the multiple missions they were founded to accomplish, but by a number of other conditions which operated at the district level. Some of these conditions were set by the board and central office, but other actors, especially the teachers' union and parents as a collective entity, played a significant part in shaping the parameters of their operation.

The teachers' union and the staffing of magnet schools

Heartland has a powerful, well-organized teachers' union to which virtually all teachers belong. Some union members feared the central administration might use the development of alternative schools as a means to distinguish among teachers on the basis of competence, however named, and to develop two classes of positions. The union therefore fought to maintain the principle of seniority in staffing the new schools and to allow the teachers who had taught in the school buildings which were chosen as sites for alternative schools to staff the new schools. The school district administration, on the other hand, wanted the right to choose the teachers for the new schools.

In the summer before the first schools opened, the two could not agree on how to staff the alternative schools, so the court stepped in to impose a compromise. The administration was allowed to select teachers for a small percentage of slots as 'super-intendent's choices'. For other slots, teachers in the schools which were transformed into magnets had first claim if they wanted to stay, provided they would take an in-service course in the school's special approach. The alternative for teachers who decided to leave these schools was unattractive. They had to enter a citywide pool of transferring teachers with little idea of where they would be placed and to lose the building seniority which was a crucial ingredient of job security in a time when steeply declining enroll-ments were anticipated. Consequently, very few teachers in build-ings chosen as the locations for magnet schools departed.

Except for a few programs which received superintendent's choices, the magnet schools operated with faculties inherited from the schools which had previously occupied their buildings. The histories of these neighborhood schools thus became part of the history of the magnet school; the common educational assump-tions and working relationships which the faculties of these schools had built up in the old setting provided a context for their new joint endeavor.

Further, the union continued to place a high priority on resisting efforts to staff the magnet schools with specially selected teachers. At the end of the first year of desegregation, in the spring of 1977, there was a strike several weeks long. Staffing for alternative schools was among the major issues. The contract eventually signed stipulated that vacancies in magnet schools were to be filled by seniority, with some preference to teachers who had training and/or experience in the special approach. However, one year of experience at any time or one in-service or university course would fill the latter requirement, as could a promise to take such a course. Thus the schools could not filter in specially selected or trained teachers as vacancies occurred, but had to take the most senior teacher in the district who applied for his or her own reasons. There were several union grievances concerning both the procedures used in staffing some schools and transfers by princi-pals based on unwillingness or inability to teach according to the specialty.

The need for haste

After the federal judge handed down his order for desegregation in January 1976 with the requirement that the first third of the schools be desegregated that September, it took some time to reach the decision to use magnet schools as a means to that end, especially as the Board was simultaneously appealing the court order and was not active in developing a plan for compliance. Then the court sent back the first plan as insufficient, including too few magnet schools, and more had to be added. Thus the first magnet schools were put into operation essentially over the course of the summer.

There was little time to notify teachers of the new design for their schools, let alone to consult them about details of the program or even to offer them training. Teachers might be angered or pleased by the change to a new program, but they were bound to feel unprepared to deliver the special approaches promised for the new schools from their opening. Because of the short lead time, it was not possible for the city to get much help in outside funds the first year. In the second year, 1977–8, federal magnet school money supplied considerable funds to order special materials and to hire substitutes while regular teachers worked on developing their schools' special approaches. But these resources appeared over a year after the launching of the plan and after the public was first encouraged to choose schools on the basis of their distinctiveness and implied superiority. The difficulties attendant on organizing a school in haste were probably most severe for those schools opened in the first fall. But as the stories of the three middle schools will show, they also occurred in other schools.

Publicity

If the magnets, or alternative schools, were to draw students, they had to have a high profile, to be very visible. They were also intended to change the public image of desegregation. In order to boost their symbolic value, they were given national publicity from the beginning. As the symbolic spearhead of the desegregation plan, they were particularly subject to inspection by agents of the court and community leaders who wanted to be sure they were not resegregated internally. As the schools shakily explored their way toward distinctiveness with little experience or training to guide them, they had to receive a train of visitors. If teachers felt they had to improvise, not only to be distinctive in their teaching, but at first to teach at all, the curtain was up and the lights were on as they did so.

The central administration, led by the superintendent, dealt with the difficulty of creating special programs on the instant by simply informing subordinates all down the line that these schools would be distinctive, that they would meet expectations, and that no one was publicly to express any doubt or lack of determination about their ability to do so. Particular needs and problems were met on a school-by-school basis as well as conditions and resources would allow. The system as a whole also had to improvise – and to do so with the newspapers, the court, and, to a degree, a national audience watching.

While the publicity to which the schools were subjected naturally created a good deal of anxiety among their staffs, especially where they felt unprepared for their tasks, it also generated some positive feelings. A long tradition of research has found that workers can respond to the experience of simply being chosen for an experiment by increasing their morale, effort, and output, because the experiment involves friendly interest from an outside audience. This response is sometimes called the 'Hawthorne effect' for an early experiment in which it emerged (Roethlisberger and Dickson, 1947). In Heartland, at least some of the staffs of the magnet schools caught the spirit of being part of a great experiment, a social adventure. Parents and children often shared and boosted these feelings which were actively encouraged by system level administrators and echoed by the print and electronic media.

Further, their prefabricated reputation for distinctiveness and excellence gave the magnet schools a little cushion of capital in the form of positive public opinion, which they used while they scrambled to create the situation which had supposedly existed from the beginning. In this way, the initially inflated claims became self-fulfilling prophecies. Though they raised the staff's anxieties, they provided both breathing room and a stimulus for the schools to fill in the outlines of the portraits already sketched of them.

Parental power

Parents in the city developed increased power at every level. The set of magnet schools had to be designed to appeal to them. Once the magnets were functioning, parents, as members of formally and informally constituted groups and as individuals, were heeded when they had complaints or suggestions lest they become the nucleus of an exodus from a school (cf. Hirschman, 1972; Barry, 1974). Parents of a race which was particularly needed at a school were specially courted; this almost always meant whites.

34

Many teachers and principals found parental involvement to be intrusive, especially when the parents expected not only to voice an opinion or offer advice but to see their wishes fairly promptly carried out (cf. Cohen and Farrar, 1977). The parents who partici-pated most in such intrusions were the upper-middle-class, often locally influential, families whose support was most needed to win over the community. The schools, and particularly the principals, expended a good deal of energy in diplomatic handling of parents.

On the other hand, when such a group of parents had been persuaded of a school's good quality, they could become powerful allies of the school in spreading its good reputation through the city, in assisting with informal channels for student recruitment, and in occasional representation to the central administration or school board of the school's need for resources or exceptions from the system's routines. Parents who held positions of formal and informal influence, ranging from positions in the media to work as managers in major businesses or partners in law firms – or who worked for the central office or were on the school board – could be especially effective in this role.

Citywide voluntary recruitment

The relations of parents with the schools were connected to the recruitment of students and the consequent composition of the student bodies.

Voluntarism

The staffs of all the schools thought that the schools benefited from the fact that someone in each family, usually a parent, had chosen the school; often the whole family had made the commitment. Therefore, even if the family were initially anxious about their choice, they were predisposed to think well of the school and to cooperate in making the student's experience a success. The beneficial effects of voluntarism were most visible in the children's attitude toward the school and in the parents' willingness to support teachers in their efforts with individual children.

Voluntarism became a more mixed blessing in the context of school policy. Some parents felt entitled to criticize practices and activities in a school which did not match their understanding of its special approach. At the other extreme, some parents made few inquiries before choosing a school and were surprised to learn of its departures from traditional patterns. The school staff sometimes had to expend effort educating such parents about their approach and persuading them of its merits after the child entered.

Student recruitment – creaming and dumping

Because voluntary recruitment of students to schools creates a fluid system, it has the potential for 'creaming' a city's school population, drawing off the best students (Levine and Havighurst, 1977). This process leaves ordinary schools coping with more difficult students and gives magnet schools an unfair advantage. Concern over this issue was one basis of blacks' and other whites' criticisms of equity in the relations of the magnet schools and neighborhood schools.

If magnet schools are made attractive, one can expect that a certain amount of creaming is inevitable. The parents most likely to notice the presence of educational alternatives, most likely to investigate them, and most willing to take the social risks and bear the logistical inconveniences of taking advantage of them will be those who care most about education for their children. Their children will be more likely than others also to care about education and to be cooperative in class and good achievers relative to their abilities. Such parents are likely to be more educated and affluent than most, or at least to be ambitious for their children to acquire these characteristics.

Creaming is partially balanced by dumping, however. If there were understandable reasons why the magnet schools drew off some of the best students in the system, there were also reasons why they drew some of the worst. Parents who might not otherwise look for alternatives are likely to do so when their children seem not to be prospering in their current setting – whether that be because they are capable and bored or because they are having academic or social difficulties (Royster, Baltzell, and Simmons, 1979). Furthermore, especially in the first years, parents' independent action was not the only impetus to recruitment for the magnet schools. In the first two years, when school personnel were asked to counsel their current students to encourage them to go to alternative schools, many school principals and counselors went first to the parents of their worst, rather than of their best, students to tell them of the bright new opportunities available to them somewhere else. Some of this process continued through the years.

This form of dumping was a particular problem for the magnet middle schools. Citywide middle schools were opened as sixth through eighth grade schools, but the move of the sixth grade from all elementary schools into all middle schools was postponed to 1985. Consequently, elementary principals could suggest to troublesome students and their parents that they would prosper better in a citywide middle school for their sixth grade year. As the years went by and jealousy of the magnet schools arose in the system as a whole, some schools seem to have intentionally dumped their more difficult children into the magnet schools with the message, 'Let's see if you look so good with *these* kids to deal with.' Two magnet school principals mentioned having had several telephone calls in the spring from elementary principals warning of the difficulty of incoming students they were sending. When asked whether these calls were meant to provide helpful information or to gloat, the principals replied that there were some of each kind.

Since it is difficult to estimate the proportions of well-motivated children compared to problem children in the city as a whole, it is impossible to know whether the magnet schools received more than their share of either or both kinds. It appeared that, on the whole, they had more than their share of both the best and the worst – with the exception of Mann, the gifted and talented school, which, because of its selective admission procedures, clearly had more than its share of the best and less than its share of the worst.

Freedom from neighborhood cliques
Especially at the middle school level, the citywide magnet schools benefited significantly from drawing children from all over the city. Since children came to the schools from many neighborhoods and many feeder schools, most had few old friends and few friends from their neighborhoods in the school. The schools thus had a much freer hand in forming the academic and social habits of the children than do most middle and junior high schools where long-established cliques provide a countervailing socializing force. Children could be more academically diligent and more friendly with children of other races than they would be under the surveillance of their neighborhood peers.

Further, the schools were less subject to the effects of the neighborhoods in which they were located than are most middle or junior high schools. The principal of a desegregated neighborhood middle school in a white area, which I visited for a week for comparison, told me that one of his most serious problems had come from white high school students who liked to come over to the middle school and hurl insults or stir up their younger siblings and neighbors to start confrontations with black students. The citywide schools did not have these problems to the same degree even when they were located in residential neighborhoods, because their students were generally not from the neighborhood and so not acquainted with the older adolescents who liked to lounge about.

The magnet schools in this study, then, were subject to a large array of special conditions in their surroundings, what sociologists call their 'environment' as organizations. They were part of a political agenda and one which was increasingly contested with the passing years. They were given multiple missions, both announced and unannounced. Their internal arrangements were directly formed by outside forces which set policy for recruitment of both teachers and students. Parents acquired the power to become more active participants in their lives if they so wished. Some of these special conditions smoothed a school's path; others made it more rocky; the balance differed as each school had a somewhat different relationship with the system as a whole. Each school was shaped by the interaction of these external influences with other influences which were generated within the schools.

Chapter 3

Organizational processes and life within the schools

Influences from the environment discussed in the last chapter set crucial constraints upon the individual schools' lives, but these conditions were taken as givens by the participants in the schools and so were not problematic on a day-to-day basis. Thus the district recruited the cast for the play, hired the hall, provided a script and props, and then, along with parents, stepped back to watch, allowing the principal, teachers, and students to improvise freely upon the script, invent the details of action not included in the dialogue, and interpret its mood and meaning in their own terms.

This chapter is meant to provide a context for understanding the typicality or distinctiveness of the traits developed in the study schools. It first discusses some patterns found to be common in the life of schools which have students like those at the study schools. It then introduces a set of processes relevant to the life of organizations generally. These processes constitute the most important influences found in the schools; they were discovered inductively as crucial elements in the lives of the schools, though they are introduced here in a deductive fashion as they are treated in the literature which analyzes organizations. Three influences will be discussed: principal–teacher relations, technology and logistics, and the development of organizational subcultures.

Relationships between teachers and students and among students

The magnet schools' mission to work with a diverse student body was particularly problematic, except at the school for the gifted and talented, because the city of Heartland, like other large central cities, has more than the national percentage of low achievers and more than the national proportion of families in poverty. Consequently, in addition to being racially diverse and having students from a broad spectrum of social and economic backgrounds, the two schools whose student bodies reflected the city had a majority of economically poor, low achieving students. The development of relationships between teachers and students and among student peers which will support learning and foster mutual understanding between races is far from automatic in such a situation.

There is a considerable literature of case studies documenting conflict between students and teachers where students are racial minorities, poor, or low achievers. There are no systematic studies of the frequency or degree of such conflict. The closest approach to one, the Safe School Study (National Institute of Education, 1978), suggests that severe conflict is more common in situations of poverty and therefore also among racial minorities, and is particularly instigated by low achievers, but that it is by no means limited to, or universal among, schools with poor children, minority children or low achievers. To anticipate the next chapters, none of the study schools had significant difficulties with classroom conflict. In order to have a context for analyzing why they did not, it will be helpful to discuss here the dynamics which social scientists have suggested are at the root of classroom conflict when it does occur.

Sources of conflict between low achievers and schools

The literature describing conflict between teachers and students who are poor, minorities, or low achievers is to be found in several unrelated traditions; it comes from both England and the United States and from both anthropologists and sociologists. Furthermore, race, social class, and achievement are intricately interwoven in the conflicts it describes. I shall not attempt to untangle the effects of the three, but shall argue that at the secondary level, achievement becomes most important even though it may be operating as a proxy on both students' and teachers' part for conflicts which stem from differences in race, social class, or both.

Several American anthropologists have described minority

students' school experiences as ones which force them to choose between the culture with which they come to school and the one presented to them by teachers representing the mainstream white culture. Looking mostly at elementary schools, they note that the majority of children pull away from the teacher's culture and set up strong peer norms and social ties which support their home culture. Not only do such children enter into expressive conflict with the teacher and the school (Leacock, 1969; McDermott, 1974; Wax, Wax, and Dumont, 1964; Wolcott, 1974), but they reject academic effort as part of the teacher's world as well.

Observers concerned with secondary schools note a different kind of dynamic which alienates minority and poor children from the classroom. By watching the lives of older relatives and neighbors they learn that their racial (Ogbu, 1974) or class (Willis, 1977) characteristics will preclude them from eligibility for the kind of work or life-style which school success promises. Such students see little point in making an effort for success, since their effort will lead only to disappointment. Working-class students may also find the kind of knowledge honored in school foreign to their experience, while that which they see their parents use at work and in domestic life receives no recognition in the school (Connell, Ashenden, Kessler, and Dowsett, 1982). Again, effort or cooperation in school may seem to such students to bear little fruit in adulthood.

Once students perform poorly in the academic sphere at school, whether for reasons of cultural and social alienation or for any other reason, their school lives are likely to become painful and unrewarding. Schools are inherently competitive contexts which rank students according to their academic performance. That ranking has profound implications for their status in the school and possibly for their status in adult life. Because school is a competitive context, students can do well only in comparison to others who do poorly; high grades and honors have value because they are relatively rare. For those students whose poor performance serves to add lustre to the comparatively able performance of others, school offers few reasons for engagement and many for resistance. For such students to maintain their pride, it may become necessary for them to make vivid to all around them their disdain for the academic enterprise. They present their rejection of academic effort as the reason for their poor record of performance. Continued lack of effort leads these students to have even poorer skills and thus to be increasingly less capable of doing the work asked of them or holding their own in competition.

There are a number of studies which show that groups of students who are labeled as comparatively less able than those around them, usually through tracking or streaming, engage in more conflict with their teachers than do other groups even when all are of similar social class and race (Hargreaves, 1967; Lacey, 1970; Schwartz, 1981). These studies also show that groups who are given the label of high ability are conforming and diligent, even though they may be of a social class and level of ability which might incline them to resist school (Hargreaves, 1967; Schwartz, 1981) in another context. There are also studies which have found that individual students who are doing poorly academically are more likely to engage in overt rebellious or hostile actions within the school (Bellaby, 1974; National Institute of Education, 1978) even though they have middle-class families (Stinchcombe, 1964).

Students who are low performers remain ambivalent about academic work. Academic learning is a highly charged area, one which draws strong reactions, not one to which they are truly indifferent. Students who expressively reject any desire to excel, or even to offer minimal effort, will criticize others both for being 'dumb' (Willis, 1977) and for good academic skill or effort (Schwartz, 1981). Not surprisingly, several studies have noted that poorly performing students show a preference for academic work which can be done alone without public interaction and which is highly structured with clear right or wrong answers (Furlong, 1977; Metz, 1978b; Werthman, 1963).

The classroom conflicts which case studies have documented are by no means solely the work of the students. Conflict is a game which requires more than one participating player. Several studies in England (Ball, 1981; Hargreaves, 1967; Keddie, 1971) have pointed out that teachers often perceive cultural characteristics which separate working-class from middle-class students, resistant or disruptive school behavior, and low academic skill as a single undifferentiated set of characteristics. If a student shows one, they assume he or she possesses all. Studies in the United States have identified a similar attitude in many teachers (e.g. Brookover, Beady, Flood, Schweitzer, and Wisenbaker, 1979; Rist, 1973; Wilcox, 1982).

Teachers sponsor children in a sense and are perceived by other adults in association with them. Thus teachers often preserve their own respectability by distancing themselves from students who engage in patterns of behavior that are not valued by other members of the teachers' reference group. They perceive the students as very different from themselves and as morally unworthy (Keddie, 1971; Rist, 1973; Schwartz, 1981). Race or social class alone may be enough to put a child beyond the pale, but often teachers make finer distinctions. Signs of a life-style which breaks the moral injunctions the middle class associates with respectability are often what leads teachers to withdraw their interest in a child; disreputable characteristics or actions of the parent may be transferred to the child.

Teachers frequently reject students who are hostile and defiant to defend their inner selves from the attack. Similarly, when students perform poorly and teachers are therefore unable to experience success in the performance of their central professional task, they may disassociate their sense of self from an effort which they think unlikely to yield progress or rewards.

By the time poorly achieving students reach the secondary school, they show the effect of years of interaction with a series of teachers. They enter a class ready to engage in behavior which dramatically expresses their distance from a situation that denigrates their skills, and often their cultural style. Even teachers who wish to change the patterns of interaction and of academic effort in classes with low achievers will find it difficult to do so (Metz, 1978b). On the other hand, students do take note of individual teachers' behavior. If they believe a teacher is seriously attempting to help them academically, they will be much more cooperative and far less likely to engage in major disruptions or active hostility, though they may still make little academic effort (Furlong, 1977; Metz, 1978a; Werthman, 1963).

Sources of positive interracial relations

Persons who resist desegregation often voice a fear of tension or open conflict between students of different races. Those who favor desegregation often speak of the need to move from mere desegregation, taken to mean the introduction of students of different colors into the same school building, to integration. Integration involves the creation of an atmosphere where students of different colors mix easily together, participate in the school's activities on an equal footing, and develop mutual understanding and acceptance of similarities and differences between racial groups. In the latter understanding of the purpose of desegregation, improving relations between children of different races was part of the mission of the magnet schools. Accordingly, arrangements which affected children's interracial relations and their effects were considered in the study of the three schools, although it was not possible to explore the relationships which developed among students in the depth appropriate to a study where these were the major focus.

There is quite a large literature in social psychology which seeks to identify the conditions which affect the quality of interracial relations between persons of different races placed in physical and social contact. It is much more systematic than the literature on classroom conflict between teachers and students. It is organized around analysis of the conditions for harmony rather than around explanations for conflict. Three influences are commonly discussed as important in creating a positive tone to these relationships.

First, students of different races need to have equal status. Equality of status is complex and multifaceted (Schofield, 1982). Clearly students have the equal status of 'student' if they are in the same classroom. But racial identities, dress and behavior which are indicative of social class, and academic skills all confer relative status which is likely to disadvantage the black group (Cohen, 1980). Other skills, such as prowess in sports or musical ability, can also affect individuals' relative status.

Second, a long tradition of work in social psychology suggests that competition reinforces tensions and encourages negative reactions towards others, while cooperation eases tensions and strengthens positive reactions. Schools are traditionally competitive settings, with academic performance and academic rewards in the form of grades a major nexus of competition. There has been a good deal of experimental work, recently reviewed by Cohen (1980) and by Slavin (1980), which suggests that when students must cooperate for common goals they develop positive relations with one another.

Finally, the attitudes and behaviors of authority figures – teachers, principals and parents – have been shown to be important to students' relationships (Schofield, 1982). The priority these authority figures give to developing positive intergroup and interpersonal relations as an educative task is as important as their own degree of personal prejudice. Several studies suggest that the expectation that positive inter-racial relations will spontaneously grow from mere proximity is unrealistic (Rist, 1978; Rosenbaum and Presser, 1978; Schofield, 1982). Adults must work to create a variety of conditions which encourage equality of status and cooperation and which symbolically express adults' active support for extensive interaction among children of different races.

Principal–teacher relations

Since in most cases the innovative programs of the magnet schools were imposed from above by fiat, the principal, who represented the school district's administrative hierarchy within the school, had the major responsibility for seeing that the ideas of the program became realities in the school. That responsibility did not quite fit the realities of a principal's role and relationship with teachers, however. Even though the relationship is a hierarchical one of clear superordination and subordination, it has collegial or consultative elements because teachers have some claim to professional autonomy. These two definitions of the relationship are inconsistent, yet both have a degree of cultural legitimacy. The combination creates contradiction and strain in this crucial relationship.

Schools as formal bureaucracies

School systems in the United States were designed at the end of the nineteenth and beginning of the twentieth century according to the same rational, bureaucratic principles which industrial owners used in constructing their businesses as tools for the accomplishment of their goals (Perrow, 1979). That rational or bureaucratic model of organizations is one with wide legitimacy in this country and, with some differences, in the industrialized world.

In simplest terms, bureaucratic organization is a social mechanism for orchestrating the efforts of many persons toward the accomplishment of a goal. Those at the top set the overall goals and tasks of the organization and conceive the design for its efforts; persons at lower levels fill in specific details. Directions for the work to be done become progressively more specific as one moves down the hierarchy toward the level where the actual productive work of the organization is accomplished. There is a well-defined division of labor and a legitimate hierarchy down which commands and responsibility descend and up which accountability ascends. Each position in a bureaucracy carries with it a role, which different individuals can be expected to play in substantially similar ways. This standardization of conduct is re-enforced by a system of explicit rules which prescribe the behavior required in frequently occurring situations.

The lack of fit between bureaucracy and the functioning of schools

From the very earliest studies of schools in the United States, it has been clear that they do not closely follow bureaucratic patterns (Bidwell, 1965; Waller, 1965 [1932]). Much of the early study of schools as organizations sought to identify the special character-istics of schools which lead to departure from bureaucratic prin-ciples (e.g. Bidwell, 1965; Corwin, 1974; Dreeben, 1973). A number of characteristics emerged as important. First, the bureau-cratic model assumes a fairly clear goal, or set of complementary goals, which can be easily articulated at the top of the organization and then conscientiously pursued by persons lower in the hier-archy. But schools do not have clear or unified goals. While everyone can agree that they exist to educate the young, as soon as one asks the meaning of the term 'educate', it becomes clear that school goals are both multiple and ambiguous. With little agreement, and frequently active conflict, over educational goals it is unlikely that policy made at the top of a school system will be faithfully followed in every school and every classroom.

Second, even where participants and interested members of the environment may be in agreement about educational goals, there does not exist a clearly effective technological process to accomplish those goals. In the absence of such a technology, strategy cannot be set at the top of the organization and then passed down the chain of command; rather, the workers at the bottom of the hierarchy, in this case teachers, often in cooperation with students, have to experiment with various technological approaches. Furthermore, the material they work with is not standardized; so that if they discover technological strategies which work with one class or one individual, these may not be equally effective with different students. As Perrow (1967) has pointed out, when technologies are uncertain and the material to be worked with not standardized, organizations generally delegate discretion to line workers.

Loose coupling between school systems and schools

The multiplicity of organizational goals and the uncertainty of school technology, along with the variable qualities of the students to be educated, lead to departures from strictly rational hierarchy in schools. Because of these organizational characteristics, principals are granted a good deal of de facto autonomy from the school district hierarchy (Burlingame, 1981; Meyer and Rowan, 1978; Peterson, 1984).[1] Under normal circumstances, they are left alone to run their schools as long as they do not violate clear system policies, there is no visible disorder, and there are no complaints from parents or students. However, this loose coupling of schools systems' hierarchical order represents an informal, not a formal, delegation of authority. It can always be revoked at the pleasure of higher administrators. Consequently, some tension and ambiguity chonically surrounds principals' rights to control goals and daily practice in their schools.

In Heartland, the introduction of the magnet schools changed the normal state of this relationship between the central office and the principals. Pressure to institute the promised programs in the magnet schools with all possible speed and to avoid situations which could anger volunteering parents made it clear that central office administrators stood ready to activate their powers of command over magnet school principals, should they need to take corrective action. Anyone who accepted a magnet school principalship accepted responsibility for implementing the special program announced for that school and was answerable to his or her superiors for showing that it had in fact been put into practice. At the same time, since the whole school system's welfare depended upon reasonable success in the magnet schools, supervisors had reason to give the principals as much tangible and intangible assistance as the needs of the system and other schools would allow in setting up their new programs and dealing with complaints.

Teachers' claims to professional autonomy and loose coupling

Just as principals have informal autonomy vis-à-vis the school system, so do teachers vis-à-vis principals (Dreeben, 1973; Jackson, 1968; Lortie, 1975), but theirs is supported by limited rights to professional prerogatives. Like members of other occupations, most notably social work and nursing, which have some advanced training and collective claim to expertise in uncertain technical situations, teachers are often called semi-professionals. They can make some arguments for formal autonomy but have made little headway with them. Despite their claims to special expertise, they remain formally line subordinates subject to bureaucratic authority.

Teachers generally are allowed to exercise some autonomy in practice concerning the content of their teaching and their classroom pedagogy, but must accept administrative directives in matters of coordination and logistics. These lines are blurred (Hanson, 1981) and variable from district to district, however. Schools live with a perpetual tension between a formally hierarchical structure, in which teachers are line subordinates, and a vaguely defined tradition of attenuated professionalism; they work out varying compromises between these two opposing principles.

Much of the actual independence which teachers enjoy on a practical level comes from informal loose coupling within schools, rather than from recognition of professional prerogatives. Thus, teachers work in rooms alone with students, shut off from the inquiring eyes of other adults. This physical isolation has led to a tradition which gives the closed classroom door a social as well as a physical reality. Principals generally give prior notice when they come to evaluate; other adults, whether other teachers or parents, usually do not enter the classroom unless they are assisting the teacher in some way. This kind of freedom from inspection and supervision is supported only by tradition, however; principals have the formal right to observe and supervise teachers' work in whatever fashion they find most effective.

Loose coupling, but not formal autonomy, within schools is also fostered by well-established patterns of granting increments in pay for seniority and educational credentials with no reference to any judgment of teaching performance. Such practices greatly restrict the power of administrators to reward and punish teachers on the basis of their judgment of teaching abilities and efforts, and thereby grant teachers a degree of freedom from supervisorial control. Still, this is autonomy by default. It grants the opportunity to deviate from accepted practice without fear of serious reprisal, but it does not give the right to explore alternative educational approaches with institutional support, nor does it give any rewards for success.

The resilience of hierarchical control in schools

There are also strong informal forces in schools which support the living out of their formal hierarchical forms. In order to act, school staffs must pursue some limited set of goals and choose a technological approach. Accordingly, traditions have grown up which define acceptable goals and technology rather firmly. Particularly at the secondary level, there are very strong conventions for organization of the curriculum into discrete subjects taught by separate teachers to groups of students who change classes according to a rigidly set temporal schedule. Further, in academic classes, the use of lecture, recitation, seatwork, and reading from textbooks (which are selected at the school or district level) is almost universal. At the elementary level, where the self-contained classroom provides more flexibility and more privacy, there is somewhat more variety in the technical processes used. Still, there have been efforts to introduce more standardization into elementary classrooms through the use of constraints such as 'teacher-proof' kits (Apple, 1983).

It is also important to remember that principals, like persons above them in the school district hierarchy, maintain full bureaucratic accountability. Where, as in Heartland, schools are given more specific tasks than usual and are more carefully scrutinized by the public and outside agencies such as the court, principals, whose accountability is underscored, will use their powers of command and evaluation of subordinates more vigorously than in more routine situations. Such action will sharpen the tension between bureaucratic hierarchy and teachers' claims to professional autonomy by changing the customary terms of informal compromise between the two.

Technology and logistics as influences in the life of a school

Sociologists use the term 'technology' to refer to the work process of an organization in its broadest sense, that is, everything which organization members do to create the kinds of products the organization exists to produce – in this case educated children. There is literature from a variety of traditions in the study of organizations which indicates that technology plays a major role in shaping the life of an organization and the behavior of its participants. Its effect on organizational hierarchy has already been discussed; it also shapes the daily experience of workers and has implications for their relationships with one another and with the organization as a symbolic entity (e.g. Blauner, 1964; Braverman, 1974; D. Metz, 1981).

The special approaches which the magnet schools were expected to implement affected their technology, and in two cases required significant departures from traditional technological patterns. The changes principals asked for were important in their relations with teachers, not only because they required teachers to make the effort to change, but because such changes concerned the heart of classroom teaching, where teachers' claims to autonomy are normally strongest. A struggle over a new technology was a struggle over teachers' professionalism and their right to autonomy.

Technology and student–teacher relations

The kind of technology which emerged in practice in each school had important effects on relations between teachers and students and among students. Though this topic has only recently been studied in detail, there is a literature which tells us something of the effects of traditional and non-traditional technologies in schools on students' relationships with their teachers and with peers of other races.

The literature on student–teacher relations already discussed shows that discouragement and feelings that academic competence

is a hopeless quest are an important source of students' participation in disruptive activities in classrooms. Consequently, a
different literature which explores the effects of classroom technology on self-evaluation is also relevant to student–teacher
relations. This literature finds that low achievers are more likely
to become discouraged when everyone is expected to do the same
work, leaving them to struggle with material it is hard for them
to grapple with, than when tasks with a variety of difficulty are
given. Also, when classroom tasks use only a few dimensions of
skill, students are more likely to see themselves as without talent
than in classrooms where learning involves a variety of kinds of
tasks. The form of academic evaluation and reward is also
important. If students are graded or informally evaluated in
comparison to one another, low achievers are likely to be more
discouraged than when students are evaluated for progress from
their past performances (Marshall and Weinstein, 1984).

Students form their own judgments that they are not competent
and can become rebellious solely in reaction to them. But their
problems become all the greater when they have to make their
lack of skill publicly visible in oral recitations. To escape such
experiences students will often defend their honor and pride
before others with imaginative hijinks or public disdain for the
teacher and the task. Some accounts suggest students often would
rather cause a disturbance and be ejected from the classroom for
discipline than read or answer questions aloud before the class
when they expect to do poorly (Herndon, 1969; Werthman, 1963).

Public performance also affects racial relations. A few children
of a minority race engaging in this kind of escape tactic can
earn a whole race a reputation for making trouble in the eyes of
conformist students of another race (Schofield and Sagar, 1979).
Furthermore, whole class recitation allows the class to see the
performance of others and to rank it, based partly on the teacher's
response. Bossert (1979) found that in elementary school classes
which used whole class recitation, students tended to form stable
friendship groups based on students' rank in academic skill, while
in classes which had more varied activities, children tended to
form more fluid friendship groups based on current common interests. Though Bossert's classes were overwhelmingly white, this
finding has implications for mixing children of different races.

The kinds of activities pursued in a class also affect the way in
which teachers interact with the class as a whole and with its

individual members. Recitation, in which a whole class is engaged simultaneously, is far more fragile and easily disturbed by an angry or restless child, than is individual seatwork or activities pursued by small groups together. Consequently teachers must bring different considerations to bear and respond in different ways when faced with disruptions during different kinds of classroom activities. As both Bossert (1979) and Hargreaves, Hestor, and Mellor (1975) point out, in a situation of whole class recitation, a teacher faced with distraction by one child must weigh his or her response to the individual in the light of its effect upon the total group with whom both teacher and student are simultaneously in interaction.

Bossert shows that teachers' disciplinary responses are briefer in whole class recitation than when students are working separately. The teacher tries to avoid interrupting the flow of activity and causing the rest of the class to wait. The rest of the class will be alert to the fairness of the treatment of different students in terms of similar punishment for similar acts without regard to the needs of the perpetrator, so discipline is more standardized during whole class recitation.

When a class is not all working together but has its attention divided on individual work or group projects, disciplinary situations can be handled differently. The whole class does not have to wait while the teacher deals with a restless or angry individual, but can work on undisturbed while the teacher talks with the offender quietly, privately, and, if necessary, at some length. The teacher thus has the time and privacy necessary to deal with the feelings underlying the student's action and can vary his or her response according to the needs of the student or the situation. The teacher can choose a disciplinary response without fearing that other class members will label the action unfair because it differs from what he or she did with some one else the day before (Bossert, 1979).

Finally, in recitation with the whole class, teachers tend to call most often on the stronger students because their correct responses help to move the class along (Bossert, 1979). When students are working separately, teachers are not under this pressure to allocate more time to high performers. In Bossert's study of a private elementary school, when the class was working at separate tasks, teachers allocated more time to low achievers than to high ones.

Logistical influences

A set of conditions in the schools which were more logistical than technological also affected the implementation of the innovations and the tone of relationships. For example, the buildings to which the schools were assigned had an effect on their programs. They could be perceived as located on black 'turf', white 'turf', or neutral territory. They varied in attractiveness and the ease with which they could be supervised. They provided varied space and amenities in classrooms requiring special facilities, such as those for laboratory science and art.

The use of time and space are important logistical conditions. The units of time into which the day was divided and the flexibility of this division was important. The kind of space available for various activities and the grounds on which space was allocated for varied needs made a difference. The assignment of students to instructional groups and of teachers to teams constituted the way persons moved through a day and the contexts in which they encountered one another.

The development of meaning in school life – faculty cultures

Persons within organizations generally develop a socially shared interpretation of the meaning of their work. In organizations like schools, where work activities cannot be closely constrained by rules, supervision, or predetermined technological routines, this shared perspective can have a significant impact on the way organization members actually carry out their tasks. Where the shared set of meanings includes broad perspectives on fundamental issues, we may speak of it as a subculture.

To understand this phenomenon one can draw on several traditions in the sociological study of organizations and upon anthropologists' treatments of subculture more generally. One relevant line of analysis takes a managerial perspective and is concerned with meaning as an element in directing the life of the whole organization. Chester Barnard (1939) argued that all members of an organization must share an understanding of, and attachment to, its purposes, if they are properly to coordinate their efforts in pursuit of common goals. Selznick (1957) advised managers that, especially where technical processes do not provide

53

detailed requirements to guide action, organizations can best be coordinated through the articulation of common goals which take on more than utilitarian worth for organizational participants, goals which are infused with value. Clark (1970) showed how such subcultural agreement can have an effect as he analyzed the way in which three private colleges had grown into successful distinctive organizations pursuing special missions.

Recently more organizational analysts have paid attention to the importance of common meaning in maintaining coordinated effort in an organization (Lodahl and Mitchell, 1980; Pfeffer, 1981; Sproull, 1981). This interest by researchers has been paralleled in a series of books aimed at organizational managers which proclaim the importance in successful firms of unified systems of meaning (Deal and Kennedy, 1982; Kanter, 1983; Pascale and Athos, 1981; Peters and Waterman, 1982). Since the magnet schools studied here were intended to be distinctive, they were settings where one might expect administrators to try to develop and nurture such a sense of meaning.

Meaning also finds its way into organizational life without managerial sponsorship. Subcultures grow up among groups of persons who work together or who share a common background and have some form of regular social contact. Such a subculture may incorporate substantial elements from the culture of the larger society or from that of subgroups such as an occupation, ethnic group, or homogeneous community to which its adherents belong (Blauner, 1964; Gregory, 1983; McPherson, 1972). An organizational subculture may also run somewhat counter to the larger societal culture, as its participants build it up in response to the common dilemmas and experiences which they encounter together within the organization (Kemnitzer, 1977; D. Metz, 1981; Spradley and Mann, 1975). In either case, such an organizational subculture will provide a coherent rationale for the way its workers direct their efforts and the level of commitment they give the organization.[2]

It is helpful in analyzing the cultures which arose in these schools to remember the qualities of culture as anthropologists analyze it.[3] Culture is not a systematic set of logically interrelated propositions about values, norms and the nature of the empirical world, but a broad, diffuse, and potentially contradictory body of shared understandings about both what is and what ought to be. These understandings are rarely articulated as abstract propositions. Rather they are elements of common sense, so well known by the persons sharing the culture that sensible adults do not need to mention them. Among initiates, cultural knowledge is too self-evident to require discussion (Spindler and Spindler, 1983).

This tacit quality of culture gives it much of its force. Because its items are not discussed, they are not debated by either insiders or outsiders. Internal contradictions are not brought to attention. Differences between the beliefs of persons adhering to the culture and others with whom they may mingle are seen in terms of specific issues and not in terms of differences over underlying assumptions.

While cultural beliefs may grow out of structural realities, they are interpretations of them and as meaning systems gain a degree of independence from them. Consequently, they may seem to outsiders to be at odds with those realities. They are perspectives through which the world is interpreted, not tentatively held empirical generalizations regularly held up for revision.

At each of the three schools studied, faculty who interacted frequently developed a common perspective. In none of the schools did every teacher share this perspective in its entirety, but in every school there was a dominant perspective which set the tone of the faculty's collective interaction with students, with each other, and with the principal. These common perspectives could be called subcultures as they included broad generalizations about the way the world works and higher order values, both of which colored teachers' perceptions of many specific events and practices. Teachers at different schools interpreted similar situations or actions differently as a result.

The three chapters which follow describe and analyze the character of each of the three schools studied. They are organized around the influences on that character introduced here in general terms. The chapters follow a single pattern in order to give the reader a constant framework into which to fit the details at each school and a comparative context within which to see the workings of each influence as it operated at the different schools.

Each chapter opens with a description of the school's history before it became a magnet school and its founding as a magnet school. This section also describes the kinds of parents and students who were recruited to the school and the formal blueprint for its innovation. The school's character in terms of the experiences the adults provided for the students is described next; the quality of relationships among the major groups in the school and the form of the program as it was actually practiced are included. The next section analyzes the effects of technological approaches and logistical arrangements on the school's character. A description of the subculture developed among each faculty and its impact follows. The final section of each chapter presents the principal's attempts to shape the overall program for the students and his or her relationship with the teachers as an influence on the character of the school.

Chapter 4

Adams Avenue School for Individually Guided Education

Adams Avenue Middle School was established as a magnet school offering 'Individually Guided Education,' or IGE, in the fall of 1976, the first fall of desegregation in Heartland. It was located on the northern edge of downtown Heartland in an old elementary school building, built before 1900.

Environmental influences

The establishment of the school

In the late 1960s, the Adams Avenue school building was rented out to a private school because the neighborhood no longer housed enough children to support it. The history of the magnet school started in 1972, when the school system took the building back in order to house a seventh grade annex to Williams Junior High School, an overcrowded black school in the poorest part of the near East Side.

Williams Annex was established in the hope that it would relieve severe problems of discipline and under-achievement at Williams Junior High. The annex was staffed by teachers who volunteered to leave the main Williams building, by teachers who were low in seniority there, and by new teachers, mostly beginners. Mrs Michaels, a former counselor at Williams, headed this young faculty as 'administrator in charge.' She functioned as a principal but was formally subject to the authority of the principal at the Williams building.

The staff at Williams Annex exercised a good deal of initiative in developing its program. They obtained district permission to follow a 'multi-unit' plan which divided the student body into three groups, each of slightly over 100 students, and each sharing four teachers of basic academic subjects. Since the teams of four teachers had the same students, they could collectively plan their program and collaborate on strategies for helping individual students.

In the summer of 1976, as the first magnet schools were being planned, administrators at the central office identified the Williams Annex site as appropriate for a magnet program. The decision was influenced by the school's easy access to the central public library, a museum, and downtown businesses, as well as its accessibility by public bus from all parts of the city. During the summer, Mrs Michaels was consulted about being the principal of the new magnet school. She had some voice in choosing Individually Guided Education, sometimes called IGE/Multi-unit, which includes a unit plan of the kind Williams Annex had had. She already had some familiarity with the IGE approach as well.

The teachers were first notified of these changes in their school in August. They were given the chance to transfer, but virtually all stayed to be part of the Adams Avenue magnet school even though many had never even heard of IGE. Before school started, they received a week of inservice training, but their workshop was shared with several elementary schools, and so was geared to elementary patterns of curriculum, staffing and scheduling, patterns which are in many ways inappropriate to a middle school program. Furthermore, the IGE plan as it had been developed by experts was designed for elementary schools.[1] The principal recommended some books on the approach, but most of the teachers found these too general to be helpful.

As a result, when school opened in September, the faculty felt themselves very scantily prepared to be IGE teachers. To compound their difficulties, teaching materials specially adapted to IGE were scarce or non-existent. Since there had previously been no sixth or eighth graders in the building, there were too few materials of any kind for these grades. Yet despite these deficits, parents, the press, and representatives of the court hovered over the school, expecting to see the distinctive and implicitly superior program which had been advertised during the summer.

In the second year of desegregation, which was Adams's second as a magnet school, the district obtained federal funds for magnet schools from Title VII. Adams received generous allowances for materials and curriculum planning. Teachers were given released time to study IGE, to plan a coherent IGE curriculum in each subject, and to review and order appropriate materials. Several teachers, though not all, found that these opportunities significantly increased their competence as IGE teachers.

The study at Adams Avenue was conducted in the last half of the school's third year as a magnet school. By that time, even the oldest students had started their middle school experience at Adams Avenue, and the school no longer seemed brand new. The teachers and principal had a sense of having hit their stride, of having a school which, despite some continuing adjustments, was developing a coherent and solid program.

Recruitment of parents

In its first year, Adams Avenue attracted a significant number of well-educated parents with professional or managerial jobs. While these parents did not constitute a numerical majority, their presence in the school was important. Many were not reluctant to give advice to individual teachers and the principal and then to note carefully whether it was followed. As suggested in Chapter 2, such parents put a lot of pressure on the school, and in fact the principal spent a great deal of her time, especially in the first year, dealing with individual parents' concerns. In addition, the assistant principal invested his energies in planning social events for parents and children, trying to generate group feeling and good will.

At the same time, parents with the confidence to give opinions and the skill to make themselves heard became an asset to the school. At the end of the first year when the central office decided that things were going so well at Adams that this small school did not need an assistant principal, the parents argued vigorously to retain the position and got the papers to cover the issue. As a result, the central administration restored a part-time position. Further, the parents were instrumental in achieving the dropping of the proposals before the school board, in the summer of 1978 and again that fall, to close the old Adams building and move the program to another building, where the resident staff would be added to Adams's and a larger student body recruited.

The number of parents with substantial education, income, and social status shrank somewhat over the years. Such parents were drawn in large numbers to the middle school for the gifted and talented, which opened in the second year of desegregation. At the same time, as students' actual experience at Adams began to give it a reputation which could be spread through the word of mouth networks of community and kinship, more parents from 'ordinary' working and lower-middle-class families were drawn to the school.

Recruitment of students

By the third year of Adams's life, the change in its recruitment was visible in the characteristics of its student body. The eighth graders, the last group from the first year's recruitment, were the only class with a significant number of extremely high achievers, according to the teachers. In both its social and academic characteristics, the student body had come to reflect the city as a whole with surprising accuracy – and that meant that the majority of children had modest economic means and below average academic skills.

Table 4-1 shows some characteristics of the students compared to middle school students in the city as a whole. Fifty-two percent of Adams's 328 students were from minority races. All but a few were black; there were some Native Americans and Asians and some Hispanics who were counted with whites for desegregation quotas. The racial ratio was very close to that for the whole city. There is some evidence that the mix of students at Adams during the year of the study included more poor children than that in the city as a whole that year. Fifty-nine percent of the lunches served were to children whose family incomes entitled them to free or reduced price lunches, while only 43 percent of the lunches served to middle school students in the city as a whole were to qualifying children in 1978–9. Thirty-four percent of the children at Adams met the guidelines to be eligible for assistance from federal Title I funds for poor children, making the school qualify to be designated a Title I school. Many of Adams's children also showed signs of poverty in their dress, and signs of a lack of parental education in their English usage.

TABLE 4–1 *Characteristics of students at Adams Avenue Middle School compared to those in the city of Heartland, 1978–9*

	Adams	Citywide middle schools
Initial enrollment	328	17,427
Percent minority students	51	47
Percent free lunches to total lunches	59	43

Source: Heartland School District *Profile of Schools*

Tables 4–2 and 4–3 present scores on nationally standardized tests of reading and mathematics achievement for the cohort of students who were seventh graders at the time of the study. These scores are for tests which they had taken two years earlier, at the end of the fifth grade, before they entered Adams; they indicate the skills with which these students entered the school. Scores for fifth graders in the city of Heartland as a whole in the same year are included for comparison. The figures for the school and the city represent the number of students in each group scoring at or below the national percentile ranking given at the left. Thus, in Table 4-2, which reports reading scores, 66 percent of Adams students scored below the point which marked the 50th percentile in a national sample. In other words, before entrance to Adams two-thirds of its students scored as low as the bottom half of a national sample of students. Similarly, 34 percent of Adams's students scored below the 25th percentile nationally, that is, a third of Adams's students scored in the bottom quarter in comparison to national norms. Math scores were similar.

Comparison of the two columns will show the reader that Adams's students' scores very closely paralleled those for the students of the city as a whole. The wide dispersion of scores was as significant as the preponderance of low scores. By subtracting the percentage below a given point from 100, one can see that, in reading, 5 percent of Adams's students scored with the top 10 percent of a national sample and 17 percent scored with the top 25 percent of the national sample. The school had to deal with a population 17 percent of whom, almost one-fifth, were in the top quarter nationally, and 19 percent of whom, another fifth, were in the bottom tenth nationally.

TABLE 4–2 *Percentages of students at Adams and citywide scoring at or below national percentile rankings on the Metropolitan Achievement Tests in reading at the end of grade 5, 1977*

Percentile ranking	Adams (N=125)	City (N=6,747)
90th	95	96
75th	83	87
50th	66	66
25th	34	36
10th	19	17

Source: Heartland School District computer data files

TABLE 4–3 *Percentages of students at Adams Avenue and citywide scoring at or below national percentile rankings on the Metropolitan Achievement Tests in mathematics at the end of grade 5, 1977*

Percentile ranking	Adams (N=125)	City (N=6,651)
90th	96	96
75th	86	87
50th	65	66
25th	33	36
10th	16	17

Source: Heartland School District computer data files

The blueprint for Individually Guided Education

Because Individually Guided Education is a specific plan developed by a specific group of persons, it is at least in theory well-defined. However, the sources which define IGE are not always specific or consistent – as those teachers who tried to read about it discovered. In practice, there is not a clear blueprint to follow.[2] Consequently, the principal was able to have broad discretion in defining the crucial elements of IGE for the school.

As the teachers came to understand IGE, the heart of its distinctiveness lay in classroom practice. In interviews, teachers consistently defined IGE in terms of two major clusters of requirements, though some emphasized one over the other. The first of these consisted of the specification of a number of discrete learning objectives for each subject in each grade. Children were to be tested on these specific objectives before instruction, and again afterwards, to verify their progress. Each child's level of performance before and after instruction was to be carefully charted. The second major cluster of elements concerned the grouping of children for instruction. After children were tested on each objective, they were to be grouped according to the progress they had already made and then instructed from the point where their current knowledge left off. Thus there were to be groups of children with similar skills working together on each objective pursued. These groups were expected to be fluid; they were to be reconstituted when a new objective was introduced.

The school maintained the multi-unit structure which had been in place at Williams Annex before the school adopted IGE. Each unit had four homeroom groups which traveled through their academic classes together. The unit teachers had an hour a day for common planning and had leaders who met with the principal regularly in an 'Instructional Improvement Committee,' which provided two-way communication between the teachers of each unit and the administration. Teachers took the unit structure more or less for granted; they did not think of it as part of IGE, but as a separate part of the school's organization.

School character

At each of the schools some issues seemed to be foremost in the minds of the staff; they spoke about these issues at length or with feeling in interviews and they spent much time attending to them. At Adams, most of the adults centered their attention on their work with the students. The teachers' energy was directed toward planning and executing classroom teaching, arranging for a variety of extra events and activities offered during the school day, and directing the extensive extra-curricular program, in which a large proportion of teachers were involved. Teachers noted with pleasure that they knew the students well and were able to work fairly effectively with them. Though they spoke of the curriculum in terms of small, discreet bits of learning of the kind emphasized in IGE, they spoke of their teaching, as a whole, more in terms of their effective relationships with students.

The school was notable for its constructive social relationships, especially between teachers and a potentially volatile student body, but also among students and among adults. This is not to say that there were not significant strains between teachers and students, among students, and among adults, but that these provided counterpoint to a situation in which harmony was the predominant theme.

Having studied desegregated junior high schools in two communities which had significant numbers of poorly achieving students living in poor economic circumstances (Metz, 1978a, 1978b, 1978c), I was immediately struck by the good order at Adams, and by the positive tone of classroom interchanges between teachers and students despite the presence of a potentially volatile student body. I also noticed more voluntary interracial mixing among students than I had seen elsewhere. The overall tone of positive relations in the school did not seem to be a spontaneous phenomenon, however, but rather seemed to take active efforts to create and to maintain, even though these were not always consciously undertaken or deliberately designed. The presence of exceptions to Adams's generally positive relations underscores this point. A few teachers had fairly serious conflict with their classes; some children avoided those of other races; and some teachers were in all-out conflict with the principal. Good relationships were a fragile construction.

Teacher–student interaction

Adams followed the district's policy of creating classes of students who were heterogeneous in ability. Within these heterogeneous classrooms, small groups of students who performed similarly on pretests worked together on similar tasks. However, during the study year, the school did have roughly homogeneous classes in the eighth grade, which had the most diversity because of a fairly sizable group of very highly achieving students. Still, even in the classes attended by the eighth grade group with the lowest skills, which was also an overwhelmingly black group, neither students nor teachers engaged in the kind of conflictual behavior described by other authors as typical of lower track classes with lower class or low caste students (e.g. Ball, 1981; Furlong, 1977; Hargreaves, 1967; Metz, 1978a, 1978b; Schwartz, 1981). Excerpts from an account of an English class with this group suggest the tone of interaction:

Mrs Pohl showed a filmstrip on how a telephone works to [one] group. They then worked on two worksheets about it. Mrs Pohl had them read aloud six statements about the filmstrip which they were to put in order. She asked them which might come first. When a student named the last for the first, she asked her to read it aloud again. The class seemed to discover together – another student pointed out – that the statement would come better at the end. As they went along Mrs Pohl reminded them of a picture on the worksheet which gave some visual evidence on the steps.

Mrs Pohl spoke of there being five items and the students corrected her that there were six. As she looked for the third item, she said there seemed to be a step missing, but two students pointed out that it was included in the second statement. The students made these corrections and Mrs Pohl responded to them in a matter of fact way centered on the task, not on the fact of a mistake.

Though the class work was simple, the students seemed involved in the task, were willing to contribute aloud, and were cooperative. They did not tease or defy the teacher when she made a mistake, and she accepted their corrections without embarrassment. In a science class, the same group of students were more active and restless, but they were serious and cooperative when they were given work. And once again the teacher took them seriously and kept the class focused on the academic task.

The students came in at 12.30 from lunch, hale and active. The students took their seats with little ado and Mr Crow called the roll out loud. They were restless and noisy during the process. Mr Crow threatened one boy that if he could not be polite he could leave. He made the same threat to a second student later, but neither time with great conviction in his voice, and he did not follow up his threats.

Mr Crow went to the board at the back corner and wrote 'How a Thermometer Works.' By 12.37, he was in full swing explaining a thermometer and the class was listening very quietly . . . [As he gave his explanation, he asked them to supply the three forms of matter, which they correctly and quickly did. He set up an experiment with unmarked thermometers for measuring the freezing and then the boiling point of water. He talked as they set up the experiments at their tables. They began to chatter and he called upon individuals for attention. But when his voice changed to give some new crucial piece of information, they grew quiet and listened. After giving careful directions for procedure and safety, Mr Crow went around checking on individuals' progress.]

Mr Crow went to the board after the experiment and summarized what the experiment had shown.

The teachers in both classes viewed the students as serious academic learners and encouraged their academic efforts. Although the students were not always quiet, they were attentive to communications relevant to the task at hand and actively engaged in doing their assigned work. For the most part, both teachers and students oriented their interaction toward academic matters, cooperated with one another, and treated one another in a friendly fashion. Neither teachers nor students expressed hostility toward the other.

In other classes at Adams as well, the tone was task-oriented, although students did engage in distracting activities. When students talked about non-academic matters while working at their desks, teachers often did not interfere as long as students were regularly completing the tasks. When students distracted others during a presentation to the whole group or failed to complete the tasks set them, teachers would reprimand them; if they persisted in such behavior, teachers sometimes lost their patience and raised their voices. But their reprimands assailed the activity, not the person involved; teachers did not assault students' pride or attempt to shame them. Disciplinary encounters were simple matters of children's interests competing with teachers' responsibility for academic tasks. They were not the dramatically loaded affairs described in the literature which details persistent conflict between lower-class, poorly achieving, often minority, students and teachers who they believe do not respect them as learners (Metz, 1978a, 1978b; Werthman, 1963; Willis, 1977).

Formal indicators also suggested an absence of conflict in both the classroom and the school at large. Adams gave few of the school system's 'yellow cards,' formal referrals of a child to an administrator for discipline, which were noted on a child's record. In May, after 165 days of school, only 239 yellow cards had been issued at Adams, an average of less than two per day for over 300 children. Through May, suspensions totaled less than one for every ten children. Adams's spare use of yellow cards and suspensions partially reflects a preference for handling problems informally, rather than an absence of problems. But that very preference and its practice were a part of the amicable relations between teachers and students.

Thus, while Adams's students were not sweetly obedient angels who never angered their teachers, the general tone of student–teacher relationships was positive. Teachers and students chatted with one another before and after class and engaged in good-humored joking and ribbing. Teachers often used humor in asking children to desist from minor distractions or to get down to work.

A number of unusual practices symbolized trust and courtesy between students and teachers. Nearly every lunchtime, students would knock at the door of the teachers' lounge in search of materials or information. The teachers welcomed them into the lounge and courteously gave what was asked. Teachers also gave students keys to get materials from unsupervised locked areas. After school, students played basketball on the playground, using school balls. In May, the assistant principal said that not one ball had disappeared throughout the year, and that the students returned the balls to the office without being reminded.

Inter-racial relationships

Students had better relations with others of their own race than with those of a different race, but there was less conflict and more crossing of the racial line than is described in many studies of desegregated schools.[3] No teacher at Adams spoke of having difficulty in getting children of different races to work together in the classroom, and I saw none. When asked about their voluntary relations, a few teachers said that some of the children had trouble developing smooth relations across the races. (Black teachers were more likely to make this observation, either because they were more observant or because the students were less inhibited in their presence.)

In the dining-room and the playground, where children chose their companions, in all three units some groups were all white, some all black, some mostly of one race with just one or two of another, and some thoroughly mixed. One person who supervised lunchtime play for the seventh grade unit every day described their spring play patterns as follows:

'Every day you'd see one basketball game that has almost all white and Latin kids playing. You'd see another basketball game with all black kids. But boys and girls mixed. Then you'd see another game – that's the biggest game out there – that has white and black kids playing in it. That's the full court game.

'And you'd see a jump rope game that has almost always all black girls in it. Then you'd see a keep-away game that would be maybe 70 percent white and 30 percent black. Then you'd see a bunch of kids standing around and talking that would be mixed racially.'

In the late spring, I interviewed nineteen students chosen within quotas for grade level, ability, race, and sex. Of these nineteen students, all but two claimed to have good friends of a different race, and some spontaneously named the friend(s). All but two preferred racial diversity when asked whether they would like their next school to be mainly of their own race or mixed half and half. Some students' responses may have been more a reflection of a cultural norm at the school that one ought to have friends of a different race, than of the reality of actually having such friends. However, even such cultural expectations have some significance. The students spoke in ways which indicated that many of them developed new understandings of race, after coming to the school from highly segregated environments.

A white seventh grade boy with average achievement explained why he would prefer a mixed high school this way:

'Well, when they first started integration I thought the black kids were real mean and all that. You know, I'd never even met a person like that. And when I came here they were real nice. Some of 'em were. So I figure if they're nice here, then they can be nice there.'

An eighth grade black girl, who was an average achiever according to teachers and who defined herself as a leader, expressed her observations on race tersely and unsentimentally. Asked if she had good friends who were not black, she named three girls then said, 'They're really nice. I don't go by the skin color. I just go by the personality.' She explained her choice of a racially mixed high school for the following year this way: 'Because I've been around too many black people for too long and I have to get adjusted; so when I get older I'll know not to just hang around blacks. To hang around blacks and whites.'

A seventh grade black girl who was a strong student said she had hesitated to come to the school because she had not had much contact with whites and was worried about what it would be like. But after she came, she had discovered, she said with a beatific smile, that 'They're just like me!'

Still, the school did not overcome all racial separation. Two students claimed no friends of another race and two preferred a segregated high school. When asked how students of different races got along, one of these, a black seventh grade boy with low skills, who had had negative experiences with whites at schools on the West Side, responded:

'Get along all right. Most of them. I don't know what they be doing. I don't be around them that much. . . . I be around the black kids a lot. Playing basketball or eating around with them. We all eat together you know. The same big old group. I don't know what the rest of them do.'

Additionally, a few students spoke of some fights in the school and of some mean and destructive individual students. Although the destructive students were identified as black, when they were identified by race at all, the respondents associated these activities with 'some kids' or a 'few kids' rather than with a whole racial group.

The students I interviewed expressed an overall contentment with the school which was striking to me, even after several months of experience in its halls and classrooms. Many positively glowed as they described it. Asked what they would change if given magical powers to change anything they liked, a few changed nothing, and most of the rest changed some aspect of the physical facility, most often the small playground.

There was more tension among the adults at Adams than

between teachers and students. There was a split between those deeply attached to the union and others, especially those who did not strike in the spring of 1977, two years before the study. Some teachers were in rather severe conflict with the principal, as well; union leaders led this faction. These relationships will be discussed in more detail in dealing with the principal's impact on the school.

The program in practice

For the most part, the teachers followed the two essential clusters of practices which they understood to be the core of IGE. They kept charts of students' progress on specific skills, and they assigned students to small groups for instruction. These practices were easily visible to visitors or to parents from walking through the school and talking briefly with teachers. The principal also could check them, by visiting classrooms and by consulting with teachers about their charts, something she did with each teacher four times during the study year.

But if one looked below what was easily visible, there was variation in the teachers' compliance with IGE. Some teachers rotated students through the same set of tasks, so that even though they were split into groups, they did not have differentiated work. Some constructed precise-looking charts on the basis of estimates of students' progress in various areas, rather than on the basis of careful pre-testing and post-testing of specific skills. All the teachers agreed that IGE required more effort from the teacher than regular teaching. Some teachers did not comply with it because they were unwilling to do the considerable work required in developing objectives, constructing pre-tests and post-tests, and setting up differentiated tasks according to students' skills.

Some did not comply as a matter of principle. They argued that the logic of their subject was ill-suited to the logic of IGE, though virtually no one questioned that it was a reasonable approach to teaching overall.[4] Others argued more simply that their subject required many demonstrations of skills, given most easily to the whole group, or that their subjects were new to most students of this age and every one needed the fundamentals.[5]

Some teachers who came to Adams from elementary schools found IGE, at least understood in a relaxed way, to involve little that was new. They said they had always grouped students for instruction according to their skills and kept track of their progress. There were also quite a few teachers who had become enthusiasts for IGE, who said that it helped them to become more systematic in their teaching and made it easier to deal with students' diverse skills.

Even the teachers who were relaxed in their approach to IGE and those who resisted on principle, seemed to have learned to teach in a special way because of it. Both in their classes and in their discussion of their goals and practices, they conveyed clear pictures of the purpose for each day's instruction and gave evidence of having thought systematically about how the instruction they planned would further that purpose. They seemed to develop fairly good understandings of each child's skills and deficits and to consider strategies to lessen the deficits. Even though the teachers as a whole followed IGE in less detail than appeared on the surface, in general it did lead those who were conscientious about their teaching to become very serious about imparting the basic skills of their subjects, to be reflective about how to get those across to the varied individuals in their classes, and to measure individuals' progress fairly carefully.

The teams of teachers for each unit, which were part of the multi-unit aspect of IGE, all took their work seriously. They met regularly and were task-oriented in their meetings. They spent a lot of time discussing individual students and how to reach them most effectively; they talked about strategies for getting them to pay attention and put out effort to learn, and sometimes about ways to explain effectively to students who had trouble comprehending the material. They also discussed social relationships between students which distracted them from work, were disruptive to the class, or generated quarrels. These meetings were also the place where they planned common special activities.

The school's program was also distinctive in the great variety of special activities which took place during the school day. Each team of teachers was expected to develop four long units of study which crosscut the various subjects and were centered around a theme. Some of these had traditional academic content, such as 'astronomy' in the eighth grade, but some were only partly academic, such as the sixth grade's study of transportation, and the seventh grade's 'Who Am I?.' Children were grouped across classes and in small groups which were not geared to ability level for these activities. The school also sponsored a lot of field trips.

Classes made regular trips to the central library and the science and social studies museum which were within three blocks of the school and could be reached for an outing of a single class period. These varied activities added spice and variety to the heavily skill-oriented curriculum encouraged by IGE and by the need of most students to catch up in their knowledge of basics.

The school also sponsored a wide variety of extra-curricular activities ranging from bowling leagues to an ambitious musical show for which students made costumes and sets. Students studying Spanish went to Mexico and the camping club went to Canada, while the camera club made their own simple box cameras from cardboard. There was a 'math track team' of strong math students which did well in citywide competitions among middle schools. These extra-curricular activities helped to provide enrichment for the stronger students, but many of them also allowed students with varied academic skills to participate together in situations where common interests and non-academic skills were relevant. All but three of the nineteen students interviewed participated in at least one extra-curricular activity.

Technological and logistical influences on school character

IGE changed the technological routines which are traditional in secondary schools. The simplest required changes, implemented even by the teachers who were not enthusiastic about IGE, had important effects in facilitating a social context which encouraged good relationships between low achievers and teachers and good relationships among peers of different races.

The effects of technological arrangements on student–teacher relationships

Curricular structure
With its injunction to test each child's level of accomplishment on all skills and its assumption that the children of any given class will perform at scattered levels, IGE throws into question the significance of a concept of 'sixth grade work' or 'eighth grade work'. It thus lifts some of the stigma of failure from both students and teachers when sixth grade students need work on skills often

included in a fourth grade curriculum. If students' post-tests indicate that they have made visible progress since the pre-test, even though their skills may still not have reached the sixth grade standard, both they and their teacher can none the less see solid evidence of the fruits of their labor together. Charts make the fact of progress more official. Such visible forward movement encourages effort and mutual respect in both parties; both would be demoralized by the same students' repeated failure on standard tasks set 'at grade level.' Teachers at Adams talked about slow students' progress with satisfaction. When they spoke to me about students, they also were less quick than teachers elsewhere spontaneously to characterize them as low achievers. In interviews, slow students spoke about their studies with a sense of legitimate participation.

The IGE plan also allowed high achievers to dispense with 'grade level' work if they were already competent in it, and to move on to new material. Thus, even though they were in the same classroom with much slower learners, they did not have to wait for them. The school also attempted to keep the most advanced students stimulated by offering them enriching experiences. Some of the strongest students had special small group activities in advanced math and advanced reading; in the latter, they learned how to use the resources of the central library to do research. They also tended to gravitate to academically oriented extra-curricular activities such as the 'math track team.'

Academic reward structure

Adams adopted a report card which emphasized effort rather than accomplishment by replacing the traditional A, B, C with two kinds of grades for each subject. One grade indicated the level at which the student was working in the subject, while the other indicated his or her degree of effort. Thus, at least in theory, a hardworking sixth grader progressing well with fourth grade skills might earn an 'I', for superior effort and progress, while a lackadaisical sixth grader who did not progress far, despite eighth grade level skills already acquired, might receive an 'E', for inadequate effort and progress. ('G' indicated adequate effort and progress.)

The honor roll was based upon the number of 'I's, not the level of work at which they were earned. This system was intended to provide rewards for effort and progress to less skilled students, and to keep advanced students from resting on their laurels. While not all teachers could bring themselves to give the letter grades for effort and progress which would put industrious but unskilled students on the honor roll and take easygoing but skilled ones off it, the system was official policy. Teachers followed it enough to change the composition of the honor roll to include many children who would not have qualified on the basis of their current skill levels ranked against their classmates'.

Thus, IGE worked indirectly to equalize social prestige among Adams's socially, racially, and academically diverse student body. Those with low skills still had a chance to earn academic legitimacy and even academic honors. They did not have to feel that to make an effort at academic learning was to embrace a role at which failure was preordained. Their teachers also had a chance to feel that they were making progress and doing legitimate teaching even with students who started well behind the average standard for middle school. Both students' and teachers' morale was supported by these arrangements; they did not have to blame and attack one another in order to disassociate themselves from the failure of their mutual efforts.

Of course, as the school did away with ranking students by their absolute levels of achievement, and equalized social prestige, it weakened the competitive rewards given to the students who not only worked hard but whose achievement was outstanding (most of whom were also white middle-class students). Some teachers feared that the strongest students were insufficiently pushed to excel because they were not given more competitive rewards than the hardworking but less skilled.[6]

Classroom activity structure
Except in the eighth grade, classroom groups were academically heterogeneous. Since the principal insisted on grouping according to skill as a crucial element of IGE, academic classes were virtually universally broken into small groups. (Eighth grade classes often were also.)

Because there was ordinarily only one adult in the room with the students, the children had to work independently most of the time. It was rare to see a teacher talk to a whole class for more than a few minutes. It was even rarer for students to discuss or answer questions except in small groups. Even within those groups, the most common pattern of activity was a brief explanation by the teacher followed by interaction between the teacher

74

and individuals as the teacher moved around assisting, assessing, and answering questions. Those not in the group being assisted worked at their desks.

This pattern of activity shaped the experience of students and the constraints operating on teachers with profound consequences for their relationship. First, this pattern of activity kept students' skill levels relatively private. Since students were virtually never called upon to perform before large groups, and rarely before small ones, those with low skills did not need to suffer public embarrassment. Nor did they attempt to avoid it by creating humorous or angry diversions from the task at hand in the pattern described in the literature cited in Chapter 3.

Second, students' rhythm of work became much less dependent on others' actions than it is where there is a great deal of lecture or whole class recitation. An industrious child could work undisturbed by others' social interchanges, while a restless child could doodle, sharpen a pencil, or chat with a neighbor without bothering anyone else but that neighbor. Such distracting activities, which could bring all students' educational activity to a halt and require the teacher's time and energy during whole class recitation, were part of the flow of individual activities and had little effect upon the whole.

Teachers took full advantage of the freedom conferred by the children's independent work to confer with individuals. During much of each class period, they could deal fairly privately with individuals in response to inattention or in giving discipline for activities which distracted others. In these discussions, as well as those on academic topics, they could get to know individuals and develop some understanding of their perspective on their experience in the school.

Furthermore, teachers did not have to call on the best students to keep the class moving in the right direction. They seemed to spend a good deal of time with those having difficulty. Both strong and weak students seemed to find this overall arrangement satisfactory. When the students who were interviewed were asked what was special or distinctive about Adams as a magnet school, one-third, mostly students whom teachers described as above average or average in achievement, said that the school allowed them to go at their own pace. Another third, all but one of them described by teachers as below average or average in achievement, replied that the teachers helped students more at Adams.

A black girl with weak skills, in a lower group in the eighth grade, described getting a good deal of assistance:

ANGIE: IGE means Individually Guided Education. That means – individualized means – one person that they guide on their own kind of education. In their own special needs, what they need to improve on . . .
INTERVIEWER: And what do the teachers actually do that makes it individually guided?
ANGIE: Well . . . like in my math class he'll sit down with me and he'll go through step-by-step instructions on how to do it, and then he'll have me do a problem to make sure I got it. And then if he thinks I do got it he'll give me a quiz. And if I don't pass the quiz, then he'll just help me all over again. Ain't no hassle about it, fussing and all that.

Angie's comments remind us that, in traditional activity structures, teachers as well as students may become frustrated and angry when a student does not perform well or when the teacher has to make the rest of the class wait in order to give another explanation to a student who did not understand the first one. Adams's teachers did not have the pressure of a waiting class to make them 'fuss' at a student who needed repeated explanations.

Student–teacher relationships as a cycle of mutual response
Because the academic patterns and activity structure of Adams's classes lessened strains on individual students, and reduced their need to create classroom disruption to distract from their academic deficiencies, they also affected the character of the classroom as a whole. Since the teacher had few such disruptions to deal with, time that might have been taken up with discipline was free for academic instruction or personal conversation. The teacher's emotional energy was also freed for encouraging individual efforts or devising new strategies of explanation. Further, these helpful activities indicated to students that teachers seriously intended to teach, and therefore increased students' trust in them. Trusting the teachers made students even less likely to engage in angry outbursts or teasing sideshows, and teachers were once again freed for positive academic and personal activities.

The effects of technological arrangements on inter-racial relations

Equality of status

The curricular structure, academic rewards, and classroom activity structure also affected inter-racial relations among the students. They worked to equalize students' status by de-emphasizing students' initial differences in academic skills. Black students, whose academic skills were on the average weaker, were not as strongly disadvantaged by this fact as they might have been. It was also helpful that there were quite a few white children whose skills were weak and a few black students whose skills were strong.

The system of grouping within the rooms did give some visibility to differences in skills. Still, the groups did not suggest a tight association of race and ability because there were usually four to five, and at least the middle ones, often all, were racially mixed. The structure of the curriculum, academic rewards, and classroom activity structure all helped inter-racial relations by lowering conflict between poorly achieving students and teachers. If some of the low achievers and teachers had engaged in more conflict, even without race itself being any part of that conflict, black children would have been in more conflict with the teachers than would white children. Such a pattern could give a reputation as 'the bad kids' to a whole racial group. Classroom conflict is both more visible and more dramatically impressive than cooperation; a few disruptors make much more impression on others than many quiet cooperators (Schofield and Sagar, 1979).

Cooperation

After students were divided into groups who needed the same level of instruction and the same kind of practice on the academic tasks being worked on at a given time, these groups were seated around tables. Children at the tables, usually in racially mixed groups, were allowed to confer about their work. While such cooperation among individuals for their separate success has less strong effects in welding solidarity than does cooperation for a collective goal, it still seems to encourage positive interpersonal relations (Schofield, 1982). This is particularly true when the persons cooperating do so as equals (Cohen, 1980), and since students were placed together at tables because they performed similarly on pre-tests, their most relevant academic skills were roughly comparable.

Teachers did not attempt to prevent all conversations on non-academic topics among these racially mixed groups at the tables, as long as the students were completing their assigned work promptly. Such conversations offered students a chance to explore the differences and similarities between themselves and children of another race. As students at the same tables came to know each other, they also developed acquaintanceships which carried over to the voluntarily structured contexts of the dining-room and playground. This carryover of crossracial association from classroom to lunchroom and playground was especially likely because students did not have continuing neighborhood and elementary school peer groups to retreat to (and answer to) in these voluntary settings.

The plethora of special activities at Adams provided students an opportunity to interact in settings where academic skills were not crucial. The children who were most skilled in special activities were not always the same ones, and not always those who did well in the classroom. Since the skill-based groups in Adams's classrooms made academic rank somewhat visible, non-academic activities were important in giving students opportunities for contact around common activities and interests, pursued in groups where academic ranking was less salient.

Authorities' emphasis on integration

The faculty, counting teachers and administrators, was 31 percent black, and the majority of aides were black as well.[7] Adams had a black principal, a black curriculum coordinator, and a greater proportion of its black teachers in academic subjects than is common in many schools. The legitimate place of numerous blacks among the staff helped to legitimate the place of black children both in the adults' eyes and in the eyes of students of all races.

The principal, Mrs Michaels, was aware of racial issues and took many steps to help the school move from mere desegregation to integration. Many schoolwide activities related to ethnicity. Speakers from every non-white ethnic group were invited to give presentations to the whole school and to be available to smaller groups. There was a week-long set of activities titled 'Afro-Americans on the Move' for the whole school, and each of the three units chose one of the largest white ethnic groups in the city for a week of study. The principal played a large part in fostering these activities.

In dealing with the faculty as a whole, the principal often treated issues which could be seen as having a racial dimension without mentioning race explicitly.[8] She used a language of concern for students' personal welfare which did not heighten racial awareness but did emphasize every child's need for respect and acceptance. She apparently had conversations with individual teachers in private where she tried to interpret black children's perspectives in situations which had racial overtones. I was observing her one day when three black girls were sent to her office to be disciplined for refusing to scrub the floor by a white teacher who was having the class clean up the room for a special show. The principal lectured the girls on the importance of cooperating for the good of the whole class and of obedience and sent them home for the day – but without suspending them. After they were gone, though the girls had made no mention of race, she told me she would talk with the teacher and explain that it was tactless, in the light of history, to assign the heaviest and most menial cleaning job to an all-black, rather than a racially mixed, group.[9] Even in speaking to me, however, she was careful to call the situation a cultural misunderstanding, not discrimination.

When the principal composed the teams each year, she placed at least one black teacher on each. Consequently, as the teams discussed individual students or groups of students, the discussion was always in a racially mixed setting which was likely to inhibit blatant expression of any individual's racial prejudices. Further, where children engaged in activities or expressed attitudes which might be more easily understood by someone of the same race, such a person was present and at least potentially able to interpret the child's behavior. I never heard teachers make such an interpretation with an explicitly racial reference, but I did hear teachers defend or interpret behavior in ways that it seemed to me came much more easily to someone of the same race than of a different race.

Some teachers, both black and white, actively promoted inter-racial understanding with topics discussed in the classroom, especially in social studies, or in activities. Most spoke in interviews in ways which took it for granted that informal mixing among children of different races was at least normal and appropriate and perhaps something for the school actively to encourage.

Logistical influences

The nature of life at Adams was affected by logistical influences which set the context for both the work process and social interaction.

The effects of the Adams building

The Adams Avenue building and its location had several important implications for its program. The location made the resources of downtown cultural resources and businesses readily available for large and small field trips. The school was located on racially neutral territory. Since everyone arrived by bus, no group could claim the school as their own turf, and, since adults on the surrounding streets were of varied races, all the students felt comfortable waiting for city buses there. The location made the school easily accessible from all parts of the city, with few bus transfers; it played a part in its recruitment of students from over eighty elementary schools. Finally, there were no neighborhood teenagers in the area who might either invade the playground and building or serve as role models for its younger students.

Adams's building also had consequences for its program. It was a small building and so required that the student body be small. As a result the teachers and administrators had a chance to know students as individuals. The building's old-fashioned elementary school design provided three floors and short, broad halls. Thus each unit had its 'own' floor and the halls easily accommodated movement between classes without the crowding, jostling, traffic jams, and din, which are common in the long, narrow tile corridors of junior high schools. The halls also provided no hiding places for truants from class, and any adult whom children trying to skip class might encounter would be likely to know who they were and approximately where they ought to be.

The building had less benign effects for the conduct of the curriculum and the life of the adults. It did not have the facilities ordinarily expected for middle school students. The third floor gymnasium had been converted to make the Instructional Materials Center (library) and the students had to walk a block to a downtown athletic club for physical education. Rooms for music, art, home economics, and shop had been converted from elementary classrooms with varied success. Many specialists, such as reading and math specialists and the Title I teachers, had to perch at desks in rooms with other activities going on. During inclement and winter weather, even teachers with their own classrooms had to vacate them over the lunch hour so students would have a place for indoor recreation. The building looked old and its heating system was sometimes uncertain. Because of these genuine deficits, as well as the potential value of the downtown land, the school board thought of closing the school and moving the program.

Despite these real deficiencies in the building, the faculty and administrators were nearly unanimous in not wanting to leave it.[10] Though the teachers who had the most need for space spoke matter of factly of the problems they experienced, they did not dwell upon them, and they too, with one or two exceptions, wanted the school to remain where it was. For the Adams faculty, the small size of the student body, which the building required, was a more valuable asset than better facilities would have been.

The Adams building had a final benefit which was largely unrecognized by the staff. Its crowding pushed the faculty into shared spaces, especially its small second floor lounge where teachers brought their lunches. There they developed cordial relations with colleagues, even with those with dissimilar backgrounds and outlooks.

Grouping of students and teachers

Because the student body was grouped into 'units' of 110 students, each assigned a single team of academic teachers, a floor of the building, and a separate turn at lunch and recreation, students spent most of their day seeing only this group of 110. Thus after the first few weeks, even the new students spent their days surrounded by familiar and identifiable faces, except perhaps as they arrived at school and left again. Such a situation made the school manageable for shy younger students and cut down hostile older students' opportunities for anonymous theft or aggression. There was little pressure on the younger students to imitate the apparent sophisication of the older ones.

The linking of a team of teachers with each unit of students made it possible for the teachers to agree on consistent rules and expectations for students and to support one another's efforts in enforcing them and in working with individual difficult children. The discussions of students in Adams's team meetings generally maintained a constructive tone and purpose.

The use of time

As part of its IGE/Multi-Unit plan, Adams Avenue arranged the time in the school day somewhat differently from standard secondary schools. Though students had the same number of subjects defined in the same terms as at other junior high and middle schools, they did not follow a single time schedule with bells signaling the whole school to change classes. Instead each unit had a partially independent time schedule. Within limits imposed by the fact that all students went to the same teachers for non-academic classes, and all went to lunch, the time schedule of the three units was worked out with an effort to give each unit blocks of time which included more than one class hour. Within those time blocks, each group of four academic teachers could work out their own schedule for instructing the students. In practice they worked out fairly standard schedules of class hours for the routine days; students moved from class to class as elsewhere.

Flexible time became important when there were special activities. The whole unit of students could participate together in a special activity for significant blocks of time without disrupting other classes. If one teacher's field trip lasted more than a class hour, the next teacher's class would simply not be held. In standard secondary scheduling, a few students on the field trip would be absent from each of several different classes and their teachers would have to help them catch up the next day.

The benefits of flexible schedules could only be realized if teachers were willing to plan cooperatively and to rearrange their individual class activities to accommodate each other. All the teams of teachers displayed such willingness, though there was some variation in its frequency and quality. Flexible time blocks facilitated, but did not ensure, the undertaking of activities which could not be accomplished in a single class hour.

Faculty culture and school character

Most technological and logistical arrangements at Adams worked to encourage the constructive relationships between students and teachers and among students which were its hallmark. While these arrangements certainly facilitated such relations, they were not sufficient causes for them. Teachers could easily have vitiated most of the benefits of the structure of the curriculum, classroom activity structures, and academic rewards by making public comments belittling poorly performing students.[11] Through racially biased comments and prejudicial treatment of students, they could have disrupted much of the equality and cooperation between blacks and whites. They could have complained about the shortcomings of the building and have scattered to restaurants nearby to eat their lunch in isolated cliques of likeminded individuals, as indeed a very few did do. They could have been uncooperative or apathetic in team meetings.

The technological characteristics of the program worked together with a subculture which the Adams faculty shared in supporting the school's constructive social relationships. The Adams faculty assumed that increasing contact among any set of persons will increase their liking for one another and the positive tone of their relations. Underlying this assumption was another – that faculty and students would treat members of their own and of the other group in a generally respectful and pleasant way unless they were given specific cause not to. Supporting both assumptions was a basically benign view of human nature which saw all persons as fundamentally good despite some foibles and faults. Consequently, good will and inventive teaching could be expected to elicit academic and social cooperation from most students most of the time, though occasional temper or backsliding were also to be expected.

The faculty considered good relations among persons in a school both an end in itself and helpful to learning. They spoke of their 'knowing the students well' as a substantive accomplishment and they said that the 'success' of the school was related to its small size which enabled them to know students as individuals. Although some noted that learning and good or cooperative behavior are not synonymous, that some children made no trouble but also no academic effort, they still considered establishing positively toned relations with students to be an accomplishment. They thought such relationships at least facilitated academic progress, and that they were able to get a sizable proportion of the students to be diligent workers.

Their shared expectation that students would routinely cooperate and be friendly with their teachers and peers set a tone in the teachers' own behavior which helped to elicit the response they anticipated. Their courtesy to students, their visible efforts to help them learn, and their willingness to extend them privileges such as coming to the faculty lounge with questions elicited trust and courtesy from the students which re-enforced the teachers' expectations.

Manifestations of Adams's faculty culture

Adams's teachers believed they got along well with their students and could work constructively with them, but most did not describe relationships at Adams as unusual or striking. They seemed disinclined to consider whether they could easily be much more difficult. When I probed for comparative assessments or suggested outright that relations at Adams were unusually good, teachers who had experience at other secondary schools generally would grant that Adams had better relations than their old school, but seemed to consider the comparison insignificant. They found good relations 'normal,' and defended this belief even in the face of some counter-evidence. Belief in the normalcy of their good relations re-enforced their assumption of a universally benign human nature upon which it rested.

The strength of the Adams teachers' cultural assumptions was also evident in their explanation of the positive character of relationships in the school. Nearly all of them explained that the school's small size was its crucial characteristic because it enabled them to know the children as individuals. But this explanation rested on the assumption that people who know each other well will get along well, an assumption which is not always correct.[12]

Similarly assuming that proximity breeds liking and helpfulness, Adams's teachers were puzzled when I commented upon the student body's friendly reception of all the acts in an amateur talent show, despite the fact that they ranged from dreadful to excellent and from purely white in cultural style to purely black. They did not understand why I should remark upon this audience response or seek its sources. 'The students know each other,' several explained with the shrug of self-evident comment.

Adams's teachers also took it for granted that teachers who were assigned to work together would attempt to work constructively – though they recognized the strains of differing instructional styles and personalities. They assumed that the existence of teams would operate to benefit the students as the teachers sought constructive strategies for dealing with students with whom one or more might be having difficulty. In contrast, the part-time assistant principal, who maintained an outsider's perspective on the school, described how teams at other schools served only to intensify hostility between students and teachers; an angry teacher would spread rejection of the student to the whole team. The Adams faculty assumed that flexible time was the key ingredient in allowing them to plan cooperative team projects or to make adjustments for one another's individual projects, field trips, or immediate needs. But it would have been possible for teachers to be rigid in these matters and to refuse to cooperate, as does happen at some other schools.

With some partial exceptions among white teachers, the teachers' positive expectations of children extended to those of all races. None of the children mentioned racial discrimination by teachers in their interviews, nor did teachers speak of other teachers' discrimination against children of a different race. In unit meetings and in the teachers' lounge, I was consistently unable to tell the race of children being discussed by name if I did not know the child – though the presence of persons of varied races in the room at most times would have inhibited any explicit expression of racial prejudice. The teachers' acceptance of children of different races probably set an example which contributed to a similar acceptance on the students' part.

The assumption that all students have some good points and all deserve respectful treatment was a subcultural one which ran somewhat counter to the larger middle-class culture. Not only children of all races, but low achievers, and children whose families engaged in behavior normally considered disreputable, or who did so themselves, remained acceptable human beings. There was a lack of class stereotyping as well as of racial stereotyping.[13] In the course of nine meetings of teaching teams which I observed, I heard, among others, of the following situations, which teachers mentioned in the course of discussion of how to work better with the children involved. A girl was returning from the Children's Home, while a boy was gone from school because he had broken probation with a minor robbery and was in police custody. A father had just gone to jail, while a mother had deserted her family and the daughter's chronic tardiness was discovered to be the result of her responsibility to see younger siblings off to school. A boy had attempted (unsuccessfully and perhaps jokingly) to pimp a girl classmate in a teacher's hearing, while another had been selling non-existent goods at a 'discount' to his fellows. The teachers spoke of these incidents in a matter of fact way which indicated that they were routine. While the teachers took vigorous steps to correct behavior such as selling non-existent goods to one's fellows, they did not find the perpetrators of such acts totally beyond the pale. They were generally sympathetic with children whose school performance was hampered by family responsibilities or by inattentive parents and did what they could to assist in dealing with their problems.

Their attitudes and behavior contrast with other authors' descriptions of teachers' active disidentification with such students (Keddie, 1971; Leacock, 1969; Rist, 1973; Schwartz, 1981). The distinctiveness of the Adams faculty's attitudes was also underscored by contrast with those of a new teacher who had worked in suburban elementary schools. In her research interview, after six weeks at the school, she spoke of some of the kinds of behavior of parents and students just described with astonished horror. She described great frustration in working with the students and referred to the school as an 'inner city' school, though no one else did. Though she had as yet had no contact with parents, she assumed that a lack of parental interest was a source of her problems.

The reader may be a little surprised that some students at Adams were engaging in an array of not-so-innocent activities in their spare time and living in families where the parents did likewise. But that is precisely the point. Some of Adams's students were 'tough kids' from 'rough neighborhoods.' But in the school they set aside much of that cultural style, and participated in the school's activities mostly on the school's terms.[14]

The literature on student–teacher conflicts cited earlier describes frequent atrophy in teachers' academic efforts in secondary classes with poor achievers, especially when teachers disidentify with students because of race, class, or a perceived lack of respectability. Adams's teachers, by contrast, remained frustrated and argued that there was something wrong in the *school* when they were unable to succeed academically even with students who had reached the seventh grade with second grade skills. As the descriptions of classroom interaction with the slowest eighth grade students indicate, they persisted in academic efforts even with the least skilled students.

The maintenance of the faculty culture

Cultures do not persist automatically. If they are to be maintained they must be reaffirmed and taught to new recruits to the society. This process was evident at Adams both in team meetings and in conversations in the teachers' lounge. Several teachers consistently threw positive comments into conversations about students which had started to turn negative. It is difficult to know how consciously they did this; it was done so casually that only someone considering the tone of interaction would be likely to notice it. When I returned to the school to give a report on my findings, I asked two teachers who often made such comments whether they were aware of participating in this pattern. They said they were not. Their response underscores once more the unreflective character of cultural patterns.[15]

The process of continual maintenance and renewal of shared cultural definitions becomes most visible when newcomers arrive. Such persons not only are ignorant of what others 'know;' they are also a threat to the self-evident character of the reality others have constructed. Through deviant acts born of ignorance they can alter relationships which both depend upon and reaffirm that reality. For example, one day in the teachers' lounge, a new teacher was complaining about how long it took a well-known eighth grade black boy with low skills to complete his product for the class project she had recently displayed to the school. Just then, the same student knocked and came in with a request for a teacher. The group, who had been joking about his lack of application, displayed no embarrassment or hesitation. Immediately one teacher complimented him upon the finished product and others followed with their own congratulations. His teacher started to say that she had been telling the other teachers how long it took, but one of the informal leaders of the faculty turned her back on the student and effectively signaled the newcomer to be quiet. After the student left, the informal leader covered over her rather stern sanction with another joke about the student's slow rate of progress. Here, the faculty as a body displayed their insistence upon building students up when they completed something – regardless of their estimation of their comparative ability.

The impact of the faculty culture on the students worked indirectly to maintain that culture. A teacher whose classes are reasonably pleasant and amenable to direction can more easily believe in the benign character of human nature and the responsiveness of students to respectful treatment, than can one whose classes are angry and raucous. It is far easier to maintain twenty-six good moods than to create them in children who enter a classroom tense and defensive from confrontations in their last class. Each teacher's respectful treatment of students supported the efforts of others through its good effects on the children, and thereby confirmed the assumptions of their common culture.

Exceptions to Adams's patterns of culture and technology

The importance of Adams's faculty culture in creating the good relations between teachers and students became evident where the culture was not shared. There were five teachers at Adams whom I observed in repeated angry confrontations with students in their classroom or in the halls. These deviant teachers also did not share fully in the faculty culture and in some cases did not share it at all. They used different technological patterns from the ones encouraged by the school in their classrooms, so that it is somewhat difficult to untangle the effects of cultural differences from those of technological differences.

These teachers confronted students in angry tones, and the students returned the anger in a manner as explosive as any I had seen in traditional schools. In varying degrees, these teachers threatened more than did others and spoke to the whole class in annoyed voices, while their students were more restless and rude and ignored the teachers' requests or statements much more than they did other teachers'. In classes run by these teachers, I saw such exceptional events as a really angry fight between two (sixth grade white) boys before class, and a black girl saying threateningly to a white girl as she passed her on the way to the pencil sharpener, 'you lucky that teacher (the observer) [is] over there.'

Two of these teachers were black and three were white; three were women and two were men. All five structured the activities of their classes differently from most teachers. Two attempted many activities involving whole group recitation. All failed to circulate among their students to help individuals when they were working in separate groups. Those who did not work with the class as a unit carried on lecture and recitation with small groups, stationed themselves at their desks while students worked at theirs, or drew an observer into conversation which distanced both of them from the events of the class. They therefore did not reap the benefits of the classroom activity structures typical of the school, and they did not have as much opportunity to become personally acquainted with their students.

These teachers differed noticeably from others in the school in their hostile manner in talking about students as well as to them. They did not share the benign assumptions and behavior of the faculty culture. Four of the five were only marginal participants in the common social life of the faculty which centered around the lunch hour spent in the small faculty lounge. Of these four, two had been in the school less than a year and another had been there less than two years; they had had less opportunity to be socialized into Adams's faculty culture than had other teachers. The fifth teacher, who was an active participant in faculty conversations and who had been at Adams since it was Williams Annex, was the least extreme of the group. She also had an illness that caused her chronic pain which may have shortened her patience with classroom problems.

First causes are difficult to discern in an ongoing situation. Since students in these teachers' classes were surly and disobedient with the teachers and argumentative with one another, they were an objectively difficult and unlikable crew from the exceptional teachers' point of view. The teachers must have considered the stiff and stentorian tones they used from the beginning of these classes thoroughly justified by the students' general behavior. But observation of other classes in the same school suggests that teachers rather than students initiated the deteriorating cycle of anger and mutual needling. The same groups of students engaged in constructive cycles of supportive behavior with other teachers in other classrooms.

Still, Adams's students were rather quick to take offense with these five unusual teachers. None of the teachers approached the extreme in acting hostile or in giving harsh or frequent discipline when compared to the range of behavior I have seen in teachers in other schools (Metz, 1978a; 1978b). The tone of interaction at Adams appears therefore to have been a fragile social construction; many students remained alienated from the larger society and potentially volatile in school. The ease with which they could be brought into conflict suggests the importance of the technological and cultural conditions which made this conflict a rarity.

The exercise of power and school character

The principal's influence on the tone of relationships

The principal exerted two kinds of influence upon the school. Her control over the tone of relationships was indirect, while that concerning the practice of the basic elements of IGE was direct and formal. Her influence over the tone of relationships will be discussed first.

The faculty's concern with knowing the students well and their implicit benign view of human nature was consistent with the principal's explicit philosophy, though they did not use her kind of language. She frequently said it was important to make students 'feel good about themselves.' She directed much of her own energies, and attempted to direct the other adults' energies, to seeing that students individually did feel good about themselves. Her own efforts involved fostering activities which would give social support to students' good feelings, and encouraging good personal relations between adults and students.

While Mrs Michaels never explicitly articulated an analysis of the social effects of the organization of the curriculum, grading, and classroom organization of instruction, she apparently had an intuitive grasp of them. She did say that teachers should not be unduly concerned with a child's accomplishments in comparison to absolute standards; it was most important for a student to have some sense of making progress in learning to motivate him or her to keep trying. While she was in sympathy with IGE's concentration on building basic academic skills, she saw a need to leaven these lessons with activities other than academic learning. She stressed supplementary special activities during the school day and extra-curricular activities after it. She quietly saw that these activities were structured to include a good deal of contact across racial lines. Because she thought explicit attention to ethnic pride was important, she oversaw a variety of programs celebrating the ethnic roots of the various groups in the school. She encouraged the teachers also to plan special programs and activities with an ethnic emphasis.

Though Mrs Michaels organized some special activities herself, she had to rely on teachers for much of the supplementary program during the day and virtually all of the extra-curricular activities. She could require some things, for example that each unit would pursue four interdisciplinary learning activities a year. But, she had to rely on teachers' own investment in these activities and in extra-curricular activities for them to become lively and interesting. She encouraged teachers' extra efforts through public appreciation of the teachers and publicity for the activities, and she allowed teachers to retain control of the activities so that they felt a sense of ownership in them. She further made sure that the teachers got the formal and informal institutional resources they needed to carry a project through.

For example, she encouraged and gave publicity to the teachers who cooperated to put on an ambitious musical production of *Alice in Wonderland*. She arranged for noontime rehearsals so that the few children whose homes were so far from city buslines that they had to ride yellow buses could participate, and she saw to it that the teachers were paid as they would have been if rehearsals had been after school. She also arranged for use of an auditorium in a nearby technical college and invited several elementary schools to a performance, so that there would be enough performances to reward the students' work. She cajoled the other teachers into freeing performers' time for extra rehearsals just before the show was ready.

A teacher who, the previous year, had taught half-time at Adams and half-time at the Atlantic Avenue gifted and talented middle school contrasted her experience at the two schools. She had proposed to both principals that she take a group of students from the two schools on a week long field trip to Mexico. She said:

'I enjoy working with Mrs Michaels. I think she has a lot of good points. If you have an idea, she'll say, "That's great, try it and we'll back you up." When I told her I wanted to take the kids to Mexico, she encouraged me. When I told him [Mr Barton, principal of Atlantic Avenue], he said, "Did I ever tell you about the time a couple of kids were killed in a plane crash?" [She makes a face expressive of disgust.]

'A lot more could have been done there [at Atlantic]. He could have at least said goodbye to the students and "We hope you have a good time." And he could have welcomed them back with some comments about the trip. Here [at Adams] the students got sent off with "bravos" and "olés" and it was an event. There [at Atlantic] I felt the school

91

wasn't backing the students up. And I needed some support. I was giving up my time and using a lot of energy and I needed backing.'

When this teacher had to choose between full-time positions at each of the two schools for the year of the study at Adams, one consideration in her choosing Adams was this support for her special efforts.

Mrs Michaels set a tone for relationships between adults and students through her own relationships with students. Her morning announcements were generally upbeat, focusing more on upcoming activities and congratulations to students than on reminders about rules or reprimands for poor behavior. She made a point of getting to know the school's most difficult students especially well, so that when the time came to discipline them she did so within the context of a broader and partially positive relationship. She left her office door open when she was not in private conferences and told students that they were free to come and see her on matters of their own choosing. Students did in fact go in to see her.

It is difficult to trace the connection between the values of the faculty culture and Mrs Michaels's values, even though there was a great deal of similarity between them. Most of the teachers accorded Mrs Michaels a certain admiration – though in some cases a slightly grudging admiration – because in their common phrase 'she cares about the kids.' But many rejected her psychological and sweetly positive language. They spoke of admiration and appreciation of her good values in the important matter of caring about the students with no hint that she was the source of their own concern with it. Her influence upon them may have been part of the lost history of Williams Annex.[16] Whatever the process by which accord was reached, by the time of the study, the principal and the faculty culture shared an emphasis on the importance of 'caring about the kids' and held the positive attitudes toward all students already described.

The principal's efforts to establish IGE

The principal's relationship with the teachers over the issue of IGE was quite different from her relationship with them on the issues just described. It was profoundly shaped by the influences from the district as a whole in the establishment of the school. The teachers experienced the change to an IGE magnet program as the imposition of an unfamiliar pattern about which they were given no choice. The district offered them neither time nor opportunity for discussion of the strengths and weaknesses of IGE in general, in particular subjects, or with particular kinds of children. Parents and the court had been promised an IGE school and the system's reputation for good faith depended in part on its delivery. In this situation, Mrs Michaels resorted to use of the formal hierarchical powers of her office. She articulated the elements of IGE which must appear in every classroom. Especially in the first year, she walked the halls and checked in classrooms to be sure the requisite groups of students could be seen. She met with teachers to discuss their curriculum and their charting procedures, and she told them to make changes if these did not fit the IGE pattern. In the year of the study, she still had four meetings a year with every teacher in which he or she was expected to appear with charts to be discussed. In faculty meetings in the first two years, she repeatedly and peremptorily reminded teachers that they were to be practising IGE or were to request a transfer to another school.

At the end of the first year, the principal issued involuntary transfers to three teachers on the grounds that they were not following the IGE pattern. All protested at first, but two were eventually persuaded to accept the move. One pursued a grievance through the union all the way to a formal hearing at the district level which took place two years later, during the school's third year. Whether the principal intended these transfers as a means to drive the seriousness of her purpose home to other teachers or not, the teachers received them as a warning that the same could be done to them. But they also resented them as unfair because they felt that no one was capable of competently teaching IGE in the first year and that the transferred teachers at the least deserved more time. The final hearing took place at the time of the study, making these transfers once more a lively bone of contention.

None the less, in the third year, the teachers were beginning to feel some degree of comfort with IGE. Furthermore, the school was receiving more applicants than it could accept in each year's round of applications for magnet schools. Anxiety, and pressure for performance as an IGE school, from higher in the school system and from parents had eased.

In this year, the principal used her hierarchical powers less aggressively and used more praise of the progress the teachers had already made, at least with the group as a whole. A teacher who arrived during the second year described the change in Mrs Michaels's behavior in faculty meetings:

'She used to really come on strong about what she expected and how we were handling it. This year she has really eased up, and even at the end of last year. Where at the other faculty meetings she would end it on a negative kind of note and just leave you hanging, now she is much more positive and reinforcing of what we are doing.'

The teachers' response to the principal's direction

It is not surprising that the principal's strong use of her hierarchical powers and her employment of a commanding tone evoked resentment in the teachers. While she was clearly acting within her legitimate rights as principal, and thus as the bureaucratic superior of the teachers, and while she was clearly acting in accord with the announced serious policy of the larger school district organization, she was none the less violating the traditional informal rights of teachers. Her commands about IGE invaded the heart of their work as teachers. Furthermore, in the first year, the teachers found those commands impossible to follow. All the teachers had genuine difficulty in obeying the command to teach according to IGE when they knew little about it and did not yet have special materials or the kind of logically ordered and tidily subdivided curriculum which it presumes. Many had principled objections to it, at least for their subjects, which outlasted the resolution of those initial problems.

Mrs Michaels also gave teachers more commands than are customary about their relations with parents. She needed their help in giving parents the image of a functioning IGE school and in keeping them generally pleased with the school, so that they would keep their children there and encourage more parents to volunteer. Teachers who had some sensitivity to the external conditions in which the school was working were not offended by her concern over parents' perspectives, but others felt that she was siding with parents against them or pandering to parents or children.[17] Mrs Michaels herself did not mention outside pressures to the teachers when she would discuss parents' desires or objections with them,[18] though if she heard that a teacher had criticized the school to a parent she would point out that such an action was impolitic.

The majority's response
As a consequence of the principal's assaults on their autonomy, and with it their professional pride, many of the teachers distrusted her on a personal level. Their comments in interviews were often long and complex as they struggled to characterize her in answer to a question about her impact on the school. A black teacher of a non-academic subject who was hardworking, engaged in extracurricular activities, enthusiastic about IGE, and a leader in maintaining the positive faculty culture – in short the kind of teacher about whom the principal should have been enthusiastic – struggled to express the grounds of the ambivalence which she felt she shared with other teachers:

'I don't think she has a good rapport with the staff now. I think that they know where she's coming from, and they work with her. I don't think she's such a bad person or anything. I think that maybe they are just wary of her. Because of what happened to those people [the three teachers who were transferred]. But I'm wary of her too [laughter], you know. Just because of the fact that you don't know where you stand.

'I really don't have any negative things to say about Mrs Michaels because she is like I said very sensitive to the special areas [non-academic subjects]. She has gone out of her way for us. But now that's in terms of looking at my program. As far as myself, I think I am as expendable as anybody else . . .

'As a staff member it's like there's a murky cloud around Mrs Michaels. I don't know where she really is. I think she really is interested in these kids and what happens to them. I really do. But I think perhaps the way that she has dealt with her staff has not [pause] led them to feel that way. Or to feel any loyalty to her. I think administrators need to have their staffs loyal to *them* and I don't know if she really does.'

Notice here, that while this teacher was criticizing the principal for creating this lack of trust and personal loyalty, in a sense she was saying that the principal was acting in the spirit of classic bureaucracy. It is the duty of a classic bureaucratic superordinate to consider the welfare of the organization and the pursuit of its goals and to be concerned with the participants, not as individuals, but as competent or incompetent performers. Consequently, it could be said that the teachers were angry that she was acting so fully in the role of bureaucratic superordinate.

Displeased as the majority of teachers were with the principal's hierarchical tone and her intrusion into their classrooms with IGE, they did not question the formal legitimacy of her right to behave in this fashion. They were willing to admit, however unhappily, that despite their informal prerogatives, as one teacher said, 'The bottom line is she's the boss.'

More important than the formal legitimacy of her demands, however, was the majority of the faculty's sense that she had very important virtues in encouraging and facilitating the kind of relationship they wanted with students and the various special projects which many of them enjoyed undertaking. Teachers who fully shared the faculty culture's emphasis on seeking the welfare of the students and who actively enjoyed developing some special activities or imaginative programs could not totally reject the principal. Even when she made them feel angry or insecure, they were aware that she too stood for many of their central values. She 'cared about the kids' and she supported their special efforts.

Some of these teachers were not angry with the principal at all, and gave her little but praise, but most were at least ruffled and some 'really mad' at her tone in faculty meetings, her insistence on IGE whatever arguments against it a teacher might present, and her hospitable treatment of parental complaints. Still, their anger was straightforward and its basis perfectly clearly rooted in her actions related to the establishment of the IGE magnet program and their impact on the informal prerogatives of teachers.

A minority's response

There was a small group of teachers who responded quite differently, however. This group criticized the principal for a list of alleged weaknesses – for example, obedience to the central office, failure to secure adequate resources for the school, failure to discipline students strongly, and failure to support teachers vis-à-vis parents or to stand up to them at all. They even accused her of lacking vigor in instituting IGE. Their criticisms differed from those of the rest of the faculty in two respects other than their severity and the difference in specific topics chosen. First, where other teachers complained that the principal ran rough-shod over them in insisting upon IGE and threatening them with transfer if they did not comply, this group said nothing of her strong use of her powers of office, but instead complained of *weakness* in a variety of her actions. Second, they were far more bitter and attacked her as a person.

The tone of their criticisms was given the most forceful voice by their leader, Mr Haupt, who minced no words in his research interview:

MR HAUPT: She has three qualifications for the job. One, she's black. Two, she's a woman.[19] Three, she's no threat to the central administration.

INTERVIEWER: Why is that?

MR HAUPT: Because she will not stand up to them. She has the Little Red Schoolhouse image of the principal as mother or father to little kids. Well, she is the little kid that people from Central Office can tell what to do. Anyone from there who comes in here can tell her what to do and she'll never think twice. She's told to do something and she acts. She does everything not to rock the boat.

Like the other teachers, these teachers had to admit that Mrs Michaels was the formal head of the school, superordinate to them. But while the other teachers complained that she did not inspire loyalty, or induce people to 'go out of their way for her,' these teachers wanted to cast doubt upon the legitimacy of her right to demand anything of them. Since the prerogatives of her position gave her the formal right to command them, whatever informal traditions might be broken, the only way to question the legitimacy of her commands was to question her competency as an officeholder. While principals in general might have the right to give teachers the kind of commands she did, if they could demonstrate that she was not competent she would lose that right, because she would then have a doubtful claim to the prerogatives of the office. It is in this light that we can understand these teachers' failure to mention the principal's insistence on IGE and her commanding tone and their complaints about actions which suggested weakness rather than strength in using the powers of her office.

The teachers in the dissident minority had reasons to be particularly critical of the principal. She was strongly critical of the teaching of three[20] of the four core members of the group and had differences over life-style issues with at least two. These teachers did not seem to share the values of the faculty culture; in their interviews they had little to say about their teaching but were preoccupied by relationships among the adults. In varying degrees, they argued strongly for literal enforcement of the level of effort required by the union contract, while Mrs Michaels implicitly expected, and much of the faculty voluntarily gave, a great deal of effort beyond that level. The dissident minority thus had less basis of accord with the principal than the other teachers and more reason to oppose not only her hierarchical stance, but much else in her expectations of them.

This group of teachers as a whole sought support for their perspective toward the principal among the rest of the faculty. Mr Haupt, the leader of the group, was the building representative of the teachers' union, the head of the school level unit of the union.[21] Three other members of the dissident minority held three of the four other positions on the 'building committee' of the union. These positions gave them a power base from which to build criticism of the principal, though only Mr Haupt and one other, Mr Minelli, really actively participated in this effort.

It was the responsibility of the building representative and committee to gather teachers' complaints and concerns and present them anonymously to the principal on a monthly basis. These persons, therefore, had a franchise to ask every teacher for complaints and then to mention them to others and ask if they shared them, thus spreading knowledge of every possible source of discontent to everyone on the faculty. Furthermore, it was evident that the teachers outside this group who became most sympathetic with its perspective were persons thrown into proximity with its members, especially its two leaders, because of common team membership, department membership, or the sharing of a room.

The minority's effect on the majority
Criticisms of the principal from the minority of teachers found resonance with the rest of the faculty because all were made uncomfortable by the principal's strong use of her formal powers. None the less, while the criticisms of the minority made the majority recognize their resentments of the principal clearly, and while they accepted some of the minority's specific criticisms of her behavior, they were not won over to the dissidents' general perspective despite the energetic persuasive efforts of the group's leaders. Many of the other teachers found the virulence of the minority's anger exaggerated and some of the issues they chose offensive. But more important was the majority's feeling that – despite their anger with Mrs Michaels over her enforcement of IGE, and perhaps over the pressures she put on them to consider parents' perspectives more than before – they shared with her a real concern for students' welfare. Her administrative support and public recognition for individual and group efforts on special projects helped to make this agreement tangible.

A teacher who defined the opponents of the principal as union members made this feeling of the majority explicit:

'I think most of the staff, if we had to stand up and be counted to go in this group or go in that group – with the union or the establishment – the majority of the staff would go with the establishment in saying they're interested in education . . . For the most part they think you ought to work within the system. They think that you ought to think positive. Most of them want to work in that way.

'I have never once heard the union people talk about the quality of our work. Never once . . . I resent their way of operating. The administration is not always wrong. They never ask what kind of a job you're doing. They never ask whether kids like a teacher. They never ask whether a teacher is doing extra things with kids. It's always your rights – "what are your rights?"

'You can't legislate dedication. I've been told I shouldn't work on my lunch hour and that I shouldn't take things home because that's not in the contract. I can't do my job to my own satisfaction, to satisfy my own standards if I work only in the hours I get paid for. I think that is part of the job which is a professional job that requires dedication.'

Though Mrs Michaels undercut the teachers' sense of professionalism and autonomy with her hierarchical and coercive insistence on IGE, as this teacher makes very clear, Mrs Michaels also restored that sense of professionalism for the majority who shared her general goals with students, as she supported their dedication to the welfare of their client/students.

Summary and implications

Life at Adams Avenue Middle School was distinctive primarily because of its constructive relationships. The school practiced its formal innovation of IGE to a moderate degree, and that practice seemed to be an ingredient in its good relationships. The simplest, most easily enforced, elements of IGE helped relationships by making legitimate learners out of students who entered the school below the standard expected for their grade.

These technological arrangements for IGE allowed students to move ahead independent of the rate of others with very different skills and still to have their progress legitimated. They also protected the pride of those who learned most slowly by giving them some privacy in performance and by giving out rewards based on effort and progress rather than on a comparative level of accomplishment. Technological arrangements in classes worked to equalize the status of children of different races and provided some limited chances for cooperation. The plethora of special activities undertaken during the school day and the full extra-curricular program of the school provided students with a chance to exercise a range of skills, and so to see one another in more than one hierarchy of skill, and gave more opportunities than the classes for genuine cooperation toward group rather than individual goals.

The technological arrangements of the school were no guarantee of its good relationships, however. The faculty culture was a crucial ingredient, with its benign view of human nature and its unspoken assumption that respect would breed respect, and acquaintance would generate good feeling. If teachers had been hostile to students or belittled them publicly the technological arrangements alone could not have given students the sense of legitimate participation in the school which did in fact develop. A few teachers who did not share the faculty culture and who did treat students in an aggressive and hostile manner, most of whom also did not follow all the technological design for the classroom, did in fact develop conflictual relationships with students in which each party drove the other toward further alienation.

The establishment of the IGE program with only a few weeks' warning, and the pressure to gain parental approval of the school, required the principal to take a sternly hierarchical approach with the teachers. Her manner, her expectation that they would be able to offer IGE before they had training and materials, and her insistence on IGE regardless of their principled objections to it, undercut the teachers' sense of control over their own work. They resented her actions around IGE, even while the majority had to admit that she was acting within her formally defined rights in making the demands she did.

The faculty's resentment stayed within bounds, however, despite the energetic efforts of a small group of really angry teachers to nurture it. In most cases, it was expressed as ambivalence, because the principal clearly worked hard for the welfare of the students, that is, for the same values the teachers did. Furthermore, the many teachers who were willing to volunteer time and effort for special projects found the principal gave them formal and informal resources and public appreciation for their work. Thus, though there was a lot of conflict and tension between the principal and the faculty, they also worked together with some sense of mutual support in a common endeavor.

Some of the most important influences on the life of the Adams Avenue School were not recognized, or at least not acknowledged, by the participants. The teachers seemed to be unaware of the contribution of their technological arrangements to the cooperative behavior of the students. In fact, while they talked about its small size contributing to the school's success because, they believed, it allowed them to 'know' the students well, they seemed actively reluctant to remark upon the school's good relationships as strikingly better than other schools'. As long as teachers and students, and student peers, know one another, they implied, they will get along well. The benign assumptions of their culture about human nature, together with their lack of self-consciousness about racial differences and lack of condemnation of conventionally disreputable behavior in families, persisted best when taken for granted. As much as possible, they left unnoticed the difference

101

of their beliefs from those of teachers elsewhere and from the values and beliefs of the larger culture.

Both the teachers and the principal also downplayed the importance of pressures from the school system as a whole in creating their conflicts around IGE and the principal's role. The teachers dealt with the principal on a daily basis and felt the personal impact of her insistent and critical tone; the needs of the district in setting up credible magnet schools were distant and abstract and thus less real for them. The principal herself did not say much about systemwide constraints. There were social pressures on her not to emphasize these constraints to the teachers. If she had reminded teachers that she had to enforce IGE unquestioningly because of the district's desire to attract parents with distinctive schools, she would have undercut her position; the person in charge then would be the distant and impersonal 'central office' which was far enough away to fool and faceless enough to betray. Further, while it is the duty of a middle manager to be obedient to superiors while being firmly demanding of subordinates, American culture is ambivalent about obedience. The dissidents interpreted the principal's obedience to commands from central office as evidence indicating she acted like a 'good little girl,' quite the opposite of the 'strong man' who commands respect and obedience from subordinates. Thus to appear in control the principal almost had to make her commands to teachers appear to originate with herself, even if that meant that she drew resentment for difficulties and contradictions which were not under her control.

Finally, the principal was subject to some of the same pressures as the teachers. Her autonomy as a principal was considerably lessened by the command from above to become an IGE school and to please volunteering parents, but just as the teachers needed to own the projects they undertook in the school, the principal needed to own the running of the school. She questioned my emphasis in an earlier paper (Metz, 1982b) on constraints on her behavior emanating from the district, and from her perspective she was right to do so. Her choice of a hierarchical style was, after all, not imposed, but a reflection of her judgment of the most effective style to use in the circumstances. While an outsider might say there were few other effective choices available, in fact she studied her situation and chose a strategy. Emphasizing her choice and de-emphasizing the constraints from outside the school contributed to her own sense of professionalism as well as drama-

tizing for the teachers that she was the superordinate whose directions they were obligated to follow.

Chapter 5

Jesse Owens Open Education School

The Jesse Owens Open Education School had been founded before desegregation, housed in a white neighborhood on the North Side. At the start of the magnet school plan it was moved into the Rodgers Junior High School building in a residential neighborhood on the northern edge of the black East Side.

Environmental influences

The establishment of the school

Jesse Owens had the only program which had been founded primarily on the initiative of school level administrators and teachers. It was initially developed, in the face of much skepticism from the central office and the school board, before the schools were desegregated or the magnet plan envisioned. In contrast to the teachers at the other two schools, Owens's teachers saw themselves as defending the innovation from incursions by the larger district organization, not as having the innovation imposed upon them by that organization.

Jesse Owens was the oldest of the three schools studied. It was founded in the fall of 1970 as an annex to an overcrowded inner city junior high school, Rodgers, to which site it later returned. The whole seventh grade was moved to the annex, which was headed by Mr Osten, an assistant principal from Rodgers, who was administrator in charge under the Rodgers principal. The school and its crew of young and inexperienced teachers were charged by the central office to do something creative.

Within the first two years, the staff had taken that directive to heart more seriously than the central office had planned. The staff requested permission to assign groups of children to groups of teachers in 'families' to allow deeper acquaintance between students and teachers and to allow teachers to share their knowledge of students. When several staff members attended workshops at the state university looking for innovative ideas, they were drawn to open education. One teacher tried it in her classroom at the beginning of the second year; by the end of that year four teachers had adopted an open education pattern. When students from a second junior high school were assigned to attend the school in its second year, the staff asked that the school be renamed Jesse Owens, a name chosen in an election among staff, students and parents,[1] and that Mr Osten be designated principal.

The original Jesse Owens program
Before the school's third year, the construction of a new high school which would accommodate Rodgers's ninth graders made it possible to reabsorb the seventh graders into Rodgers. The staff proposed that Jesse Owens be designated a special school offering open education to students from all over the city. With the help of a committee including some parents and central office staff, they wrote a proposal which had as its centerpiece the open education philosophy and distinctive curriculum, schedule, and overall program which, with various changes, characterized Jesse Owens up to the time of the study.

Their plan for the school also had several other features which were to become models for magnet schools. Students were to be drawn on a voluntary basis from throughout the city and the school was to be intentionally desegregated, with slots filled according to quotas for race and gender. Finally, it was to serve sixth through eighth graders, rather than the seventh through ninth graders served by the city's junior high schools.[2] The school board initially adopted the plan on a one-year trial basis.

Jesse Owens drew a good deal of attention. In its first year, there were 3,000 inquiries and 700 completed applications. The school level staff handled the selection process; they required a statement on the application giving the student's reasons for wanting to attend an open education school. According to common memory, most of the students genuinely wanted to be in an open education school, and a sizable proportion possessed advanced academic skills which supported their efforts in independent work. Those who became severe discipline problems or persistently failed to apply themselves to their studies could be asked to leave.

At the time of the study, the staff of Jesse Owens recalled the years from 1972 to 1976 as a mythic Golden Age. These were the years when the staff worked together intensely to develop a viable form of open education for their circumstances. Teachers and administrators attended workshops and discussed classroom practices in depth in small 'support groups,' which met on a regular basis. They stayed after school for staff meetings, informal discussions, and work with students.

They also went time and again to the central office, and often in appeal from there to the school board, to ask for exceptions to standard district procedures. Meanwhile the program was under nearly constant evaluation from the district, and its very existence was negotiated virtually every year. The teachers and especially the administrators, often with the support of active parents and a few sympathetic board members, were constantly at the barricades fighting to create the school's distinctive design and defending its very life.

Incorporation into a group of alternative schools and a move
In 1976, when the court order for desegregation was handed down, the new superintendent, Dr Stewart, cited Jesse Owens as an example to show that whites would be willing to volunteer for desegregated schools if the schools offered educational rewards. In the rhetoric used in the planning and the first publicity for the magnet schools, Jesse Owens was suddenly an exemplar instead of a maverick. According to the principal, the school's relations with the central office dramatically improved.

Incorporation into a group of magnet schools was by no means simply a boon for Jesse Owens, however. In the planning for the first year of desegregation, central administrators decided to close Rodgers Junior High School and move the Jesse Owens program into its building. Administratively, this idea made a good deal of sense. It gave the open education program better facilities and a larger building which would allow it to admit more students. At the same time, it helped systemwide desegregation by scattering the black students who had been attending Rodgers Junior High, most of whom could be expected to volunteer to attend outlying white neighborhood junior highs.

The change created serious problems for the internal life of the school, however. Because there were objections to closing Rodgers from its community, the final decision to move the school was not made until three weeks before school was to open in September. The physical move was rushed. The sudden doubling of the student body which accompanied it, led to the recruitment of many students who had neither an interest in nor an understanding of open education. Owens's practice of integrating new students into the school's approach partly by relying on the example of old students broke down as a consequence of the large influx of uninformed newcomers.

Furthermore, as the student body doubled, so did the faculty. Because of the union contract, teachers from Rodgers could stay if they simply expressed interest in open education and a willingness to take an inservice course in it. Many of the Rodgers teachers were attached to the building and loath to take their chances in a citywide transfer pool. They stayed at the school but let their disapproval of open education and their resentment of its 'takeover' be widely known. Some teachers from the old site, experienced in open education, were excessed from the program, because they had less seniority than the Rodgers teachers certified in the same subjects.

Most of the Rodgers teachers, especially those most at odds with open education, stayed only one year. When told by the principal that they would have to go back to college to earn elementary certification, now that their classes included sixth graders, most of the former Rodgers teachers found that prospect more unpleasant than a transfer and left the school. The few who remained were for the most part teachers of non-academic subjects, whose certification was good for both elementary and secondary schools. The rest were replaced by new teachers, however, not by the teachers from the old site who had been excessed during the move. Most of these new teachers had no previous experience in open education, and some had not even requested Jesse Owens when transferring. This new group had to be trained in open education and socialized into Jesse Owens's values.

As Jesse Owens became one among many alternative schools,

new problems arose. The teachers' union, which sought to prevent the magnet schools from acquiring a special status, took a new and lively interest in Jesse Owens's staffing formulas and teachers' schedules, and threatened to become a new source of constraint on the school's distinctive arrangements. It liked neither the privilege of Owens's relatively long teacher preparation periods nor the burden of its expectation that teachers would spend extra time in meetings and with students.

Jesse Owens was now one among many special schools with reason to make special claims on district funds. It had been staffed relatively generously by the system in its early days, but now its student–teacher ratio was governed by the union contract's formula for all magnet schools together. Jesse Owens qualified for a share of federal magnet school money in the second year of desegregation, but then officers in Washington decided that open education did not meet their definition of magnet schools and no more federal funds from the magnet schools grant were available. In the fourth year of desegregation, the year of the study, 1979–80, it also lost its share of funds from the federal basic grant for desegregation. All of these losses of support for staff and materials were sorely felt.

Since other schools were being cut back as well, it was difficult for Owens to follow its old pattern of mobilizing support and making a dramatic appeal for its distinctiveness to the central office or the board. It was now part of a larger group of distinctive schools which shared a common fate. Jesse Owens could not argue that any of the single cuts which it suffered was devastating to its program, yet together they eroded resources and pushed a smaller school staff toward pedagogically less open patterns. The principal spoke of the pattern he experienced as one of chipping away the school's capacity to be distinctive. There was no single dramatic cut around which the staff and parents could rally and fight. For Jesse Owens, then, incorporation into the larger group of magnet schools was a mixed blessing.

At the time of the study, 1979–80, the fourth year of desegregation, the required number of schools in the city had become desegregated. The magnet schools had accomplished the most important part of their work, and it seemed that systemwide thinking was moving more toward consolidation than new invention. I interviewed personnel at the central office a year later. When asked about the magnet schools in general, some curriculum supervisors were critical of Jesse Owens. One unguardedly referred to the school as 'flaky,' then asked not to be identified with that comment. Another spoke clearly though with a careful reserve about supervisors' feelings:

'Now I don't know if you know that that school is a real sore point among the supervisors. They're really frustrated, that they can't work there. I do what I can, and if they won't take it, well . . . there's nothing I can do . . . We're all in content areas and that's our concentration, our interest. And for us it was just devastating to see the whole sequence that we had worked on thrown out.'

The resistance which the Jesse Owens staff had encountered at the central office was beginning to build up again now that the crisis of desegregating the system seemed to have passed. However, personnel there with administrative responsibilities spoke with some appreciation of Jesse Owens as offering a genuine alternative to traditional schools for families who desired one and as dealing effectively with some very difficult students.

Parent recruitment

As Jesse Owens became one of a group of magnet schools, its recruitment was affected in several ways. First, the central office selected the students using the standard simple form for all magnet schools. This form did not ask students or parents to state why they were interested in open education. Further, all applicants were accepted up to the quota for their race and gender, with selection by lot in oversubscribed categories. Consequently there was no way of knowing before students arrived whether they had any interest in or understanding of open education.

Apparently many students and parents did not know what they were signing up for. When I interviewed students, sixteen out of twenty-three, or 70 percent, said the school differed from their expectations and most of these were completely surprised by its approach. Several of these said later in the interview that an older sibling had attended the school. When I asked if the sibling had told them what it would be like most said he or she had not. After the interviews were over, I realized that these students for the most part lived near the school and the older sibling had probably gone to the same school in the sense of the same *building*, that is to the old Rodgers Junior High School, not to the same *program*. During orientation at the beginning of the year, teachers posted a map and had students put in pegs for their houses. The vast majority were in a fairly small circle close to the school, with only a few in each class scattered around the rest of the city. Many of the students interviewed said they walked to school, which meant they lived within two miles. Thus the school seemed to be drawing voluntary enrollments from families in the surrounding working-class area who chose the school because it was close and convenient with little or no understanding of its special educational approach.

As a consequence, the school staff said they had to spend a good deal of energy in simply explaining open education to both new parents and new students. With some, they had to spend further energy persuading them of its worth. A few could not be persuaded but still did not want to withdraw their child from the school; they remained to create conflict.

There was a small but active group of parents who were strong supporters of open education. They met in a group combined with parents at the two open education elementary schools as Parents for Open Education. However, many of the Owens parents in this group were long-time supporters of the school who were seeing a last child through middle school.

The school lost enrollment from middle-class families for three fairly visible reasons. First, open education was becoming less attractive to the middle class on a national basis as the 1970s turned into the 1980s. More directly, the title of Mann School for the Gifted and Talented had enormous appeal for middle-class families, and many who would have chosen Owens previously, or who had chosen it for older children, applied to Mann instead. Furthermore, though no one talked about this issue, because students at Owens rode city buses, they had to wait on street corners in Owens's predominantly black and somewhat shabby neighborhood. Many white parents in particular may have been discouraged from sending children to the school by this fact. At Adams students waited for buses on downtown streetcorners, and the site was served by more lines so that fewer students had to transfer and wait on a corner somewhere else. All of Mann's students, as we shall see, were served by yellow buses. Owens suffered in competition.

The comparatively small number of middle-class families under the new conditions gave the school a smaller cadre of influential parental supporters as it dealt with the school board and central office. It also gave it less word of mouth advertisement in middle-class neighborhoods; this fact depressed the number of its middle-class recruits and lowered the number of skilled students among its entrants. The small proportion of high achievers and middle-class students then made the school yet less attractive to middle-class parents.

Finally, the school suffered as it had to compete for sixth graders with elementary schools, and especially two open education elementary schools created at the time of desegregation. The consequence was a small sixth grade and an influx of new students at the seventh grade level each year. This pattern allowed only two years for the students to learn the ways of open education. It also provided only roughly half, rather than two-thirds, of a student body already familiar with the school and so able to teach its customs to younger peers.

Student recruitment

Jesse Owens enrolled 380 students in 1979–80, the year of the study and the fourth year in the Rodgers building. Table 5-1 compares Jesse Owens to Adams and to the city as a whole in size, racial composition, and proportion of free or reduced lunches. Forty-eight percent of the students were racial minorities, all but a few of them black, and 52 percent of the students were white. Seventy-one percent of the lunches served were to students who qualified for free or reduced price lunch, compared to 59 percent at Adams and only 50 percent in middle schools citywide. The school qualified for Title I funds on the basis of having a preponderance of poor children.

Teachers and administrators agreed that the academic abilities of the students decreased markedly after the move to the Rodgers building. The loss of a large proportion of the middle-class families formerly attracted, and the attraction of many from the neighborhood eventuated in a student body whose scores before entrance were lower than those of fifth graders in the city as a whole. Tables 5-2 and 5-3 give the distribution of scores on standard tests

111

TABLE 5-1 *Characteristics of students at Jesse Owens Middle School compared to those at Adams, and in the city of Heartland, 1979–80 (Adams Avenue, 1978–9)*

	Owens	Adams	Citywide middle schools
Initial enrollment	377	328	12,400
Percent minority students	48	51	54
Percent free lunches to total lunches	71	59	50

Source: Heartland School District *Profile of Schools*

of reading and mathematics at the end of the fifth grade for students who were in the seventh grade in 1979–80, the year of the study at Owens. The scores are reported as the percentage of students scoring at or below each of several national percentile rankings. Scores for Adams and for the city as a whole are supplied for further comparison. The reader can see that Jesse Owens's entering students scored lower than those at Adams and those in the city as a whole. In reading, 71 percent, almost three-quarters, scored below the 50th percentile nationally, and 47 percent or almost half scored in the lowest quarter compared to a national sample. Scores in math were very similar, except that 'only' 40 percent scored in the bottom quarter. However, the school could not simply gear itself to remedial efforts, since 11 percent were in the top quarter nationally in both reading and mathematics. Students representing every level of skill were present.

The large number of students with poor skills in reading and basic mathematics was especially problematic for Jesse Owens because of its special character. Its open approach involved much work in which students were expected to read directions and proceed independently. For this reason, the school asked the central office to allow it to set a floor of a fourth grade reading level for admission. The request was denied. While no reason was given except a reluctance to set special admission standards for magnet schools, it seems probable that the central office was responding to accusations of elitism in the magnet schools of the kind discussed in Chapter 2. Fourth grade skills for entrance to the sixth or seventh grade do not set a very elite standard, but any admissions criterion could have been read as elitism without consideration of its details. Further, some other school would have had to deal with the unskilled students turned away from Jesse Owens.

TABLE 5–2 *Percentages of students at Owens, Adams and citywide scoring at or below national percentile rankings on the Metropolitan Achievement Tests in reading at the end of grade 5, 1978*

Percentile ranking	Owens (N=129)	Adams (N=125)*	City (N=6,081)
90th	96	95	96
75th	89	83	87
50th	71	66	66
25th	47	34	36
10th	16	19	17

*Adams data are for the spring of 1977.

Source: Heartland School District computer data files

TABLE 5–3 *Percentages of students at Jesse Owens, Adams and citywide scoring at or below national percentile rankings on the metropolitan achievement tests in mathematics at the end of grade 5, 1978*

Percentile ranking	Owens (N=125)	Adams (N=125)*	City (N=5,982)
90th	99	96	96
75th	89	86	87
50th	72	65	64
25th	40	33	32
10th	18	16	13

*Adams data are for the spring of 1977.

Source: Heartland School District computer data files

Recruitment was also affected by the fact that many parents, school counselors, and psychologists saw open education as a place for children who had difficulty coping with traditional schools. The staff thought that some such children did indeed shed their school difficulties upon leaving a traditional environment. The school was also helpful to others with emotional problems, but it could absorb only a limited proportion of such students without unduly affecting the character of the student body. This problem had existed throughout the life of the school, but the school's greater visibility as part of a list of well-advertised alternatives somewhat increased the proportion of students with problems. Furthermore, under the new regime associated with magnet schools the school could not require a child whom the staff thought was not improving to leave. They could only try to persuade the child's parents that he or she might do better elsewhere, but many parents of such children would not transfer them because they were at least doing better than they had anywhere else.

Owens's student body, then, was one which could be expected to engage in conflict with the school on the basis of poverty, low achievement, and the previous school behavior patterns of a sizable minority of its students – including some of its white middle-class students with reasonably good standardized test scores.

The blueprint for open education

The Jesse Owens staff developed their own blueprint for open education out of workshops and reading.[3] They continually revised its details. The principal and curriculum coordinator had the most opportunity formally to articulate the approach, but a group of respected teachers also had a good deal of influence. The principal was emphatic that Jesse Owens was an open education school, not a free school. Its primary goal was to help students to become 'responsible for their own learning.' Once that lesson was learned, the Owens staff maintained, all further learning would be accessible, even under adverse circumstances. Basic skills were important for their usefulness in the service of autonomous learning, not the reverse.

Other special educational goals were part of the school's approach but received varied emphasis from the school's formal and informal leaders. Some leaders stressed the importance of integrating different subjects into a unified intellectual experience, and some stressed the importance of fostering students' affective development as a necessary underpinning for their intellectual development. Some emphasized the development of social skills, whether in the form of civility and cooperation or of fostering

114

understanding across lines of ethnicity and gender. All of these aims were discussed to some extent in formal presentations of the school's approach.

In the pursuit of its goals, the school developed an unconventional curriculum, organization of classroom groups, and temporal schedule. In principle, each student, under the guidance of a teacher, was supposed to construct his or her own curriculum around his or her own interests. The teacher had a responsibility to stimulate interests, as well as to facilitate the pursuit of pre-existing ones, and to see that the student did not neglect important areas of learning such as reading and mathematics. More concretely, each classroom was expected to be equipped with five basic 'learning centers' which supplied self-guided materials in essential areas of learning. These could provide complete activities for weaker or less imaginative students and a starting place for adventurous ones. Students were to be encouraged also to design projects which would integrate various subjects in the pursuit of a topic of interest to the individual child.

To facilitate this process, students were assigned to a single self-contained classroom or 'center' instead of having different teachers for different subjects as in other middle schools. These self-contained classrooms included students in all three grades from the sixth through the eighth; ideally a student worked with the same teacher for three years so that the teacher came to know his or her skills and interests in some depth. The older children could both serve as models of industrious independence and help to instruct the younger children in the intellectual and practical strategies required for the open education approach to learning.

There were several resource centers staffed by adults in the school where students could find additional ideas for activities, information, and materials beyond those in the individual self-contained centers. The school was also an active participant in a citywide program of field trips for small groups of students to business and cultural centers in the city.

To ensure structure in students' efforts, much attention was given to 'goal sheets' and 'activity sheets.' Each student, in consultation with the self-contained teacher, was to state a series of goals for every two-week period. Each morning, every student was to fill out an activity sheet listing activities planned for the day which led toward those goals. Before the student could leave his or her self-contained center for work elsewhere in the school, the teacher was to read and initial the activity sheet as adequately detailed and appropriately related to the student's goals. Students were to sign out of the room and to have their folders containing goal and activity sheets with them, ready to show to interested adults wherever they went in the school. At the end of the day they were to write down a brief evaluation of the results of their day's activities.

The adults in the school had become increasingly aware over time that children need to be taught and to practise how to structure their time and focus their efforts to take advantage of a system such as this. Consequently, there was a two-week orientation early in the year in which children were instructed in the resources available at the school, in ways to organize their time, and in how to plan a project. Further, most teachers were more directive early in the year; they assigned group tasks and common projects with common deadlines, and provided more limited choices than they would later in the year. They wanted to prevent students from being paralyzed by the breadth of their freedom and to teach them in incremental steps how to set goals and structure their efforts in pursuit of them.

There were structured activities for students outside their self-contained centers. The school day was broken into four time blocks in addition to the lunch period. During the first block, all students were to be in their self-contained centers for announcements, planning their day's agenda, and activities in which the whole class would share. During two of the other three blocks, students made individual decisions with their teachers concerning whether they should work in the self-contained center or elsewhere in the school. During the third, all of the students in a self-contained center left the room for a variety of 'specialized centers' while the self-contained center teacher had a preparation period. These specialized centers offered specific subjects, such as art, music, home economics, wood shop, physical education and laboratory science. Students selected one of these courses for a six-week period, then had a chance to move to another. Once they were placed in a class, they had to attend that specialized center every day for six weeks during the time block that their class left the self-contained center.

Finally, the school had a reading laboratory, a math laboratory, and two remedial 'academic support centers.' In all but the math laboratory, students received group instruction at regularly scheduled times, based upon tests which demonstrated that they needed assistance with particular basic skills.

Owens's program then departed from most traditional structures and practices in its curriculum, time schedule, and grouping of students. But it did not substitute a lack of structure. Instead, it developed new structures for the work of the school as a whole and attempted to teach students how to create and follow a structure of their own in intellectual endeavors.

School character

The tone of the school

At Jesse Owens, the special purpose of teaching students to take responsibility for their own learning permeated the school's life. Most teachers guided their efforts by this goal; the few who gave more emphasis to traditional practices at least used its rhetoric. When I asked each self-contained center teacher to recommend two students for me to interview, one with strong academic skills and one with weaker academic skills, they looked at their rosters and discussed possible interviewees in terms of the extent to which they had developed responsibility for their own learning. In research interviews with children, when strong students complained about other students or expressed their sense of superiority, they spoke not – as at the other schools – of students who learned slowly or could not understand academic material, but of students who took advantage of the system to do little work, who failed to develop responsibility.

The teachers were philosophically self-conscious and most were able to articulate rather readily and clearly a detailed set of their priorities and the specific activities they had designed to serve them. They were also able to talk about the problems they had encountered in realizing them. They remarked upon their interdependence; no single teacher could insure students' personal, social, and intellectual growth without the cooperation of the body of other staff members. The staff consensus on the value of open education and the perceived need for cooperation from the whole set of adults put pressure on the less enthusiastic to keep their doubts mostly to themselves.

If Jesse Owens staff members were constantly aware that they

117

were part of a special school, they also knew that their ability to be special rested on a precarious base. They felt they were swimming against the cultural mainstream and were often misunderstood. It seemed that the wider system only provisionally provided the special resources and special structural arrangements they needed, and that they could not count on public support. They feared being eliminated by vote of the board with little notice or being subjected to administrative constraints which would eliminate the real essence of their program.

A shared sense of the program's distinctiveness, isolation, and fragility wove a strong net of loyalty among the staff despite vigorous debate over real differences of opinion and practice. Furthermore, at Owens, as at neither of the other schools, the history of the program provided an organizational saga (Clark, 1972) which created a standard for members' endeavors in the present. The school had established its values and goals in the early legendary days; faithfulness to them was at least one important measure of their current degree of success.

There also developed, as happens in many free schools (cf. Deal, 1975; Kozol, 1972; Swidler, 1979), a certain sense of sectlike separation from the rest of the world (Firestone, 1980b). The principal and curriculum coordinator regarded outside visitors somewhat warily as they believed one could only understand the school and judge it fairly if one had an understanding and appreciation of open education. On the other hand, all but a very small group of teachers were quick to note emphatically that Owens was an open and not a free school. They accepted a public school's responsibility to serve a broad clientele who were not selected for their agreement with, or even readiness for, open education. Further, as public school employees, they accepted the legitimacy of general administrative guidelines from the central office, though the principal occasionally had to remind them of this fact of life.

Teacher–student interaction

The Jesse Owens staff noted that they had very few confrontations with students. They attributed the low level of classroom conflict to the school's approach which allowed teachers to come to know their students well as persons and to work with them toward the development of self-control and social responsibility. The near absence of conflict was especially remarkable since Owens, even more than Adams, had a student body with a high proportion of the kind of students most frequently involved in classroom battles with teachers.

In general, students' cooperation was good. The corridors and bathrooms were generally neat and clean, with only occasional graffiti or an excess of paper in the bathrooms. At the time that classes were to begin, the students were usually in their rooms, writing out their activity sheets with plans for the day's activities. One or two students might arrive late, but usually not very late, and then with an excuse. There were a few specific students who seemed to wander the halls with little purpose; other teachers blamed the permissiveness of their self-contained teachers for their behavior.

Thus, while all of the students did not follow all the rules and procedures or feel cooperative and friendly all the time, the majority of students followed school procedures; those who did not engaged in fairly minor infractions which had little impact on other students. There was tension between teachers and some individual students but this remained between individuals and was not a covert expression of the relationship between the teacher and the whole class. In addition, many, if not most, of the self-contained teachers pointed out one or more students who had come to Owens with a history of severe conflict with adults in their previous schools, and who through their years at Owens had become diligent students and cooperative members of the classroom group.

Inter-racial relationships

Inter-racial relations at Owens were not quite as comfortable as at Adams, but were better than those described in most of the literature on desegregated schools. Neither students nor teachers complained of prejudice on the part of teachers. Students sat in groups of one race in the cafeteria, but did not use separate parts of the dining-room. The several long tables which ran the length of the dining-room each had a checkered pattern of alternating small groups of different races. In the playground, groups playing games were sometimes of a single race, but often well-mixed, and some of the groups of students standing talking at the borders of the playing area were mixed. In short, in voluntary settings, most students chose same race companions, but they did not actively avoid contact with the other race.

In classrooms, many Jesse Owens teachers let students choose their tablemates, with the consequence that the tables in the rooms were separated by race and sex as students began the day in their own seats. However, as the day wore on and students moved around the room to use resources and sometimes stopped to chat or confer about a project with others, they often crossed color lines. Again, same race students were preferred where choices were made for companions over the long term, but there was a good deal of voluntary interracial contact in moment to moment interaction. Some teachers assigned students to tables and consciously mixed them by race and gender in doing so.

There was cultural pressure in the school toward accepting desegregation as a proper arrangement. When the students interviewed were asked whether they would prefer their next school to be mostly of one race or mixed half and half, all but one preferred a mixed school. When asked why they preferred a mixed school, some students said because it was fairer, others said they weren't prejudiced, and yet others said a school which is all one race wouldn't teach people how to get along with other races. A few, apparently with experience in mixed schools where one race predominated, said it was important to have an equal mixture so one race did not dominate and put the other at a disadvantage. It is hard from these comments to distinguish between students' true feelings and the influences of adult expectations upon them.

A better measure of students' spontaneous feelings about race came from a question in which they were asked to think of their five best friends and were then asked several questions about those friends, ending with a question concerning how many were of the same or a different race from themselves. (The question was not asked at Adams; so comparable data are not available.) Table 5-4 shows the pattern of answers. More than half the students interviewed had at least one friend of another race, and the proportion having such friends increased from 43 percent among those in their first year at the school to 66 percent among those with three years' experience there. These numbers cannot be considered directly representative of the student body, however, because the sample was small and the method of selection not random.

TABLE 5–4 *Student interviewees with friends of another race at Owens by number of years in school*

	1st year	2nd year	3rd year	Total
No friends of another race	57% (4)	43% (3)	33% (3)	43% (10)
One friend of another race	14% (1)	0% (0)	22% (2)	13% (3)
Two or more friends of another race	29% (2)	57% (4)	44% (4)	43% (10)
Total	100% (7)	100% (7)	99% (9)	99% (23)

There was a good deal of variation in interviewees' perceptions of generalized relations between the races. Those who had friends of another race themselves tended to answer affirmatively when asked whether black and white children generally mixed in the cafeteria and playground, while those who had best friends only of their own race answered that the races kept separate in those settings. Most students found odd a question concerning whether other students of one's own race would be critical if one had friends of another race; they said there was no such pressure and seemed to find the very idea surprising. A few, however, said that some students did exert such pressure. One white girl gave an example of a black friend of hers who was teased and pressured by other black girls because she jumped rope inside in a mixed group instead of going outside to jump rope with an all black group.

Thus there was evidence that children of different races were comfortable in one another's presence at Owens and that some developed a friendship with at least one individual of another race. Still, race did maintain some salience as a criterion for association or friendship. There was clearly more friendly contact within than between races; some children, though not a majority, stayed protectively within their own race, and a few even encouraged others to do likewise.

Open education in practice

Not only the ethos of the faculty as a body, but administrative arrangements, such as the way students were grouped and the time schedule, pushed teachers actually to practice the school's official educational approach. Direct administrative pressure for visible manifestations of the expected education – such as learning centers in the self-contained center rooms and the regular use of goal and activity sheets by students – also had an impact on teachers who might have had doubts about open education, and upon those who were reluctant to make the extra efforts its active practice entailed.

Still, there were noticeable differences among the teachers. At one extreme was a teacher whose philosophy and practice verged on those of a free school. He rarely insisted on the use of goal and activity sheets, did not have fully developed centers in his room, made decisions on activities by vote, and taught according to the flow of immediate interests. There were also one or two teachers who gave the class little structure, not out of conviction like the first teacher, but apparently more out of inability or disinclination to make the considerable efforts required to create structure for thirty separate individuals with thirty intellectual agendas. At the other extreme were some teachers who introduced a good deal of traditional structure and many common activities of traditional kinds into the classroom. Between these extremes, there were enough differences to give an observer a sense that each self-contained classroom developed quite a distinctive flavor and offered a noticeably differentiated experience to its students.

The specialized centers and laboratories were expected to have somewhat different patterns of teaching and learning, since they were charged with teaching specific subjects or remedial skills. Additionally, their teachers had only a third as long to see three times as many students – and the faces changed every six weeks. Furthermore, almost all the specialized center teachers said they had to give some demonstrations to the whole class because students often started the classes needing to learn the rudimentary skills of the subject. Still, just as among the self-contained teachers, there were marked differences among the specialized center teachers in the way they structured their classes. Some allowed much more opportunity for individual choice of projects and worked more closely with individuals than did others.

Differences between teachers interacted with differences among the students, so that students' accounts of their school experience showed considerable variety.[4] Students with lower skills were likely to cling to the language of traditional subjects as they talked about their experience and to give accounts of their days in terms of 'doing' a series of subjects, much as they might in traditional schools. They seemed to seek out the kind of short, well-defined, closed-ended tasks which literature on low achievers suggests they prefer. Students with higher skills described more complex activities and spoke of enterprises which required some definition and initiative of their own.

All of the students were asked in interviews to describe the goals they had set for the current period and their activities on the day of their interview and the preceding day. Two replies to these questions convey a little of the flavor of the variety of their responses. Christine, a black eighth grade girl, was described by one of the teachers in the academic support centers as possibly needing the 'shelter' of a program for the mildly retarded when she moved into a big high school. Her teacher, Mr Koenig, considered her one of his success stories because in three years she had overcome a fiery temper and become a respected member of the class and a diligent worker, despite very slow progress in improving her skills, which were still at about the third grade level.

INTERVIEWER: You have to write goals and an activity sheet each morning. What were your goals and activities for today?
CHRISTINE: Finish two lessons in my math folder and read fifteen pages. Finish spelling, write my sentences and look up the meaning first and then write the sentences to them. My writing – I do writing for my English goals – to do two pages of English for homework. And [the activity for] my project was to have a conference with him to find another way to do maps for my project. And that's about it.

An eighth grade white boy who was capable but unambitious according to Ms Layne, his teacher, illustrates the greater complexity with which the more skilled students describe their days. His statement also illustrates how Ms Layne dealt with such a student.

INTERVIEWER: What are your goals right now?
MIKE: Well, one is to work through my algebra book, in the next couple of weeks if I can. Or do it as fast as I can. And one is to go to the reading lab to try to get my study skills.

123

And one is to set up a center in the class for the other students' use, and one is get done with my autobiography which I have to have done by April 1st.

INTERVIEWER: What's the center you're setting up?

MIKE: I'm not really sure yet because I just made the goal last Monday and sort of . . . Well, I was thinking about like setting up a human body center with the help of Ms Layne. She suggested that I do that for the class 'cause she thought the class isn't doing very well in that and she wanted to set that up. So she asked if I would do that.

INTERVIEWER: What do you need to do that? What kind of materials and so forth?

MIKE: Well, I guess that I would have to get down to the curriculum center and check out some books on it and read up on it before I could set it up because I'm not that great on it really.

Changes in Owens's philosophy and practice

Owens's character, especially its educational philosophy and practice, was undergoing some change during the time of the study. The dwindling resources in staffing and moral support from above as the magnet plan was consolidated, the change in the student body which accompanied the move, and the blending of the faculty from the old program with newcomers all contributed pressure toward evolution in the character of the Owens program. More will be said of this change in discussing each of the influences which shaped the school.

Technological and logistical influences on school character

As Owens encouraged open-ended curricular tasks which integrated subjects, the spirit of its curricular changes was in some senses diametrically opposed to Adams's emphasis on the acquisition of discrete skills in each subject. None the less, the two schools had several similarities in their technological arrangements which had similar effects on their potentially volatile students. The schools were alike in assuming that students in the same grade would begin at very different starting points, in judging them according to individual progress rather than according to rank in a group, and in instructing them individually or in small groups most of the time. At both schools, these practices encouraged positive student–teacher relationships and positive relationships among students of different races.

The effects of technological arrangements on student–teacher relationships

Curricular structure

At Adams, it was assumed that children in the same grade would come with different skills; at Owens it was assumed in addition that they would come with different interests which would affect what they were to learn in their year with a given teacher. Students were not compared to a standard of 'sixth grade work' and found wanting if their skills were low. Both teachers and peers at Owens judged students according to whether they seemed to work conscientiously and to participate responsibly in the common life of the class, not according to whether or not their skills met an absolute, presumably age-appropriate, standard.

Further, at Owens, because classes were multi-aged, differences based on grade level or age melted into those based on students' rate of progress. Grade level was not a salient public identity which set up expectations for performance; both students and teachers paid little attention to it. When I asked teachers the grade level of particular students, many had to consult their rosters in order to answer. The multi-aged basis of grouping made both slow learners and fast learners less conspicuous than they would have been in classes with only one grade level. Thus, stigma, and with it social pressure toward rebellion, was lifted from students with low academic skills. Hard work and progress from their starting point could earn them a reputation as solid academic citizens.

Academic reward structure

Owens's grading system included no numbers at all; so students could not even rank themselves based on inquiries about others' numbers. There was no honor roll. Students received progress reports in the form of narrative paragraphs describing their progress or difficulties in areas the teacher found important.

125

This system, like Adams's, gave a student whose skills were poor a chance to earn a good report through diligence and progress in remedying his or her weaknesses. Further, because the school valued taking responsibility for one's own learning as an end in itself, even a student who was genuinely slow or who was not adept at academic learning could earn praise for effort and improvement.

Owens's system also lifted the stigma of failure from the teachers. At Owens, since students were supposed to be responsible for their own learning, the teacher's role became, as one teacher put it, like that of a gardener. The teacher could plant and water and weed but could not force the plant to grow. If he or she supplied appropriate and stimulating materials, explained, encouraged, and cajoled, but still the student did not learn, the failure was partly the student's responsibility, not solely the teacher's. Not having to bear as heavy a burden of guilt when students failed to learn as do traditional teachers (Lortie, 1975; McPherson, 1972), Owens teachers were not as easily moved to anger with them. They were therefore freed to work supportively with the students, trying their best to help them progress.

Classroom activity structure

As at Adams, the activity structure in Owens's classrooms allowed students to keep their level of skill private most of the time. Thus low performers were not driven to rebel or to bate the teacher into expelling them from the room in order to hide their inability to read aloud or to work a problem on the board. The activity structure at Owens differed somewhat from that at Adams as most self-contained centers, though not all, made more provision for oral reports and for discussion of various sorts than was made at Adams. Thus even though students could keep much of their work private, in most classrooms they did get some practice in speaking before a group and in exchanging ideas in a formal setting. Since children usually had an opportunity to plan oral reports around their strengths and to contribute to discussions on a voluntary basis, these occasions did not put the students who performed less well too severely under pressure. At the same time, they gave students with good skills an opportunity to display their prowess.

Because the class worked individually or in small groups much more often than as a whole group, students who were not in a mood to work ordinarily distracted only those students seated near them, just as they did at Adams. When a student did require discipline from the teacher because of an angry outburst, an infringement on others' rights, or a simple failure to concentrate on the work in hand, teachers could deal with the infraction quietly, one to one, without the rest of the class as an audience. Teachers thus could take their time in responding to the individual needs and situation of students as they disciplined. They also did not have to give standardized punishments in order to appear fair to other students. At Owens, if either the student or the teacher were really angry, sometimes the teacher would take the student out in the hall where their conference could be even more private. These arrangements clearly made it easier for teachers and the students most given to nonconformity to relate fairly constructively to one another.

If the Adams teachers knew their students well because of the activity structure, the Owens teachers knew theirs intimately. As thirty students and a teacher interacted in a small space, with activities at least some of which required cooperation, through a large part of the day, they were bound to get to know one another personally. When the same teacher worked with students for three years, their bond was considerably deepened. Further, as one teacher said, the students' ability to direct the curriculum around their interests and the informality of the classroom routine allowed feelings to 'rise to the surface like cream.' Students expressed their feelings; they acted like fully rounded human beings rather than persons playing the formal role of student.

This intimacy did have one negative implication for student–teacher relations, however. Intimacy can breed irritation as well as empathy. The intensive and extensive contact between teacher and student which Owens fostered led to some personal antipathies when students were chronically uncooperative or student and teacher together created a combustible combination. In these situations, a reservoir of anger grew up which was quickly and easily tapped by minor incidents. The school allowed either a teacher or a student to request a change of self-contained center for the student, at any time, though preferably between school years, so that pairs who were not interacting constructively could be separated.

In general, interaction in the classroom had a relaxed and personal tone; the formalized style of exchange in traditional classrooms was nearly absent. Even though it was clear that the teacher was in charge and could make demands upon each student, exchanges took place between full persons who were semi-equals. When teachers chastised students it was generally for lack of effort or for distracting others, rather than for not following directions or being disrespectful. Teachers responded especially strongly to slights or insulting comments directed by one student at another. Even when a teacher was across the room from such an exchange, he or she would often correct the perpetrator and later follow up the correction at some length, in private. It was infractions of this kind that most often led teachers to real anger and strong punishment. This response did not come simply from teachers' sensitivity to feelings and interpersonal ties. Teachers worked hard to build up students' confidence as a way of getting them to learn more effectively. Thoughtless or cruel teasing from peers could undercut the fruits of the teacher's labors.

Not all teachers had the interpersonal skills to take advantage of the opportunities offered by the school's educational approach and activity structure, however. As at Adams, there were teachers whose different behavior generated different responses in the students and highlighted the importance of the patterns followed by the majority in affecting relationships. For example, one self-contained teacher, who had been with the program since before the move, confronted the students with an oppositional tone which led to a contest of wills throughout the day I observed her. She nagged students to work from the front of the room so all could hear. She created confrontations, threatened, and sent several students to the assistant principal. Students whispered to me that they were a bad class and that they did not like their teacher, a common occurrence in conflictual traditional classrooms.

One of the specialized center teachers created conflict with his classes with his desultory instruction, criticisms, and ostentatious locking of the cabinet each time supplies were taken. His classes were noisy and restless. A few other teachers had difficulty in maintaining a flow of constructive activity. Neither the philosophy nor the technology of the school guaranteed pleasant and constructive relationships, if teachers did not exercise the skill and insight needed to benefit from the opportunities they offered.

Student–teacher relationships as a cycle of mutual response
In the majority of classrooms at Owens, as at Adams, however, it was clear that technological arrangements reduced students'

need to initiate conflicts with their teachers. The teachers used the energy which their counterparts in many traditional schools spend on conflict and public confrontation in helping students academically. The help teachers gave and the good spirits they maintained in turn inclined the students to treat them civilly.

The effects of technological arrangements on inter-racial relationships

Equality of status

At Owens, the rarity not only of public academic performance but of skill-based groups made it difficult to compare the skills of black and white students as groups. This situation helped to equalize the classroom status of the races, as did the fact that there were not large differences in skills between blacks and whites. There were many whites with poor skills at Owens and only a few of either race who were performing far above average.

The varied activities which were legitimate aspects of learning in Owens's classrooms also allowed a variety of skills to come to the fore in the course of a day. Students thus had more opportunity to display some strength which could gain them respect from others than in classrooms dominated by the teacher with a limited set of activities considered to be of any importance. Since concentrated and consistent academic effort and improvement were considered important virtues, even low achievers had one path to respect open to them.

In almost all the self-contained centers there were one or two students whom teachers described as persistently difficult in their behavior. Some of these children were very visible; they tended to wander around the room or to sit staring into space. They often seemed isolated from other students and in some cases their overtures for conversation were rejected. They talked to the teachers more than other students did, and in some but not all cases entered into conflict with them. These students were disproportionately white. Thus, not only did the black children escape low status from low academic performance, but they also escaped the 'bad kid' label which often goes with the conflict in which low performers engage. Instead, predominantly white children who had trouble adjusting even to Owens's flexible demands bore that label.

129

Cooperation

Owens students' experience with cooperation in racially mixed groups was uneven, depending on the self-contained centers to which they were assigned and the specialized centers they selected. When teachers allowed students to choose their own tablemates and groups for work on joint projects, most groups included only one race. When teachers assigned seats and teams for projects, these groups provided an opportunity for cross-racial acquaintance and occasionally for cooperation; tablemates did not regularly have work in common.

Authorities' emphasis on integration

Owens laid less stress on ethnicity as a part of identity and on inter-racial activities in its life as a whole school than did Adams. Though the school did celebrate Jesse Owens's birthday, and the events of his life were discussed, there were fewer special events or common curricular activities which made any reference to ethnicity.

The assistant principal and counselor at Owens were black, but they were considerably less visible to either the staff or the students than were the white principal and curriculum coordinator. The staff as a whole, not counting the aides, was 28 percent black. The aides were about half black. Four of the thirteen self-contained center teachers were black. All had come from the old site and were well-respected by the administration and other teachers. There were also three black teachers among the specialized center teachers; all had formerly been part of the Rodgers staff. Thus blacks were visible among the faculty and their presence was a legitimating force for the black students, though they were not as strongly represented in the school's leadership as at Adams where the principal was black.

Students' experience with authority figures who legitimated the worth of members of ethnic minorities and discussed openly the importance of developing social contacts beyond one's own ethnic group varied according to the self-contained center and the specialized centers in which they participated. Some self-contained teachers devised learning centers which touched on ethnicity and some put up pictures or displays which celebrated the accomplishments of members of minority ethnic groups. Others did not. Some spent a fair amount of time in class meetings discussing relationships across ethnic lines and the need to get to know members of a different race from one's own. Others did not deal with these issues or did so only fleetingly.

Jesse Owens's students varied considerably in their attitudes toward race; this variation may have been affected by the variable influences on racial attitudes exerted in different self-contained centers where students spent most of their time and received their fundamental orientation to the school. Students had less to say about the subject of race when it was raised in the interview than at either of the other two schools. If they had a common ethos, it was one which regarded race as one of several individual characteristics. Many students clearly chose their major associates within their own race, but apparently more as a matter of practice than of principle. As already noted, many engaged in casual friendly interaction and even formed friendships across racial lines, in most cases without exciting notice or comment from friends of their own race.

Technological sources of change

During the year of the study, there began to be visible changes in the staff's technological actions and their thoughts and plans about technology. Externally generated changes were steadily increasing the difficulty of following their previous technological patterns. Direct external pressures for change were also having an impact.

The technology of the Owens program made unusually high demands upon teachers, especially upon teachers in self-contained centers. To be successful, they needed to ensure that interaction flowed smoothly when the class worked together and was appropriately limited so as not to interfere with productivity when students were working alone or with a small group. Teachers had to remain aware of the activities of many persons at once so that they could help everyone to stay on task. Teachers had to be both empathetic and firm in their work with individuals. They needed to be supportive of students who were uneasy planning their own goals and budgeting their own time, but to be firm and demanding in setting high standards for students who preferred to socialize or were lackadaisical in their efforts. They also had to be both knowledgeable about many subjects and their interconnections and inventive in finding ways to fire students' imagination and

131

enthusiasm for learning. In order to help each individual child to develop in taking responsibility for his or her own learning and in the substantive development of that learning, they needed to remember – with the help of a well-organized notation system – each child's progress in a variety of specific academic skills and subjects and his or her stage of personal development.

Some teachers had the capacity and the will to rise to these challenges more adequately than did others. Those who lacked the required capacities tended to move in one of two opposite directions, becoming either more laissez-faire or more teacher-directed than the school expected. The former group gave the students less direction and pressure to keep productive than they needed, while the latter gave them less scope for individual initiative and variation than open education promised. Given Owens's unselected faculty, it was remarkable that most did not succumb to one of these alternatives, but taught in some version of the style that the school's leadership expected. For these capable and dedicated teachers, it took enormous energy to direct a class, exercising all of the required skills in kaleidoscopic succession day after day, year after year.

The demands of the open education approach had initially been kept within reasonable limits by the board's granting Owens a smaller than average class size. However, when Owens became one of the set of magnet schools and fell under union rules concerning student–teacher ratios in all magnet schools, its ratio rose from twenty-five to twenty-eight to one. During the fall of the study, after the school lost federal funding for a teacher for its math laboratory at the same time that one of the self-contained teachers resigned for personal reasons, the faculty and administration decided that the math laboratory was important enough to their program for each self-contained teacher to take two of the students in the departing teacher's class, making it possible for the math lab teacher to continue his work. Teachers therefore had ratios of thirty to one. Further, the same cuts eliminated two aide positions which, because of union rules on seniority, meant the loss of two talented aides who had major responsibilities. Teachers felt the impact of the larger number of students and the slimmer supporting services intensely.

Further, because the move to the Rodgers building had led many children from the neighborhood with very low skills to apply to the school, the approach and the student body became somewhat ill-matched. A student body many of whom had less than fourth grade reading skills and needed further instruction in fundamental arithmetical operations simply did not have the capacity to direct their own activities through the extensive use of written suggestions, directions and information which the program's technological structure demanded. Furthermore, students who had come to Owens because they experienced conflicts with traditional schools often at least initially had emotional reasons to be unwilling to work consistently in Jesse Owens's style of independent industry even when they had the skills to do so. Jesse Owens's system thus became far more labor-intensive for the teachers than it had been with its original population.

Finally, Owens students did not do well on the standardized tests administered by the district. Their scores created political problems for the school and for the district. They fed the image of open education as all play and no work, and, since they were published each spring, they at least potentially discouraged families from enrolling their children at Owens, especially those who were ambitious and whose children were capable. Furthermore, black parents in the district as a whole were focusing their disappointment with the desegregation plan in new pressure for improvement of educational quality as indicated by improved test scores.

At the March faculty meeting during the study, the principal told the faculty in blunt terms that the scores of the previous year's seventh graders on standardized tests of reading and especially mathematics had been very low in comparison to national and even to city norms. He said that the school simply could not afford to let this situation continue. The majority of the teachers agreed with little argument that something had to be done for the welfare both of the school as a whole and of the children whose files would carry these low scores with them through the rest of their school careers.

As they discussed possible methods to improve the scores, teachers analyzed the sources of the problem. Some suggested that the school's open-ended, integrative approach to learning did not well prepare students to take tests. Some teachers looked at the students' scores on subsections of the test and noted that the Owens students had done better on the supposedly more difficult word problems, which require the kind of complex thinking the

133

school encouraged, than on apparently simpler problems. Others pointed out that Owens students were unused to thinking in discrete categories in the ways demanded by multiple choice questions. Teachers noted further that without tests as part of the school's regular program, students were not accustomed to considering them important events worthy of special concentration nor were they habituated to the burst of energy and rapid activity required to do well on a timed test.

In sum, then, pressure for change in the school's technological approach came both from the outside and from the teachers' experience with the technological process. The inherently high demands of the school's technological approach were increased by growth in the number of students per teacher and loss in supporting services. The low academic skills of the students, and the presence of an increasing minority of students with emotional problems, made it difficult for students to develop the capacity and willingness to use learning centers and resources outside the classroom to work independently. Poor standardized test scores promised to create political problems for the school and career difficulties for students.

Teachers were under enormous pressure to retreat to less labor-intensive, less individualized, methods of instruction and to concentrate more narrowly on the development of basic skills as primary ends. They began to look for ways to teach skills to groups. They began to schedule more common tasks so they could be sure that everyone was working on important skills and so they could follow their progress more economically. Self-contained teachers looked toward the staff of the reading laboratory and the academic support centers – whose appointed tasks were to take small groups at regularly scheduled times for work on basic skills – for more assistance and more results. At least some began to think in the more conventional categories of skills and subjects and to think of education as the process of moving students to higher levels in these skills.

Logistical influences at Owens

Though the school was in a black neighborhood, it was near the edge of that neighborhood. None the less, Owens's turf was not as neutral as Adams's. Still, Owens drew students from over seventy schools.[5] Thus, as at Adams, students were freed from the norms of their previous schoolfriends and of friends in their neighborhoods. They could become engaged with the school's curriculum or could idle their engines, as they could not if peers' norms either discouraged engagement or encouraged competition. They were also free to make friends of a different race.

The Owens building aroused little comment from the staff. No one praised it, but only a few condemned it for being oppressively institutional. It was in some ways well-suited to the program, despite dark halls and an institutional feel to its public spaces. Its spacious classrooms, well-lit by large windows, could in most cases accommodate the stations for learning centers and the many materials in the rooms, and still allow for easy movement as the students used resources. Further, the building was large enough in relation to the size of the student body to provide space for laboratories and rooms stocked with resources for students and teachers.

Owens's time schedule and method of grouping students were important in supporting its special educational approach. The time schedule and the method of grouping also fostered deeper than usual relations between teachers and students and provided students with a chance to know the peers they encountered during most of the day very well. This intimacy could provide a shelter for some students who found the size and changing faces of traditional schools difficult to deal with. At the same time, because students were allowed to travel through the school and to use community resources, students who did not need shelter could encounter a stimulating array of adults and other students as they pursued their educational goals.

Faculty culture and school character

The Owens faculty, unlike the faculties of the other two schools, shared an explicit ideology. Furthermore, they and the school's administrators were in acknowledged agreement upon it. Together, the whole staff had a self-consciously distinctive view of education which they used to justify their special practices. According to their ideology, their primary goal was to teach children to be responsible for their own learning. They agreed that they were teaching in a holistic fashion. The curriculum was based on the integration of subjects, and children's personal and social development was seen as inextricably bound to their intellectual learning. Teachers varied in the primacy they gave to the elements of this ideology and in the strength with which they endorsed it, but all of them recognized it as the credo of the school.

There were, in addition, less explicit shared assumptions and attitudes common to the Owens faculty which contributed to a distinctive style in the teachers' relations with the students and each other and a distinctive atmosphere in the school. The teachers were accepting of both students and other adults and shared a sense that Owens was a special place, a place where good education was happening.

Faculty culture and teachers' attitudes toward students

Both their ideology and this deeper consensus, which can be called the culture of the Owens faculty, were concretely expressed in the teachers' statements about their students and also in what they did *not* say about them. The categories which teachers constructed for talking about the students reflected their understanding of learning and their own values. They labeled as exemplary those students who had learned to work responsibly and diligently, even if they were not high achievers. They criticized children most often for being unwilling or unable to work consistently without close supervision and for distracting the class from their serious pursuits. Several teachers complained that the children the school had received since moving to the new building had less understanding of open education and weaker academic skills than those who were admitted at the old building, but they did not mention that these children were economically poorer.

Teachers did not talk about students in terms of their families. One almost never heard about drunken fathers, single mothers, too much responsibility for siblings, or older brothers in jail, although, judging from the neighborhoods from which students came and from the poverty reflected in the percentage eligible for free lunch, many families must have had such problems. The teachers talked about parents as problems only as they directly affected the school or the child's school participation. Thus teachers told me about parents who were unconvinced of the worth of open education, or who refused to insist that a truant child attend school, or who encouraged a child in rebellion against the teacher's requirements for her. But they did not talk about parents' own problems or their breaches of propriety.

In short, the teachers were more concerned that a child make an effort to learn from his or her starting place and show some initiative and persistence in the effort, than that he or she display the highest skills in the class without effort and initiative. They were more concerned that a child show courtesy and consideration toward other individuals and the class as a whole, than about the respectability of his or her family.

This attitude led them to take students with low skills seriously as academic learners and to treat students who were poorly dressed, used crude language, or were defiant as capable of learning courtesy and consideration. As at Adams, this cultural perspective was a necessary supplement to the school's technological arrangements in creating constructive relations between students and teachers. If teachers had publicly exposed or derided the academic efforts of students with low skills and had treated students who arrived in the school with rough manners angrily and contemptuously, the constructive relationships which predominated in the school could quickly have been transformed – as they were in the classrooms of individual teachers who did not follow the general pattern.

Faculty culture and teachers' relations with each other

The Owens staff also treated one another distinctively. They interacted more as full persons than as narrow role players, and they offered one another an acceptance which was striking. In part, this acceptance may have represented an alliance which resulted from the fact that they felt the rest of the school system and many parents misunderstood and failed to appreciate them. But this acceptance also included me as an outsider uncommitted to their approach, with remarkably few tests of my perspective except some initial ones by the principal. It seemed that the teachers accepted one another as they did the students, simply for their personhood.

To say that the teachers extended one another acceptance is not to say that there were no significant disagreements among the faculty; in fact there were several. For example, self-contained center teachers and teachers from the specialized centers and labs had different kinds of responsibilities and differently structured roles which re-enforced differences in their educational priorities. Differences in prior experience among teachers from the old building, from Rodgers, and new teachers led them also to have identifiably different perspectives on their teaching. There were further disagreements among teachers which did not exactly follow the lines of current responsibilities or past experience. These divisions were sometimes expressed in strong statements of differences openly voiced in large meetings. In smaller support groups, teachers criticized others, often absent, if not by name then by clearly identifiable description of their actions.

The faculty felt no compulsion to address one another in tones of sweetness and light. On the contrary, the Owens faculty were easily the most blunt and fractious of the three faculties in their public dealings with each other. In several of their faculty meetings teachers addressed pointed questions in annoyed tones to the principal or curriculum coordinator. Still, their quarrels, open and genuine as they were, were not duels to the death. No one questioned another's right to be part of the faculty or his or her fundamental integrity. These were quarrels over specific actions or patterns of actions, not personal attacks. It was assumed that differences should be aired and discussed. Compromises would be reached, one side would be persuaded of the other's logic, or the conflict would continue, but in any case relationships would not be ruptured. Like a large family, the adults at Jesse Owens had vigorous open arguments, but, like a family, they did not question their attachment to one another – or to their students – or everyone's right to belong.

This mutual acceptance seemed to be related to an aspect of their attachment to the special program. The teachers at Owens felt that they were on the right track in their approach to teaching and in their treatment of the students. They had doubts and worries about specific aspects of their pedagogy and they experimented with various changes. They expressed many frustrations with the conditions of their work, especially the large numbers of students, the low skills of many, the proportion of students with emotional problems, and the lack of public understanding and support of their efforts. But despite all that they felt they were good teachers. They saw evidence of the quality of their teaching and experienced rewards for their efforts in the response of some, even if not all, students.

Their security with their teaching, as well as their openness to further learning, was expressed in their unusual custom of observing one another in the classroom. This pattern had started early in the school's history, and it continued even after eight years. A new teacher brought in to replace some one who resigned said that he was learning about open education mostly by observing other teachers. Veterans also continued to observe one another, although as they learned about differences in philosophy and style, they generally observed and were observed by other teachers with whom they had a good deal in common.

Evidence for the relationship of the teachers' sense of competence to their positive attitudes toward one and another and the school is supplied by two different contexts in which both were absent. The first exception involved individuals who differed from the rest of the faculty. Two teachers were fundamentally critical of the basic forms of the school and of the other staff overall in their interviews. Their tone implied rejection, not just frustration over specific differences. Two other teachers were nearly as negative. Three of these four teachers seemed to be the least successful of those I observed in the classroom; they lacked either the skill or the effort to develop an industrious and harmonious classroom.

The other exception affected the faculty as a whole. In the weeks following the increase in the number of students in each room to thirty, a teacher in the reading laboratory resigned to leave the city. As a consequence, the reading laboratory was temporarily closed much of the time while the remaining teachers reorganized. Therefore, there were both more students all told in each room and a greater proportion remaining in the room during each hour. The self-contained teachers felt the strain of a crowded classroom and foresaw increasing pressures of this kind ahead of them. The result was a great deal of tension and some emotional confrontations between self-contained teachers and the reading laboratory teachers. These confrontations had a more acrid tone than others had. External pressures on the school were cutting resources to the point where self-contained center teachers, especially, were not only feeling harassed but questioning whether they would be able to continue to feel effective in the classroom.

The immediate consequence was sharpened conflict among the faculty.

Pressures for change in the faculty's meaning system

Jesse Owens's teachers manifested an infectious sense of dedication to the school's special approach and an acceptance of the fundamental worth of children and other adults. I found myself thinking of images from family life in trying to characterize the quality of relationships among the adults. The teachers treated their students with some of the non-judgmental fundamental acceptance ideally offered by parents, and they sometimes got into angry wrangles with the most difficult which had an intensity that reminded one of the family. Much of the strength of the way the faculty could deal with the potentially difficult student body stemmed from this family-like quality in their relations, as teachers accepted, listened to, prodded, and assisted students as unique individuals.

Furthermore, there was a remarkable lack of class-based consciousness among the teachers. They did not remark upon families' behavior when it violated conventional norms of respectability, and they did not seem to be critical of children with working-class dress and speech or interests, as long as they made progress in organizing and carrying through an academic agenda and treated others with basic courtesy.[6]

In displaying these qualities, the Jesse Owens faculty exhibited behavior which many critics of traditional education have described as virtuous in dealing with any students, and especially with low achievers from working-class backgrounds. None the less, one of the functions of the school is to move the children out of the family and teach them to cope in the impersonal public sphere; another function is to promote success in a world where working-class dress and interests can make it more difficult to gain access to middle-class jobs. The qualities which can be called strengths of the Owens teachers disinclined them singlemindedly to push students toward actions and behavioral styles most useful for middle-class success. The teachers tried to teach students to think for themselves, to be considerate of others, and to become more fully and genuinely themselves. In so doing, they sometimes forgot about the weight the rest of the world would place upon students' ability to make a good showing on standardized multiple choice tests, and to display the symbols and style of middle-class life.

They were not oblivious to the societal value on limited academic skills and a polished self-presentation, however. The readiness of the majority of the faculty to search for strategies to improve students' test scores when the principal reported on the previous year's weakness at the March faculty meeting reflected movement within the faculty toward more emphasis upon traditional school skills and more direction from teachers in shaping students' goals. Pressures from outside the school and from technological problems provided an impetus for this change in attitude. But there was as well a slow change in the faculty culture, or at least its ideology, which supported or complemented these pressures.

As one of the highly respected informal leaders ruminated aloud on his understanding of the school's goals in an interview, he gave expression to this process of change. Directly and indirectly, he showed its roots in changes in thought about education in the larger culture, in mutual socialization between new teachers and old ones like himself, and in the more pressing importance of concentrating on basic skills when students are tardy in mastering them.

INTERVIEWER: What do you see as the goals the school is ideally trying to reach?

MR KOENIG: Well, we're here to help kids become self-directed and I don't know if everybody agrees on that . . . Certainly my view has changed. I used to think that meant helping kids do what they wanted to do to the best of their ability. [Now] I think there's more to learn. They should be doing some of the things that I think they should be doing. I think that adults have experiences that kids don't have. We ought to be able to recommend certain ways in order for them to pick up skills that it would be awful for them not to learn even if they don't see the value right away . . .

INTERVIEWER: Well, did you come to the conclusion about the importance of saying to children, 'Look, here's a skill you're going to need,' by yourself? Or is that something that the faculty has been moving toward together?

MR KOENIG: I think that people who are more traditionally

oriented, who maybe have no open ed background, pointed out to the rest of us that there were some things that weren't being learned that were important. And why not? So that led me at least to evaluate what was going on in my classroom. To try to figure out why weren't kids taking homework with them. Why do some kids not read at all or as little as possible?

And then I started to realize that most of the kids really weren't setting goals. The goals they were setting were so mundane and, oh I don't know, piddling. They weren't exciting. They weren't meaningful. They didn't have any relationship to what the kids wanted to do in the future, near future or distant future. They were just goals that they set because they had to set goals.

Whereas I think that if a kid says, 'Well I read at the fifth grade level and boy I'd like to read at an eighth grade level by the end of the year,' that's a challenge. That's a real challenge and it's something that they can work for. So that when they start setting their daily goals and their daily plans, they have a target they're pushing for. Something that's worthwhile. . . .

I don't think that kids need to set in concrete what their values are. And I think that's a danger if we lead them to believe – or lead ourselves to believe – they're going to have some clear-cut values. You want to move in that direction. Keep them going that way, rather than saying, 'Well, life is whatever happens to you today.'

There were three groups of teachers whose beliefs were gradually pushing the culture of the whole faculty in the directions this teacher described. First was the group of teachers who joined the faculty at the beginning of the second year in the Rodgers building, most of whom were from traditional elementary schools. Though they were delighted with the depth of acquaintance with their students and the possibility of helping them mature personally provided by Jesse Owens's approach, they maintained a sense of urgency about ensuring the development of basic skills from their earlier experiences. The teachers in the laboratories, whose job was to teach remedial skills, and the teachers in the specialized centers, whose job was to teach specific subjects – and many of whom came from the subject-centered Rodgers Junior High program – also stressed the acquisition of skills as an end in itself.

Finally, black teachers who had been with the original program were more active than many others in offering instruction in basic skills and ensuring that students paid attention to them. They thought children who were members of racial minorities or who had families which could give them few economic and educational advantages could not afford deficiency in these skills under any circumstances. These teachers and the teachers from the original Jesse Owens, who were the core carriers of the school culture, mutually influenced one another and moved toward one another's positions after they were brought together in the Rodgers building. The conditions the teachers faced in the years in the Rodgers building with increased numbers of students overall and more students with very weak skills added weight to the perspectives of those who advocated a change in emphasis in the program.

The exercise of power and school character

The principal at Owens had been with the program from the beginning and many teachers said they thought it would not exist without him. They doubted it could long survive without a principal similarly dedicated to open education.

The principal's effect on the program

The principal's representation of the school to the district hierarchy
The teachers were virtually unanimous in saying that the principal did an outstanding job of interpreting the school to outside audiences and in getting what it needed, whether in resources, such as staffing, or in exceptions to standard school procedures. They described him as persistent and indefatigable in his efforts on behalf of the school and as brave and determined in the face of pressure and criticism from his superiors.

The principal's impact on students
Several of the faculty also praised the principal for the role he played directly with students. He made an effort to get to know students individually, to stay in touch with them as a group, and to be personally available to them. He supervised the lunchtime recreation in the playground every day in all kinds of weather,

watching how both individuals and the students as a whole were acting and interacting, and making himself accessible to students who wanted to approach him. Two or three teachers mentioned that he helped them with individual students who needed encouragement in learning how to plan and then to follow through with their daily activities; he read the child's folder of goals and activities on a daily or weekly basis and returned it promptly and regularly with helpful comments. Many teachers were impressed that he always responded reliably to requests for help and that he was available to both students and teachers seemingly whenever they needed him. Several teachers commented on how hard he worked for the school and observed that his hard work set an example for others.

The principal and curriculum coordinator as a team

The principal was assisted in shaping the school's program by the curriculum coordinator, Ms Vogel. At Mr Osten's request, she had come to the school, in its first year as an annex, from the local branch of the state university. Ms Vogel was a woman of enormous energy and force of character with a thorough-going dedication to open education. She played a large part in forming the original shape of the program within the school and in orchestrating many of its battles for permission to do things its own way. She had become the conduit for all curricular materials which came into the school; she was constantly in search of new materials and actively informed the faculty about them. In the year of the study, she took a major role in planning the two weeks of orientation sessions for students which defined open education for them and showed them steps for learning how to practise it. These sessions also reminded teachers of the school's blueprint.

Ms Vogel's energy and dedication to open education were without doubt an important ingredient in Jesse Owens's becoming a truly distinctive school. These qualities also created a few problems, however. In her zeal for open education, she sometimes forgot to be tactful with persons from the central office who had given their working lives to other approaches. She thus contributed to some of the tension between the school and the central office, especially the curriculum supervisors there. Similarly, particularly in the earlier years of the program, she alienated some teachers with blunt advice to change their teaching so it would conform better to open education as she understood it. While some teachers appreciated her comments and learned that she responded respectfully to firmly stated reasoned replies, other teachers became angry or defensive. By the time of the study, she carefully acknowledged that it was not in her job description to evaluate teachers in any formal way.

The principal and Ms Vogel worked as a team and made good use of their complementary strengths. Mr Osten was more diplomatic than Ms Vogel and slower to take forceful action. While the difference between them may have been partially one of personality or philosophy, his responsibility for regular interaction with the larger school system made him aware of the myriad of small but important issues which arose in that relationship and of the limit on the number of battles which the school could mount and win. He was more tolerant of variable practices among teachers, because, as the responsible administrator, he knew how difficult it was to have them transferred; he therefore attempted to work as constructively as possible with those whom he would not have chosen.

Still, it was partly because Ms Vogel played the role of zealot both outside the school and within it that Mr Osten's actions seem relatively moderate. The fact that she provided much of the impetus and the sense of urgency for establishing open education in a truly full and distinctive form, even though her role did not clearly give her the power to do this, freed him to use a more diplomatic style both outside the school and with the teachers.

Relations between the principal and the faculty

Mr Osten minced words with his faculty less than did the other principals about the fact that they were bureaucratic subordinates within the structure of the larger school system. He repeatedly made explicit to the faculty the fact that life in public schools requires following some commands from above which may not suit the needs or desires of the school. Unlike Mrs Michaels, Mr Osten would say to the faculty that the central administration had made a decision or policy with which they had to comply, like it or not. He made it clear that compliance was obligatory, but he also sometimes made it clear that he did not like the policy. Thus, while he made the hierarchical nature of the district as a whole more vivid for this faculty than it was for others, there were some

145

cases where he defined himself only as the conduit and not as the source of demands which were uncongenial to teachers.[7] Because the faculty knew that Mr Osten often argued successfully with his superiors, they did not take his acceptance of some orders he and they did not like as a sign of weakness, of his not being a 'strong man in charge.'

Mr Osten supervised his teachers far more closely than did either of the other principals. He made an effort to stay in close personal touch with the teaching and learning in each classroom. Whenever there was a special schoolwide activity, such as the orientation, or later 'fractions week,' he would try to spend some time in each room. He also tried to visit on a regular basis to keep in touch with ordinary activities there. If he needed to speak to a teacher about something, he was likely to walk to his or her room.[8] Students apparently found his entrance into a classroom commonplace; they did not pay much attention to him or change their behavior because of his presence in any way that I could discern. At the beginning of the year, the principal asked teachers to give him copies of the students' goal and activity sheets, so that he could get a sense of their performance on these important tasks. He also asked teachers to write a statement of their own goals for the year for his perusal. Later, in individual conferences with teachers, he could take these as a point of departure.

Despite the close supervision, the teachers made no complaint that they were being closely watched or monitored. On the contrary, some praised the principal for 'knowing what's going on.' It seemed that the lack of complaint may have reflected in part the ways in which the principal used his knowledge. He dealt with his concerns about teachers' actions in conferences with individuals. He seemed to encourage them for their strengths and to try to nudge them where he felt they had weaknesses – though there were a few with whom this nudging took a fairly directive form.

The teachers who probably received the most pressure to change did not say much about such pressure to other teachers or in interviews, but those who diverged most from the school's ideals toward either a free school or a traditional pattern were more likely to be critical of the principal about something. They did not mention his close supervision, however, just as those most in conflict with Mrs Michaels at Adams did not mention either their individual conflicts with her or her strong use of her formal powers. Unlike the dissident teachers at Adams, these teachers did not develop a set of common criticisms; there seemed to be little solidarity among them and almost no group-based orchestration of discontent.

There was a union building committee at the school which included some of the principal's stronger critics, though also some supporters. Members of this committee occasionally raised issues among the faculty as matters for concern or even for grievance. One issue which angered some of them involved an incident when the principal rang the bell for the end of a lunch hour two or three minutes early one day in late October. A rain shower had started and the students outdoors were getting wet. This issue failed to gain resonance with the faculty as a whole – though in some schools a violation of the reliability of the bell schedule would be a major issue. A member of the union building committee, who was in general supportive, though not uncritical, of the principal, seemed to sum up faculty reaction as he talked informally about it with a few other teachers. His final statement, which captured the feeling of the conversation, was that the principal's action was reasonable because, after all, 'The kids were getting *wet*.' Since the principal's action supported their dominant value on students' welfare, the inconvenience to teachers was tolerable.

The majority of teachers not only did not complain about the principal's close supervision, but spoke very positively of their relations with him. They found him to be supportive, ready to help them, and respectful of their efforts. They spoke of having freedom to make their own decisions about their work in the classroom. However, he allowed so much autonomy to teachers that several, especially those who leaned toward more traditional patterns, felt that he did not set an unequivocal direction for the staff. One of these teachers, a leading black teacher from the old building, seemed to go to the heart of the principal's pattern and the fact that he was dealing with a set of contradictory imperatives:

'I have been with him in a lot of instances when he has represented the school dealing with central office and dealing with the community. He's really astute in dealing with outside groups. He can handle them well. He's very strong . . . And he's very firm. Now if he could transfer that and be that way

147

with the staff. And on a constant basis – sometimes he is – but on a constant basis. The staff is split with one ideology in this group and another over there. To bring them together you'd have to be more authoritative, more directive.

'On the other hand, it would have to be more Osten's philosophy on open ed than it is mine or someone else's. So that's what would happen and I don't think he wants to see it go that way. He wants you to read and wants you to practise and do the things that you feel would best enhance open ed in your setting. Now that's the kind of leeway I'm talking about. That kind of makes him seem like he's not authoritative or he's not the kind of principal that really takes charge. 'Cause he's giving you that opportunity. You couldn't ask for more as a teacher. I wouldn't want anything less. But on the other hand, it hurts sometimes.'

Mr Osten was able to supervise his teachers very closely and to underscore for them the necessity of complying with central office directives even when they found them repugnant, and yet to face no organized opposition and little grumbling. He could do this partly because he also gave them significant freedoms. But, more important, he stood as a champion of their collective and individual purpose.

Principals are simultaneously participants in their schools and representatives of the higher school system hierarchy. They function as ambassadors in both directions, but usually are perceived as belonging more in one world than the other. Just as Mrs Michaels was resented for imposing IGE in a hierarchical fashion, but also ambivalently accepted by most of the faculty because she facilitated their most valued efforts to work effectively with children, so Mr Osten was perceived almost totally as identified with the teachers' collective efforts to offer an effective distinctive form of education. He also provided assistance and a positive model in working directly with students, an activity which was at the heart of the teachers' value system. Because Mr Osten was unmistakably one of 'us,' not one of 'them', and because most of his directives seemed based in a semi-cooperative search for improvement or else in inescapable external pressures, all but a small minority of teachers accepted his direction and supervision without resentment.

Pressures for change in the school and the principal's role

Several of the teachers remarked in interviews that the principal was acting in a more directive fashion in the year of the study than he had previously. While the goal and activity sheets had been used before, he insisted in this year that they be used by every teacher and he checked their use. He also insisted that students moving about the building always carry an activity sheet signed by the teacher with their purpose and destination or a wooden paddle with their self-contained center's number on it for trips to the bathroom. He was, in short, tightening the procedures for developing skills in open education and for controlling students' purposefulness and diligence. He told me in several of our conversations that he had decided that open education requires autonomy for students, but not necessarily for teachers, and that he felt more willing than he previously had to be directive with teachers.

As the year progressed, it became clear that he was responding to strong pressures from the central office and board for tightened procedures at the least and, increasingly, for more traditional activities and for evaluation of students in terms of more traditional criteria. His presentation to the faculty in March concerning the need to improve students' test scores was a reflection of this pressure.

I returned to the school in November 1981, a little over a year after the close of the study, to discuss with Mr Osten a draft of the description of the school in the first report on the research (Metz, 1982a). Mr Osten wanted to make it clear to me – for the sake of any possible local readers – that the school had changed considerably. A curriculum had been developed for the whole school which stated skills to be taught in every classroom during each six-week period of the year. All teachers were expected to give group instruction in reading and math skills to all students. In the light of these changes, Mr Osten said that my observation that teachers judged their students by their progress in developing the capacity to direct their own learning more than by their progress in academic skills was now historical.

He said that he had acted ahead of systemwide initiatives in inaugurating these changes. He thought that the fact that Jesse Owens had made such changes voluntarily put it on firmer ground in its struggle to remain politically viable within the system. He said, however, that he thought the school had now gone about as far as it could go in making these kinds of changes without ceasing to be a distinctive open education school.

In this conversation a year and a half after the study, Mr Osten spoke about the faculty as his subordinates, subject to his control, much more than he had during the study. His description of the process of implementing the new arrangements made it clear that most of the initiative and direction had come from him, despite participation by some committees. It seemed his situation was now approaching that of the other principals in the study as he was required by the central office to initiate a new program at the school. The difference was that, ironically, the new program was a return to more traditional practices.

Summary and implications

Owens developed the most distinctive program of the three schools. This program issued from the initiative of the school's staff before desegregation and the establishment of magnet schools. They had to argue and lobby for alterations in standard practice in curriculum, grouping of students, and the use of time in order to institute their program as they thought it should be run. They were deeply attached to it and perceived themselves as an embattled few representing a better vision of education. Their relations with the hierarchy of the larger school system were always somewhat difficult, although with the advent of magnet schools these improved markedly at least for the first years.

Owens resembled Adams in having cooperative and courteous relations between students and teachers, despite the fact that it had a student body which could have been expected to be even more inclined to engage in conflict in the classroom than was Adams's. Although the schools differed a great deal in their understandings of the nature of knowledge and therefore in the content of the curriculum and in the way students were encouraged to approach it, the technology at Owens supported constructive relationships in much the same way that Adams's did. Both schools had a curricular structure which allowed students to start at varied points according to their current skills. Both gave academic rewards on the basis of improvement rather than comparison to a group standard. And both used activity structures

which allowed privacy to low achievers and saved them embarrassment while they made efforts to improve shaky skills. The activity
structure also allowed teachers and students to come to know
each other well, and enabled teachers to discipline students
privately, with a discussion of the disruptive act and punishment
fitted to the miscreant's needs.

The technological arrangements which Adams and Owens had
in common encouraged friendly interaction among the races.
Relationships seemed to be almost as good at Owens as at Adams.
At both, the technological arrangements which took away reasons
for students to create conflicts with teachers also protected their
pride in front of peers. If black students had lower skills than
whites, classroom groupings and activities did not make this
obvious. It was also helpful that, at Owens particularly, there
were not large differences in academic skills between the races.
At Owens, varied activities in the classroom allowed students to
display varied strengths and to earn respect from peers, despite
weak academic skills. Opportunities for cooperation between the
races and encouragement of inter-racial contacts by authorities
varied a good deal between the self-contained centers, where
students formed their primary orientation to school. There was a
corresponding variation in students' racial attitudes and experience of friendly inter-racial contact among the Owens students.

The faculty at Owens shared an explicit educational ideology,
though with many variations on the theme, and a common sense of
being a beleaguered minority. They also shared a deeper common
culture which was less readily articulated; they gave students'
welfare a high priority and expected to work with their students
as whole persons. They displayed an unspoken acceptance of each
other despite their willingness to quarrel with one another over
specific issues. This acceptance seemed to rest in part upon each
one's sense of being a competent teacher, of deserving to feel
pride in his or her efforts. When that pride was absent or threatened, so was the acceptance. Like the Adams teachers, the Owens
teachers' pride in their work was supported by their good relationships with the students, which were in turn supported both by the
technology and by the faculty culture. Patterns of causation were
circular and self-reenforcing.

Relations between the faculty and the principal were closer and
more positive than at Adams. As at Adams, the majority of the
faculty shared a sense of the important mission of the school with

the principal, but this sharing was much more clearly articulated at Owens and was not shadowed by the principal's hierarchical imposition of the formal innovation. The faculty saw the principal as the defender of their special approach as he dealt with representatives of the larger district, and they felt that their way of teaching depended on that defense. They also felt that he appreciated and facilitated their individual development of teaching strategies. When he exercised close supervision and occasionally required them to follow policies they found repugnant, they did not mind because these acts took place in the context of a relationship in which he was essentially supportive of them; his close supervision did not threaten their sense of professionalism or their pride as persons.

By the close of the study, Jesse Owens was a school in change. A variety of pressures converged to put consistent pressure upon it to adopt more traditional patterns. First, resources from the district were dwindling. Federal and union regulations and local financial exigencies combined to reduce its staff. At the same time, the move to the Rodgers building, together with the competition of the other magnet middle schools, encouraged neighborhood students with low skills to attend and discouraged middleclass whites. Apparently fearing charges of elitism, the central office refused to set a floor of fourth grade skills for entrance. The increased proportion of students with low skills needed more, not less, adult assistance, in working with Owens's goal setting, learning centers, and projects, but staff positions were cut as federal funds were withdrawn from the district. Such students also needed more intensive instruction in basic skills than had previous students before they could become equipped really to operate as independent learners. Owens also became a visible alternative where parents and counselors could send students who could not adjust to other schools. Like slow students, these children needed intensive assistance to learn how to work constructively in Owens's system. These additional demands for intensive assistance overloaded the teachers and encouraged them to search for methods of instruction which would lighten their burdens.

At the same time, open education had decreasing support and legitimacy in the society as a whole. Further, the new teachers who had not worked in the intense solidarity at the old building or experienced its student body, along with black teachers deeply concerned that students master traditional skills, argued for the introduction of more traditional patterns, especially for weak students. The debate among the teachers led to mutual socialization. The school culture and ideology were changing along with changed conditions outside and inside the school.

Ironically, while Owens was an exemplar to show the viability of a magnet program for Heartland, and while it was the one among the magnet middle schools which best institutionalized a genuinely distinctive educational experience, district policies were steadily undercutting its distinctiveness. Consequently, instead of drawing a student body which was well-suited to its program, as magnet schools were expected to do, it had to alter its program to fit its student population, as traditional neighborhood schools do.

Chapter 6

Horace Mann School for the Gifted and Talented

Heartland's middle school program for the gifted and talented was opened in the Atlantic Avenue Junior High School but after one year was moved to share a building with the Horace Mann High School for the college-bound. Atlantic Avenue School was in a black neighborhood on the northern edge of the downtown area. Horace Mann High School was thirty blocks from downtown in the black East Side; its neighborhood consisted of modest but well-built and well-kept houses.

Environmental influences

The establishment of the school

Horace Mann Middle School for the Gifted and Talented was deeply affected by its history and by the circumstances surrounding its establishment. Mann's complex history made it heir to the traditions of two other schools, Atlantic Junior High School and Peach Street Elementary School for the Gifted and Talented. Peach Street was founded in the first year of desegregation as a school for fourth through sixth graders who were identified by teachers or parents as gifted or talented. It was staffed with 'superintendent's choices,' mentioned in Chapter 2, slots for which the court allowed the administrators to select teachers regardless of seniority.

Parents who were well pleased with the school asked the central administration to extend the program for gifted and talented

154

students into the middle school years. They succeeded in getting board approval for such a program at Atlantic Avenue Junior High School, a school which offered both easy access to downtown cultural facilities and businesses and to students from all over the city via city buses. Atlantic Avenue had a declining population and a black student body with a reputation for neighborhood vandalism and aggressive behavior. The school board had already considered closing the school; it seemed that no one would vigorously protest its loss as a neighborhood school, and no one did.

During its first year, 1977–8, there were seventy seventh graders, mostly from Peach Street, in Atlantic's gifted and talented program. The previous year's seventh graders, drawn from the neighborhood, composed the eighth grade. Plans were made for three grades of gifted and talented students at Atlantic for the following year and students were recruited.

Then, without warning at a meeting on August 1, the school board closed Atlantic Avenue Junior High School and transferred the middle school program for the gifted and talented to the Horace Mann High School. This was a building which had been closed to neighborhood attendance and remodeled. It was to reopen that fall as a citywide high school for college-bound students. The number of students recruited at Mann had been disappointingly small and disproportionately black. Moving the middle school for the gifted and talented into the building balanced its racial ratio and filled the building in one step. Balancing the racial ratio helped the high school's progress toward desegregation, since racial statistics were reported for the building as a whole so that the high school's initially small number of whites became much less publicly visible. Additionally, the board, which had promised to save a million dollars by closing schools that summer, both accomplished savings by closing the Atlantic building and spared itself the embarrassment of operating a newly remodeled building at Mann half-empty.

The board expected the 'transfer' of the gifted and talented program to be a fairly non-controversial matter. They were wrong. Atlantic parents felt the board had broken faith with them in changing the building, location, student body, and principal of the school they had chosen for their children to attend. They were further angered not even to have been given an opportunity to voice their views on the matter. A few of them reached and organized a large number of parents, something of a feat in

August. Within a couple of days, parents as a class were in court asking for a restraining order on the grounds that the action violated the state's open meetings law, since the closing of the school had not even been on the agenda of the board meeting. The restraining order was issued and stayed in place for two weeks until the board was able to meet, hold hearings, and reaffirm its action with due notice.

As a consequence of the board's late action and the parents' restraining order, which forbade preparation for the transfer, the school year began chaotically. The class schedule for the Mann building was hurriedly constructed; initial class sizes ranged from five to fifty-five and students did not have many of the classes they should have had. The schedule then had to be done again and students shifted from one class to another. Supplies were inadequate. There was insufficient time to move materials from one building to another, so that many classes had no books well into the school year. To make matters worse, packages were not clearly labeled and were simply stacked wherever there was room, many under the stands in the gymnasium. The union told teachers they should not be asked to unpack, and several refused to do so for several weeks even though they did not have necessary materials. Further, the remodeling was not complete; there was a shortage of rooms with special equipment. Middle school science classes spent most of the year without running water, let alone other laboratory facilities. All those connected with the school had their nerves rubbed raw by these experiences.

By the second year at Mann, the year of the study, the confusion caused by the sudden move and by the logistical problems of opening two new schools in one building had lessened considerably. None the less, memories of the previous year were fresh and the schools rested uneasily together. When the board and central office staff began to speak of their combination as temporary, a parent committee was appointed and met all fall to discuss criteria for a new site for the middle school. No action resulted, however, as proposals fell prey to complex political maneuvering among parents at Mann and other schools, central office staff, board members, and outside pressure groups.[1] Thus at the time of the study, the middle school for the gifted and talented had the status of a transient guest in the building, but it was not clear when it could be moved. (As it turned out, it became rapidly harder to close schools and so find a new building for the program. The sixth grade was moved out in the fall of 1982 and the whole school in 1983, after five years in the Mann building.)

Recruitment of parents

The parents of Mann's students included a lot of college-educated, middle-class people, both black and white. Those who were working-class were probably more aware of education and ready to support their children's efforts at school than average working-class parents. Children of city civic leaders, school board members, central office administrators, and teachers elsewhere in the system were present in notable, if objectively small, numbers. Many of the parents had been active in Parent Teacher Organization affairs in various schools for years. In sum, the parents as a group were unusually knowledgeable, experienced, and influential in dealing with individual schools and with the school system as a whole.

Teachers commented on two noticeable consequences of the characteristics of the parents. First, they were very supportive of the teachers' efforts to get students to work. Many helped to guide their children through long projects and others at least helped to monitor the observation of deadlines. Second, as they were so involved with their children's education many parents – perhaps not a large number but enough to make an indelible impression on teachers – considered themselves qualified to judge teachers' work in detail. They did so frequently and vociferously, both directly to the teachers and to the administrators.[2]

In the first year of the program, many parents had transferred their considerable anger with the board for moving the school to the staff within the school. These parents were omnipresent and extremely critical of the school even in public settings. According to teachers, in PTO meetings that year, a few parents voiced scathing criticism of individual teachers' methods or even their intellectual capabilities, with several teachers present. In the meetings of the parent committee convened during the fall of the study to discuss criteria for a new site, which I regularly attended, some parents kept moving the discussion to their perceptions of teachers' inadequacies and the question of whether it were possible under union rules to change the staff of the program as part of moving it. They felt no inhibition because of the presence of the counselor, who represented the teaching staff at these meetings.

The parents who were most vocal in this way were mostly men and women with graduate degrees in families where one or both parents had professional careers.[3] They considered themselves fully qualified to assess both the school's curriculum and teachers' pedagogy. They also spoke with a sense of entitlement. They felt that they had helped the school system to make the magnet plan a success by being willing to risk their children's education to new programs. They expected consideration in return.

Despite the board's rather rough treatment of parents in moving the school without warning, it was clear that their expectations were not unheard at the central office. Administrators there were well aware of the importance of maintaining the good will of parents who were, or who mixed with, community leaders active in school affairs. To meet their objection to mixing younger children with high school students at the time of the transfer, the central office had the school administration stagger the high school and middle school bell schedules (in the first year) and set up separate bathrooms to keep the two student bodies apart. These arrangements took a good deal of the school staff's energy to administer. The central administration also provided yellow bus service for all Mann students to meet the objection that the new site was too inconvenient to reach by city bus from some parts of the city. It is hard to know whether this move was also a concession to underlying racial fears of white parents, and a sign of administrators' sympathy with them. In any case it meant that children did not have to wait for city buses in Mann's black neighborhood.

Student recruitment

During the year of the study, there were 984 students in the Mann building and approximately 450 of them in the middle school. Table 6-1 compares figures on size of school, racial composition, and free lunches for the three schools studied and for citywide middle schools as a whole. The figures for Mann middle school are all estimates because all official figures were reported for the building, with no breakdown for the two programs. The student body as a whole was 47 percent minority, including all minorities.

The figure in the middle school was lower, about 43 percent, all but a few black as at the other schools. By several indices, it appears that the children at Mann were better off economically than were those at the other two schools and in the city as a whole. Thirty-two percent of the student body in the school as a whole received free lunches. I have estimated 25 percent for the middle school alone, because the high school had more poorly achieving and more black students, two groups generally associated with low income families. Mann was not a Title I school. Many more parents of the students interviewed at Mann than at Adams and Owens were in occupations which require a college education.

TABLE 6–1 *Characteristics of students at Horace Mann Middle School compared to those at Adams, Owens, and in the city of Heartland, 1979–80 (Adams Avenue, 1978–9)*

	Mann	Owens	Adams	Citywide middle schools
Initial enrollment	450	377	328	12,400
Percent minority students	43*	48	51	54
Percent free lunches to total lunches	25*	71	59	50

*Estimates based on figures for the total Horace Mann building

Source: Heartland School District *Profile of Schools*

Students were selected for the school from a pool of those nominated by former teachers. The students' parents also had to request that they attend the school. In some cases parents, rather than teachers, nominated the child as gifted or talented. Children from Peach Street, already selected by this process for entry to that school, were automatically admitted. Criteria for nomination were those promulgated by the federal (then) Department of Health Education and Welfare. They specified seven forms of gifts or talent, including not only general or specific intellectual abilities but outstanding achievement or potential in leadership, visual or performing arts, or psychomotor ability. Teachers were given brief descriptions of these endowments and asked on a short form to rate the abilities of the children they nominated.

This process left much discretion to teachers in the selection or

159

omission of students, and led to unevenness in the talents of the students selected. It further encouraged the choice of students who please teachers. As one teacher put it, the student body was '95 percent nice kids.' A few, but only a few, students were 'dumped' to relieve the sending school of their presence. In the interviews, I was struck with the self-confidence and articulateness of the students in comparison to that of the students at the other schools. Even those the teachers picked out as having low skills were willing and able to give full, well-expressed answers.

If one looks at the students' fifth grade scores on standardized tests of reading and mathematics – which of course do not measure many of the abilities for which they were selected – it is clear both that the students entering Mann achieved far better than did students in Heartland as a whole, and that they were not a group which would conventionally be labeled as 'gifted.' This pattern is clear if one looks at Table 6-2, which reports scores on standardized tests of reading, taken at the end of the fifth grade before entrance to Mann, by the cohort of students who were seventh graders during the study. Compared to Jesse Owens, we see that only 24 percent of Mann students scored below the 50th percentile, while 71 percent of Owens students did. In other words, three-quarters of Mann students scored above the median on these tests and almost three-quarters of Jesse Owens students scored below it. Sixty-five percent or two-thirds of Adams students scored below it. Only 5 percent of the Mann students scored below the 25th percentile, but 47 percent of Owens students and 34 percent of Adams students did. Mann, then, had only a handful of the low achievers who formed the majority at the other two schools. The figures for the city as a whole were comparable to those at Adams; Mann's students did not reflect the city.

However, if one looks for gifted students at Mann, one notices that 80 percent of the student body scored below the 90th percentile, that is, out of the top 10 percent. Furthermore, in this context, fully, rather than only, 24 percent scored below the median. Fifty percent, or half, scored below the 75th percentile. Table 6-3 on math scores shows even fewer students scoring extremely high, though slightly fewer, only 20 percent, were below the 50th percentile mark. Compared to the other schools and to the city as a whole, Mann had a student body which was the 'cream.' Compared to its label, and therefore to the expectations of some outsiders, including some parents, its student body did not live up to its gifted name.

TABLE 6–2 *Percentages of students at the three schools and citywide scoring at or below national percentile rankings on the Metropolitan Achievement Tests in reading at the end of grade 5, 1978*

Percentile ranking	Mann (N=155)	Owens (N=129)	Adams (N=125)*	City (N=6,081)
90th	80	96	95	96
75th	50	89	83	87
50th	24	71	66	66
25th	5	47	34	36
10th	2	16	19	17

*Adams data are for the spring of 1977.

Source: Heartland School District computer data files

TABLE 6–3 *Percentages of students at the three schools and citywide scoring at or below national percentile rankings on the Metropolitan Achievement Tests in mathematics at the end of grade 5, 1978*

Percentile ranking	Mann (N=153)	Owens (N=125)	Adams (N=125)*	City (N=5,982)
90th	88	99	96	96
75th	58	89	86	87
50th	20	72	65	64
25th	5	40	33	32
10th	1	18	16	13

*Adams data are for the spring of 1977.

Source: Heartland School District computer data files

According to several black teachers, and one white one who had been involved with recruitment, capable black students were under-represented in the student population compared to their numbers in the city. They argued that there was furthermore a noticeable difference in the overall abilities of the black and white students. They were upset that some black students were admitted who were far weaker in skills and less endowed with ability than their white classmates. These students had a very difficult time not only academically but psychologically and they served to confirm their white and black classmates' stereotypes about the lower abilities of blacks in general.

There was some evidence that teachers and principals in other schools were eager to keep their strongest black students as exemplars for others and to make the performance record of blacks and whites in the school – which the central office noted but did not make public – as equal as possible. They consequently often failed to nominate strong black students for Mann.

Staff who had been involved in the recruitment process held also that black parents were more reluctant than white ones were to request entrance to the school once a child had been nominated by a teacher. They were hesitant to transfer a child away from a setting which had generated success or away from a sibling. Social class as well as race were probably at work here. Fewer blacks are middle-class, and working-class families are traditionally more reluctant than middle-class ones to send their children far from home.

The blueprint for gifted and talented education

Gifted and talented education does not have a clear blueprint. It is education for a particular kind of student, not education of a particular kind for all students. Furthermore, the students for whom it is intended may not have educational needs in common. For example, students who have 'specific academic aptitude,' 'leadership ability,' or ability in 'visual and performing arts,' three of the federal criteria for classification as gifted and talented, may have quite different special educational needs. In practice, however, gifted and talented education tends to be distinctive in one of two broad ways. The first is an enriched approach which gives students a variety of experiences and kinds of instruction, adding breadth and perhaps depth to the curriculum traditionally given to children of a certain age. The second approach is acceleration, which takes students more quickly through traditional material. It assumes that their special abilities render the material appropriate for their age peers unchallenging and so offers them more advanced material.

Central office staff in Heartland planned to stress enrichment in the program for the gifted and talented, especially since many of the students had talents other than general intellectual ability. As they worked with the principal at Peach Street Elementary School for the gifted and talented, they institutionalized this approach in the program of that school. Students made many trips to cultural events at the downtown performing arts complex, which was within walking distance. A majority of the children took instrumental music lessons. There was a vast array of cultural and athletic activities over the lunch hour. Computers were introduced to the curriculum long before they were common in other elementary schools. But teachers were discouraged from advancing to standard learning activities which were more than a little above grade level.

Formally, Mann Middle School's program was continuous with the one at Peach Street; it was simply housed at a different site and included an added cohort of students. Students and parents who came from Peach Street entered Mann with expectations for a similar program. However, even though Mann Middle School's only formal link with Mann High School was the sharing of the building and administrative staff, the high school program none the less influenced the middle school one. The high school, defined as one for the college-bound, stressed acceleration. Its centerpiece in relations with the public was a program which allowed students to complete the first year of college work in the four years of high school. Though there were no formal ties between the programs, a large proportion of Mann middle school students went on to Mann high school.

As it tried to define its purposes and practices, Mann Middle School was caught between these two schools. It was pulled toward enrichment by the expectations of the central office and by those which half its students and parents brought from Peach Street. It was pulled toward acceleration by the constantly visible model of the high school with which it shared a building and administrators and for which many of its students would need to be prepared.

Mann Middle School was caught between the two schools also because it was literally a 'middle' school. Middle schools are expected to provide a bridge between the 'child-centered' approach associated with elementary schools and the 'subject-centered' approach associated with secondary schools. At Mann, enrichment became informally identified in many teachers' minds with a child-centered approach and with elementary education. Acceleration became identified with a subject-centered approach and with secondary education. The two sets of tensions with which the school lived thus became entangled with one another.

The balance between these influences was tipped by the influence of yet a third school. The staff of the Atlantic Avenue Junior High School had remained to become the staff of the gifted and talented middle school in its first year and had been transferred with the program.[4] Because the student body had been small in the first year of the program, the newer Atlantic teachers had been 'excessed'; those who remained to staff the gifted and talented program had virtually all been at Atlantic ten years or more. Atlantic had been very explicitly a secondary school; the teachers from there continued to identify themselves as secondary teachers.

Virtually all of Mann's academic teachers, except those in the sixth grade classes, were certified to teach a secondary subject in grades seven to twelve and had experience in those grades in junior high schools or high schools with a clearly secondary orientation. In accordance with secondary patterns, these teachers identified themselves as teachers of a subject, rather than teachers of a group or age of children – as elementary teachers more often do. Accelerated education was more compatible with their self-conception as secondary teachers than was enriched education. To be teaching well was to teach a lot of mathematics, English, or art. To learn well was to show rapid progress through the skills of mathematics, English, or art.

The principal and administrator in charge of the middle school also had experience primarily in high schools, not even junior high schools. (The principal had served for a few years as principal of a junior high school.) They also strongly identified with secondary patterns of education and considered it an important part of their task to prepare the students to meet the expectations of a high school. However, while they stressed secondary patterns, they also urged the teachers to introduce enrichment, as the central office desired. These multiple and varied influences created pervasive tension and ambiguity around the definition of the blueprint for the school.

School character

An analysis of Mann's school character in the context of discussions of Adams and Owens is bound to develop a somewhat skewed picture. Mann had clearly the least distinctive program of the three and it had the most difficult personal relationships, especially between the races and among the adults. However, if accounts of teachers with experience in other middle schools in Heartland are to be believed, in comparison to them, Mann would appear modestly distinctive and its inter-racial relationships relatively cordial. It is important, then, to remember that the following description of Mann is colored by implicit comparison with Adams and Owens. This caveat is important in fairness to Mann for those who know its true identity. More important, it helps to underscore the significance of the sources of Adams and Owens's distinctive relationships. Mann differed significantly from them because it used traditional technological and logistical arrangements and because of its different culture. Comparison to traditional schools would bring out different facets of Mann.

The tone of the school

The tone which permeated adults' conversations at Mann and their research interviews was one of frustration. This frustration centered around the actions of other adults more than those of students. The administrators were frustrated because they felt the teachers were reluctant to move toward a distinctive program, while the teachers felt misunderstood and belittled by the administrators. They were also frustrated with the selection of the student body which they did not consider sufficiently gifted to warrant its gifted and talented title. Vocal parents were critical of both teachers and administrators.

Most of the students interviewed did not seem to be directly aware of these conflicts or tensions, though some had some sense of them. However, the students had a competitiveness in their relationships with one another and a certain high-strung, intense quality[5] which may have reflected a generalized anxiety generated by the adults' displeasure with one another. However, this quality might also be part of the home-generated personalities of

165

successful children, or a reflection of the organization of instruction, which encouraged competition.

Teacher–student interaction

On arriving at Mann, I was immediately struck with the copious resources expended on the maintenance of order in the halls. Aides and teachers were posted at the junctions of the corridors so that every part of every corridor was under supervision at all times. Students in the halls during class or lunch periods were always accosted by aides and challenged to show a pass. At least at the beginning of the year while rules were being established, students who were found in bathrooms marked as belonging to the other school in the building were suspended. Attendance was reported immediately to the office from every class; most of one aide's time was spent in circulating to rooms collecting attendance lists each class hour.

In addition to these firm controls over traffic flow in the halls, there was a tone in adults' interaction with students which assumed that they were likely to cause problems for the school unless they were strictly regulated and closely supervised. The following account illustrates this tone. The teacher talking was responsible for supervision of recreation after lunch. She was explaining to half the student body assembled in the gymnasium the procedures for spring outdoor recreation which was about to begin.

'Mrs Morley [started by telling them] there was to be no food taken outdoors: no fruit, no cookies, no milk, no sandwiches. She said, "You know where you are supposed to be: not in the parking lot, not on the track, you stay behind the –" She glanced at the curriculum coordinator who was standing against a wall at the back of the group and said, "I was going to say cage. That's not quite what I mean. You stay behind the fences."

'She told them if they bring a frisbee or jump-rope to put their name on it and keep it with them. If they let it go or lose it, that is their responsibility.

'Then she talked about there being no pushing or shoving or hitting anybody either outside or inside . . . She told them if they line up at the water fountain and are late for class, that is no excuse for lateness. . . .

166

'This talk lasted only about five minutes. Her voice was very calm and quiet, but the tone of what she said was all, "don't, don't, don't." The description of outside recreation was a description of things they could not do.'

Individual teachers also were very concerned with discipline and control of the students. When I came to Mann after being at the other two schools, I was surprised that teachers did not talk as much with each other about students' general behavior or character as at the other schools, but talked a great deal about students in terms of the exigencies of maintaining discipline. Students and sometimes whole classes were characterized as discipline problems by teachers and discussed in that context.

Teachers took more disciplinary action at Mann than at the other schools. If one looks at a quantifiable indicator, the number of the school district's official 'yellow cards,' which are used when a teacher sends a child to the school office for administrative discipline, there was a noticeable difference between their use at Mann and Adams. In May, there were a total of 738 yellow cards on file for middle school students at Mann for the year of the study, an average of 1.64 for each of the 450 children. At Adams in May of the study year, there had been 239 or .73 for each of the 328 children. (Owens did not use yellow cards, but rather their own informal blue cards which did not necessarily go in students' files and were not available to be counted.) Despite the selected character of Mann's students and their relative academic success compared to Adams's students, they were drawing more than twice as many official disciplinary sanctions per student.

The meaning of these yellow cards is ambiguous, however, except in showing conflict between students and teachers. It is not clear whether Mann's students were behaving worse than Adams's, or whether Mann's teachers were quicker to respond to similar behavior with official action. The counselor spoke of her efforts to get teachers to use a separate card for referral of students who came to class without pencils or other necessary supplies. She also found that black students received a disproportionate number of yellow cards. She thought this occurred because some white teachers used them for actions a black teacher, like herself, might take less seriously, such as the use of street language or outbursts of anger when students thought they had been unjustly accused of something.

The Mann teachers spoke of their students, both as individuals and as groups, in far simpler, less detailed, less personal terms than did the teachers at Adams and Owens. They also more often treated the students' difficulties in learning or in their personal development as a matter for referral to other experts. Thus it was at Mann, rather than at the other two schools, that I heard the most discussions of individuals as potentially eligible for special education programs, despite Mann's academically and behaviorally selected student body. It was at Mann that teachers mentioned that students had been referred not just to the counselor but to the school psychologist, a figure I heard mentioned rarely, if at all, in the other schools.

The students seemed to respond to the teachers somewhat impersonally as well. Teachers were not highly salient in the students' world. When asked in interviews what classes they liked most and least, and in which they learned most and least, Mann students mentioned teachers less often, and the subject and activities of a class more often, than did Adams students who were asked the same questions. (The question was not asked at Owens where students did not change teachers in the same way.)

Despite the teachers' concern with discipline at Mann and the greater number of yellow cards than at Adams, no one experienced in schools for children of this age with socially and racially diverse clienteles would have described the students as being serious discipline problems. The conflict which generated the 738 yellow cards which rested in the files, and disproportionately in those of black students, reflected only 4.4 yellow cards per day for a student body of 450. A student or an observer could easily go through a whole school day without seeing a conflict which generated one.

In most classes, students were cooperative and businesslike, even though they did not seem deeply engaged. They listened when teachers talked and they performed the tasks assigned them. In a few classes which permitted active student participation, and in the selected and accelerated pre-algebra and algebra classes they even seemed intense in their involvement. Attendance at Mann was higher than at the other two schools: 92 percent for the study year, compared to 90 percent at Adams, 84 percent at Owens, and 85 percent in the middle schools of the city as a whole.[6]

There were a few classes where students entered into conflict with teachers. In some classes they became passively withdrawn, requiring the teacher to drag responses to questions from them. In a very few classes, they became restless and active, ignoring the teacher. They chatted while the teacher was talking and made jokes at inappropriate times, so that the teacher had to call repeatedly for their attention. Still, even these classes rarely directly challenged, let alone teased, a teacher or grew so disorderly as to ignore him or her while engaging in uproar – though there were isolated groups that did each of these things. There was no single group of students in terms of race and sex that was most disorderly on a regular basis, though one group was often most responsible in a given class.

I was struck on a few occasions with the good order which classes maintained in the face of insults or openly hostile behavior by teachers, often substitutes. Black students tolerated hostility and racial slurs which would have sent students elsewhere, even at Adams, into angry rebellion. The most striking example involved a white teacher, whom I had seen on other occasions acting aggressively hostile toward her classes, especially toward black students. After asking students to go home and ask their parents what country their family was from, she gave all students a slip of paper on which to write their country of origin. She then blatantly ignored the black students as she called on white students and pinned their slips on a map. When she finally recognized a black boy's raised hand, he cautiously observed that all the slips were in the northern hemisphere. She replied by 'informing' him that the black students were from Africa, but said they could put no slips there because she had no extras. She assumed none of these black sixth-graders would know, even after being told to ask their parents, that their ancesters were from Africa. In response to this treatment, the black students in the class simply became very quiet. It seemed that the students selected for Mann were able to refrain from conflict even when provoked.

On the other hand, high status white students from the South Side sometimes initiated conflict with their teachers with an arrogant condescension, which was, however, difficult to discipline. For example, a boy in a high status eighth grade clique who could not answer questions in a French class responded to his teacher with questions which clearly implied that she was asking him things she had not taught – even though other students were responding competently. A seventh grader, whose father was prominent on parent committees, responded to a science teacher's challenge about the progress of his science report – when he was inattentive to another student's presentation of a completed report – by telling the class, in an authoritative voice, that he wanted examples of paper airplanes for his report 'by the end of this hour.' The class obediently set to work making paper airplanes with rustling paper; then *they* were chastised by the (black) teacher. Some white children were strikingly insensitive to the feelings of adults, especially when they were black. They loudly criticized the cafeteria food as they were served by the people who had prepared it; one spoke of his father's 'dumb secretary' to a secretarial aide who had been disconnected on the telephone by his father's office. Several black teachers commented on some white children's arrogance.

Inter-racial relationships

There were several indicators that relations between the races were more strained at Mann than at the other schools. The first was the greater presence of graffiti around the school, much of which was racially insulting. Sentiments such as 'Honky go home' and 'Black sucks' appeared on doors and walls. Since the middle school and high school shared a building, it was usually not clear which group of students was responsible for these writings. Their presence in the middle school girls' bathroom, which high school students entered only on the peril of suspension, suggests that at least some were the work of middle school students. It is important, however, that teachers who came from other middle schools in Heartland commented on the lack of graffiti and especially on the lack of defacement of bulletin board displays.

The graffiti were matched by students' comments in interviews. Both black and white students spoke more about being insulted or teased, sometimes for their race, than did children at either of the other schools. They also made more frequent references to incidents of conflict. For example, a white eighth grade boy said that, though he had gotten along with blacks at Peach Street, he had been hassled by black students at Mann, especially early in his career. He now would prefer a mostly white high school. He explained somewhat guiltily:

'not to seem prejudiced or anything – but I sometimes feel

that a lot of black students are hostile towards the white students. And the white students toward the black students. But at least the white students don't say it out loud. They don't call them anything like nigger or something. While the black students I think feel more free to just call us honky or something like that or start something with us.'

A black eighth grade boy, when asked what he would change about the school if given magical powers, replied:

TIM: The prejudice.
INTERVIEWER: What do people do that's prejudiced?
TIM (*mumbling*): They write 'Black sucks' on the walls.
INTERVIEWER: Does that kind of thing stay up there?
TIM: They wash it off, but then it's there again the next day.

It would be a mistake to draw the conclusion from this evidence that black and white students regarded each other hostilely in general, however. Teachers agreed that they cooperated in class without difficulty. Most black teachers and some white teachers thought they mixed fairly well in voluntary settings, though many white teachers thought they separated. Children interviewed tended to see others as mixing or not according to whether they did themselves. These varied interpretations suggest that there was not a single pattern of racial mixing or avoidance.

According to my own observations, in classrooms where seating was voluntary, there was a good deal of racial (and gender) separation. In the dining-room, visual sweeps suggested that the tables were more mixed than at Owens, but less so than at Adams. There seemed to be several tables which were predominantly of one race, but included a couple of students of another race. However, when I had a chance to watch the children carefully at the dining-tables for the half hour duration of a tornado warning, it appeared that conversations at these mixed tables were taking place within races.

The overall figures from students' replies to interview questions about race were similar to those at Owens. All but three (out of thirty-one) interviewees said they would prefer a high school racially mixed about half and half to one all their own race. When asked to think of five best friends and to answer several questions about them, ending with their race, 60 percent of the Mann students interviewed named one or more students of another race among their best friends, compared to 56 percent of the Owens students. However, if one looks more closely at these figures some intriguing patterns emerge.

First, if one breaks down the interviewees according to length of experience at the school, Table 6-4 demonstrates that the number of students with friends of another race was lower, the more experience students had had at the school. At Owens by contrast, the number of friends of another race was greater the more experience students had at the school. Experience at Owens seemed to foster inter-racial friendship, while experience at Mann broke up initially high rates of such friendship as recorded in December of the sixth grade.

TABLE 6–4 *Student interviewees with friends of another race at Mann and Owens by number of years in school*

	Mann			Owens		
	1st year	2nd year*	3rd year*	1st year	2nd year	3rd year
No friends of another race	18% (2)	40% (4)	60% (6)	57% (4)	43% (3)	33% (3)
One friend of another race	9% (1)	10% (1)	30% (3)	14% (1)	0% (0)	22% (2)
Two or more friends of another race	73% (8)	50% (5)	10% (1)	29% (2)	57% (4)	44% (4)
Total	100% (11)	100% (10)	100% (10)	100% (7)	100% (7)	99% (9)

*At Mann, students indicated as second and third year students are students in the seventh and eighth grades, respectively. This is not an exact measure of years they have attended Mann. At Owens, where more students enter after the sixth grade, the year in school indicates length of time at Owens, regardless of grade.

Second, when Mann students were asked whether students could get in trouble with friends of their own race for making friends of another race, nearly half, fourteen out of thirty-one, said they could. These students often specified that black students were more likely to insist that friends be made within the racial group and that black girls were especially likely to require this of each other.[7] However, 78 percent of the blacks interviewed included students of another race among those they thought of as their five best friends compared to only 44 percent of the whites.

High ability whites were particularly unlikely to have friends of another race. Many high status whites when asked how many of their five friends were 'white, black or something else' responded uncomfortably saying they had friends who were black or got along with blacks, but when pressed admitted that all of the five best friends they were thinking of were white. It is reasonable to wonder whether whites may have had norms favoring inter-racial friendship but have acted exclusively in practice, while blacks, especially the girls, responded to their practical exclusion by whites by creating protective norms for racial solidarity. Girls were only half as likely to have friends of another race as boys.[8]

The program in practice

The curriculum and the round of daily activity at Mann differed from both the other schools in being much closer to traditional junior high school patterns. The school day was divided into a traditional eight-period day; the whole school changed classes at the sound of bells. Students took the courses prescribed for regular middle schools in the city except that they could elect a foreign language in the seventh and eighth grades.

In practice, the program included little of either enrichment or acceleration. Most teachers followed traditional teaching patterns; they used lecture, recitation, and seatwork as the primary class-room activities. Occasionally the routine of the class was varied with a film or a trip to the school library for work on reports. The entire class, though heterogeneously composed in academic achievement, worked on a single task, whether that task involved recitation, individual seatwork, or homework. Non-academic classes also followed patterns traditional for those subjects, with the whole class working on a standard task. A few individual teachers allowed whole classes to engage in more varied activities or allowed individuals to work independently at different rates.

Many teachers did introduce some enrichment of the curriculum through long projects assigned for homework which allowed students considerable room for individual initiative within a common theme. For example, they might be asked to write or artistically design a project of any kind relevant to the novel *Tom Sawyer*. Adult direction for these projects came primarily from parents, however. There was also enrichment in 'exploratory

173

classes' scheduled during the last period of the day. These could offer non-traditional subject matter or remedial or advanced work and often allowed more active participation by students than did other classes. But these classes were part of a middle school plan for all Heartland middle schools mandated by the central office; they were not designed at Mann nor were they a distinctive element in its program. Further, several teachers actively resisted departing from their accustomed subjects and methods when they had to teach these classes.

One special characteristic of the school was the emphasis it put upon sending teams and individuals to competitions outside the school. Like most other middle schools the school sent teams to a citywide 'math track meet' where students competed both as a team and individually in solving math problems. The school also fielded debate and forensics teams which sometimes were pitted against high school teams. It sent an orchestra to a citywide contest. It sent individuals to a metropolitan area science fair and to regional and state competitions in French pronunciation. The students performed successfully in all of these contexts. While other schools participated in such competitions, the Mann administration gave these teams special support and visibility. In preparing for these activities students were given some work which might be called accelerated.

Extracurricular activities at Mann were severely limited, however. Fewer activities were offered and fewer interviewees participated in them than at the other schools.

Technological and logistical influences on school character

Since Mann's program was organized like that of the 'traditional' middle schools in Heartland, and the classroom teaching followed patterns which are customary in junior high schools, it provides a contrast between patterns typical in schools for this age of child and the unusual patterns at Adams and at Owens.

The effects of technological arrangements on student–teacher relations

Curricular structure
As already noted, with a few exceptions, teachers at Mann moved all students through the same curriculum at a single pace. Inevi-

tably, some children found the work rather easy while others had to strain to master it. Supervisors in the central office's department of curriculum and instruction played a role in determining the level at which the whole class worked by selecting the texts to be used. Teachers in one department – where they were chosen especially for the school – complained that they were above the students' heads. Members of another department complained that their texts – which were used throughout the city – were too simple for the students.

Academic rewards
Mann gave traditional letter grades for performance plus a grade for conduct. As is customary, these measured a student's grasp of the material relative to other students rather than his or her individual progress. Comparison of accomplishment by and among students was encouraged by the fact that each student was given a numerical grade point average. Naturally, students who entered with stronger skills had a great advantage in getting good grades.

Classroom activity structure
Most classes consisted of lecture, recitation, and seatwork. During seatwork, with a few exceptions, the Mann teachers did not circulate as did the Adams and Owens teachers but sat at their desks doing paperwork. Students with questions could either raise their hands or line up in front of the desk. Consequently, it was up to the student having difficulty to take the initiative in asking for help and the asking was publicly visible to other students.

This activity structure of shared public learning and semi-public seatwork led teachers to ignore children who were having difficulty in order to spare them embarrassment as well as to allow the rest of the class to move onward. One black teacher articulated this pattern. She blamed the teachers who recommended children for admission who could not keep up with the general pace:

'You end up not calling on those children because you don't want to embarrass them in front of the others. They just can't read it. And the punishment they take is just impossible to measure – being among all these children and not being able to do the work. It's a dreadful thing to do to a child.'

When teachers did not ignore such students, the activity structure highlighted their shortcomings without allowing an opportunity for teachers to take time really to help them. Consider for example the case of the following child in a sixth grade class in the fall:

> 'Mr Dietrich had them give the answers to the [math] homework. He called on volunteers and most of them gave the right answer. . . . He called on Randy. Randy was the boy who was sitting in the corner looking pathetic and tuned out [during a previous English class]. Randy didn't know the answer, so Mr Dietrich explained again what was meant by finding factors. Randy just looked puzzled. Mr Dietrich asked the next problem and several hands went up.'

Such attempts early in students' careers to give them assistance apparently left the students knowledgeable about one another's skills. This fact became visible in an English class where a substitute used the teacher's plan of having students read a play aloud. The substitute simply matched names from the class list to parts.

> 'Both the major characters were black students. The boy was a poor reader. Another black boy who got a smaller part said when it was assigned, "I can't read." The whole class laughed. After the parts were assigned one of the white girls asked the teacher, "If they're slow readers will you change the parts?" The substitute said no. . . . [The poor readers stumbled through their parts, occasionally prompted by other students, for the whole period.]'

The students in this class clearly were not used to poor readers being asked to read aloud. Everyone knew who the poor readers were and neither they nor the rest of the class wanted them to perform publicly.

It is important that it was not only black students with very low skills who were embarrassed by their poor performance at Mann; some students, who had formerly done well, felt ashamed of accomplishments which earned only Bs or Cs. When I asked the counselor to name students' most common problems, she said the students experiencing the greatest difficulty were those who had done well at previous schools but could not at this school.

If Mann's traditional curricular structure, academic rewards, and activity structure did not protect the students from embarrassment and public discomfort, as those at Adams and Owens did, why were there not more overt discipline problems at Mann? The

176

answer seems to lie in the fact that Mann's were ambitious students with ambitious parents and enough skills to give them hope of success. At least two studies (Bellaby, 1974; and National Institute of Education, 1978) have noted that students who fail to achieve, but who have not given up hope of doing well or whose parents hold high expectations for them, do not engage in the disobedience and open classroom conflict characteristic of students who have given up. However, they attack the school in covert ways, such as vandalism. The graffiti in the school would certainly qualify as one such form of covert expression of hostility toward the school. It seems that Mann's structures did take a toll on all but the stronger students, though they expressed it in other ways than classroom disobedience. The competitive, highstrung character of the students as a whole, mentioned earlier in connection with conflicts among the adults, may have been most directly a reflection of a competitive atmosphere which the conditions of classroom performance engendered among ambitious children.

The activity structure at Mann also had an effect on teachers' practice. Given the necessity and difficulty of retaining the attention of every student in a recitation-based classroom, teachers had reason to fear and to deal summarily with discipline problems. Additionally, since they often had to discipline publicly, discipline had to be similar in all cases so as not to appear unfair, and swift so as not to disrupt the flow of events (Bossert, 1979; Hargreaves, Hestor and Mellor, 1975). These situational pressures partially explain the Mann teachers' greater preoccupation with discipline, in comparison with the teachers at the other schools, and their greater readiness to turn students with problems in learning or classroom cooperation over to other staff experts. Of course, teachers could have circulated during the time when students worked at their desks – indeed a few did – and thus have lessened some of these pressures, but their generally shared vision of a secondary teacher's method of work did not include this practice.

The effects of technology on inter-racial relations

Inter-racial relations at Mann seemed to be significantly affected by the strains generated by the school's technological approach. Despite the fact that the black children at Mann were for the most part academically more able than those at the other schools, more likely to speak consistently in standard English, and in general more socially like mainstream whites, there was a stronger under-current of racial tension, and students were more likely to punish others for inter-racial friendship. In a study of a desegregated school where whites had much stronger academic skills than blacks, Schofield (1982) found that blacks perceived whites as conceited and experienced their displays of knowledge in class recitation as attempts to show off. Some of these dynamics may have operated at Mann as well. Furthermore, insults toward students of another race, especially those given outside the hearing of adults, can function like vandalism as a covert expression of hostility toward the school.

Equally important, Mann did not provide the conditions which social psychologists suggest foster good inter-racial relations as well as did the other schools. Its traditional technology tended to prevent the equalization of status between the races and to discourage cooperation. Authorities in the school did not visibly endorse good relations between the races as a significant school goal.

Equality of status

The preceding discussion makes it clear that students at Mann became fully aware of their relative skills in academic matters. The weakest students were black and the black students as a group were weaker than the white students as a group. Ironically, then, since the majority of blacks had skills adequate to their grade level and a sizable minority of them were definitely academically skilled, the black students were visibly academically weaker than the whites.

The traditional academic focus of classes allowed only a narrow range of strengths to be displayed in the classroom. The small number of extra-curricular activities and the low participation in them meant that these provided only a limited scope for the display of other skills which might have lent black students high status. Many of the extra-curricular activities which did exist, such as the debate team and math 'track team,' trained teams for competitive activities requiring academic skills. Most were dominated or even monopolized by white students, though a few black students participated and won prizes up to the state level.

Inter-racial cooperation

Mann's classrooms physically expressed an expectation that the class would relate as a unit to the teacher. Rows of chairs with arms for writing faced forward toward the blackboard where the teacher stood. Teachers expected students to participate together in teacher-led recitation, which was more competitive than cooperative, or to work separately on seatwork. There was little in the daily routine to encourage cooperation among students.

The seating arrangement did not encourage inter-racial cooperation or acquaintance as it did at the other schools, where students sat around tables. Mann's chairs with broad arms for writing placed in rows made it difficult for students to confer during seatwork, except with one or two others. They had to lean across an aisle or turn around toward the student sitting behind them. This movement was toward a space between seats which was accessible to no more than two to four persons. Further, students could choose the direction in which to lean and were likely to turn toward the student they knew best, usually someone of their own race. Assignment of students of different races to the same tables was much more likely to result in conversation, acquaintance, and eventual cooperation among them than was assignment to adjacent chairs in the rows at Mann.

The dearth of extra-curricular activities at Mann also cut down opportunities for cooperative activities in which children of different races could participate.

School authorities' emphasis on integration

Mann had fewer blacks on its staff and fewer in leadership positions than the other schools. The principal and administrator in charge were both white. There was a second assistant principal for the high school who was black, but his role with the middle school was limited to overseeing busing. The counselor was the only black who might be considered superordinate to the teachers. The whole middle school staff was 23 percent black, not counting the aides. (The Adams and Owens staffs were 31 and 28 percent black respectively.)

Mann's administrators and teachers did not place much emphasis on the development of multi-cultural understanding or the building of friendship across racial lines as part of the school's mission. The administrators fostered very few outside speakers or performances, and few special activities of any kind, for the school as a whole. My observations and questioning of adults about activities which dealt with race uncovered only four. There were readings from Martin Luther King's writings during the morning announcements in the week of his birthday, and the whole school was shown a film featuring Bill Cosby which used humor to show that prejudice depends on narrow thinking. A sixth grade class performed a play about stereotypes among red, blue, and green people, and home economics classes learned to prepare a variety of ethnic foods, then invited parents to an ethnic luncheon. Two of the four activities preached against prejudice; only two dealt at all with understanding different cultures. The two which did deal with cultural content to some degree were fostered by black teachers.

When white adults discussed the mandate of the school as an 'alternative school' they spoke only of its being for gifted and talented students. They made no reference to encouraging multi-culturalism or fostering inter-racial understanding as part of its mission. Indeed white adults at Mann made no reference to race except when I asked them direct questions about it. At Mann, as at Schofield's (1982) desegregated middle school, there seemed to be a taboo on the public mention of race, at least among whites.[9]

In response to direct questions about race, white teachers expressed some attachment to racial separation though they spoke somewhat indirectly. When they were asked how children of different races got along, several talked about children who preferred friends of another race with slight disapproval. Several also made it clear that they did not want to encourage racial mixing by emphasizing that they did not assign seats. (As Schofield points out [1982], when teachers say they do not have a seating policy, they actually have a policy that students should choose their seatmates according to the criteria they bring with them when they enter a school.) These teachers made statements such as the following:

> 'I'd say most separate unless you have a seating chart and make them sit together. And I don't do that. I think if they are going to mix it should be voluntary.'

The most striking statement along this line came from a teacher who recognized, as many did not, that black and white children had interests in common and could become friends. She still thought it would be inappropriately 'forcing integration' for her

to assign seats so they could get acquainted, except when she did
so as punishment for misbehavior. She said:

'I gave the children their choice the first few days. They could
sit where they please and it was basically by race and gender.
All the black boys sat together; all the white boys sat together.
The white girls sat together; the black girls sat together. I'm
still not forcing integration socially in the classroom. However,
there is some mixing because of kids having problems with
certain children in certain areas so that I move them to another
area. So now . . . [they] are [more] racially mixed.

'If they do sit near each other[10] they tend to become fairly
good friends and then they tend to sit together at lunch time
also. But unless it's forced at this early age, they simply tend
to stay apart as far as I can see. So it almost has to be forced
social integration at this point. That they need to sit next to
a person and get to know them and find out that they have
similar interests.'

Other teachers thought that the races were simply incompatible
and no amount of contact would lead them to mix voluntarily. A
teacher expressing this view also made clear the white teachers'
reluctance to express their views on race lest they be labeled
prejudiced:

INTERVIEWER: A school like this is established in part for
desegregation. How would you characterize inter-racial
relations?
MR STRASSER (*slight hesitation*): . . . I haven't seen any
animosity certainly. Any direct hostility. They accept each
other. I haven't seen them put each other down because of
their race. But by and large they congregate together with
their own race. Their close friends are with their own race.
And I think that's because of background and attitudes and
maybe things they like doing. If you look in the cafeteria,
you'll see the tables are almost all separate. They're either
white or they're black. And I think that's just the way it is.
It's not prejudice. They just pick their friends in that manner
within their own race. You can push them together all you
want and make them do things together but eventually it will
come back to that.

Not all white teachers took such a jaundiced view of inter-racial relationships. It was those from Atlantic Avenue or other central city black schools who took the dimmest view of racial mixing. Some other white teachers thought the students needed more activities which would give them a chance to mix. Others said they thought they mixed quite well already. Several of these assigned seats on bases that mixed the races.

The black teachers at Mann without exception spoke of ways that black students were not treated equally with whites and of ways in which the school created special difficulties for blacks. Some spoke forcefully, while others spoke in a restrained and measured way. Still, all saw themselves as in some degree interpreters, if not champions, for those students.

Most mentioned that black children were sent out of class for discipline more often than white children and suspended more often. The problem of unequal suspension was accentuated by a policy of 'pre-suspension' which allowed a suspended child to be readmitted without the punishment going on his or her record if the parents would have a conference on the telephone or in person before the start of classes on the day following the incident. Some black teachers pointed out that white parents are more likely to have jobs which allow them to be reached by telephone and allow them to come to the school during business hours. Some even felt that less energetic efforts were made to reach black parents. All agreed that pre-suspension allowed white children to have their cases closed without a permanent record far more frequently than did black children.

Black teachers also agreed in questioning the school's judgment in sending at least one all-white team to a citywide competition. Some of the black teachers spoke of practices and incidents which led them to conclude that black students were excluded from activities because of their race or received less attention and assistance in class. Their accounts of incidents were very difficult to assess, as were a number of small acts and statements by white teachers I witnessed myself which, while appearing to involve differential treatment or judgment of black children, contained no explicit reference to their race. As Clement, Eisenhart and Harding (1979) observe, in their careful analysis of incidents which became controversial in a southern desegregated school, there is often no clear evidence with which to determine whether behavior which may appear racially motivated is so in fact.

Two black teachers from Atlantic Avenue said that they thought the change to the gifted and talented program had brought with it a rejection of blackness. One teacher said she no longer felt it acceptable to wear her own hair in an Afro. Others pointed out that programs Atlantic used to run on black heroes and the black heritage had been dropped when the gifted and talented program was introduced. They said angrily that black students were treated as unfortunate baggage, reluctantly brought along into the new program.

Relations between black and white teachers were also considerably strained. Some black teachers described white teachers as not even civil toward them. Two spoke bitterly of seeing several white teachers ostentatiously throwing out the handout one of the black teachers had passed out when presenting her department's program to the assembled faculty in a monthly faculty meeting. Some white as well as black teachers said this estrangement went back to a deep split between white and black teachers at the Atlantic Junior High School. Others, notably whites, attributed it to most black teachers' unwillingness to join the teachers' strike three years before.

While it is difficult to know how much the faculty, both white and black, communicated their racial feelings to the students, it seems safe to say that the students would not have learned from the adults that authorities gave a great deal of active support to inter-racial understanding as a school goal.[11]

Logistical influences at Mann

Logistical influences seem to have been important in shaping the character of the program at Mann. The student body in the building as a whole was just under 1,000, more than twice as large as that in the other two schools. Sharing the building with the high school increased the middle school staff's concern with security, dictated a rigid time schedule, limited the facilities available, and gave students a feeling of being 'just' middle school students in comparison to the larger, dominating high school students.

The large size of the student body required more effort for supervision than at the other schools, since adults could not know all of the students they might see in the halls. Further, the older age of the students increased the possibility of more serious forms of delinquency – or at least parents feared that it did; the school administrators felt they had to use copious resources in supervision in part to reassure the parents. Teachers with previous experience in other senior high schools in Heartland remarked upon the *lack* of staff resources used in supervision.

The building's location also contributed to the concern with supervision. A middle school parent who was a policeman warned the administrators that the neighborhood was the scene of a good deal of trouble. One aim of the security was to keep outsiders out of the school – though in practice few problems from the neighborhood materialized. The use of yellow buses for all students – which was a result of both the physical location and the reputation of the neighborhood – inhibited the extra-curricular program, since it was not until halfway through the study year that staff and parental entreaties to the central office succeeded in getting a system of 'late buses' to run after extra-curricular activities two days a week.

The size and complexity of the two schools combined required a highly formalized use of time and space. Thus everyone changed rooms at once according to a bell schedule, and spaces were strictly regulated. Classes could not borrow more appropriate space, nor could they have flexible time for special activities. Except in the sixth grade, where students traveled as class units, any special activity or field trip which spilled over the temporal confines of a forty-eight minute class disrupted other classes by removing some students who would have to make up the work missed the next day. As a result, the sixth grade teachers and team were much more active in planning field trips than those in the other two grades.

The building was remodeled with the expectation of serving only a high school. As a consequence, special facilities such as science laboratories, art rooms, and rehearsal space for musical instruments were in short supply for the two schools together. The high school had first claim on what was available. There was a single public address system, so both schools had to listen to announcements intended for the other. Middle school students heard about many attractive activities in which they were not allowed to participate. They became very aware of being just middle schoolers, smaller and less important than the high school students – who sometimes called them Munchkins.

Logistical problems did not create their effects alone. They had effects as they were filtered through processes of interpretation.

For example, teachers at Mann declared their teaching was hobbled by the facilities until the program could be moved to another building. But the facilities were superior to those at Adams where teachers were staunchly opposed to any move of the program. It is to the question of socially constructed meaning in the school which we now turn.

Faculty culture and school character

The Mann faculty, or at least a large and dominant group within it, developed a distinctive subculture which shaped their behavior toward both students and adults. It had important continuities with the subculture which the teachers had developed at Atlantic Avenue. Its most obvious manifestations were an insistence that the conditions in which the teachers taught were overwhelmingly difficult and chronic anger with the school administration. The teachers exhibited less interest in their students as persons and in the teaching process than did teachers in the other schools. They seemed almost peevishly to cast aside opportunities for constructive and imaginative efforts in the classroom. To an outsider their behavior seemed perverse, since other teachers in the city considered their situation thoroughly enviable. But if one tries to get inside the teachers' collective perspective, then their behavior forms a consistent response to their experiences and the meaning with which they endowed them.

The faculty's behavior and beliefs

We can begin to reach an understanding of the Mann faculty's behavior and the culture which lay behind it by considering how they defined education for the gifted and talented. When teachers were asked what they did differently because Horace Mann was a gifted and talented school, many replied that good teaching is the same in any school.

> 'There was an inservice class . . . that first year, but I couldn't take it because I had a time conflict. But I don't think there is much need for it. As far as I'm concerned kids are kids and they need structure. They need the basic fundamentals. You

find out what they know and what they need to learn from
there and then you start teaching that.'

When teachers were asked in an interview how they would
ideally run a gifted and talented school, most responded that they
would screen children carefully and identify their talents clearly.
They implied that adequate selection of outstandingly gifted and
talented students and labeling at entrance were both necessary
and sufficient for a gifted and talented program.

One teacher expressed this philosophy very clearly:

'First of all you should have children who are really gifted and
talented. And then secondly you should be able to group
them. Grouping should not be a bad word . . . They ought to
be able to be grouped together to go as fast as they can go
in math. And if a child is talented in music, he ought to be
with other people who are talented in music . . . Teaching
for the gifted and talented is simply good teaching.'

These teachers took it for granted that acceleration, in the sense
of standard subjects taught faster, is the essence of gifted and
talented education. But they also were responding to pressures
from administrators and parents to make the program for gifted
and talented children distinctive, as they insisted that the key to
their mission lay in being able to work with distinctive groups of
children. Any deficiencies in the program lay in the selection and
grouping of students, not in the way teachers worked with them.
They were vehement in saying that the selection and grouping of
the children in the school were inadequate. They insisted over
and over that the children were 'average', an ordinary group of
children.

Their insistence that Mann's students were merely average
appeared to be an item of subcultural belief because it was so
frequently repeated and because it violated common sense. If
Mann's students were not all clearly gifted and talented, three-
quarters were above the national median in basic skills and 90
percent or more were above the city median which fell at about
the 33rd percentile nationally. Further, the teachers also
complained, not entirely consistently, that the student body was
so diverse that they had to teach to the middle and ignore the
needs of the most gifted or talented students. A teacher in an

academic subject expressed both beliefs about two paragraphs apart in the full transcript of her comments:

'There's very little difference between our student body, as I perceive it, and any other middle school that I know of. . . . Perhaps the basic skill areas, like the reading levels, are generally higher than some other places. . . . I have a few [seventh grade] kids that read at the fourth or fifth grade level, but those are fairly rare. Most of the kids are within a grade level or so of their current assignment. . . .

'Their behavior is generally better. . . . But in the classroom – the quality of work that they do – the whole range is there. There are kids who could be doing beginning college work all the way down to the kids who can barely cope with what we are doing on a day to day basis.'

Given the percentage of Mann's students who scored above the city average, it seems that an academic teacher, like this one, with experience in a poor black and a middle-class white high school in Heartland, would have difficulty not noticing the difference between the students in this group and others, unless she were seeing their performance through the veil of a cultural interpretation.

The belief that Mann's students were average provided teachers with a justification for giving them average teaching. The adverse conditions for teaching created by the presence of 'the whole range' of students reinforced this justification.

As the teachers understood their situation, they could not begin to develop a gifted and talented program unless all the students were gifted, and unless students were grouped homogeneously according to their gifts in each subject. They felt helpless and misused in the face of expectations that they develop a special program without these arrangements. The faculty held that they were doing the best that could be expected, considering the students they were given. They were saying in effect, 'We are good teachers, but what can you do with these students?'

Teachers were critical not only of the screening of the students, but also of the administrators. A pall of resentment hung in the air. It became palpable in little matters. For example, the teachers seemed poised to leave the building at the first legal moment at the end of each day. At faculty meetings they sat in stony silence and refused to chuckle politely in response to the administrator-in-charge's pleasantries. In research interviews, many not only expressed anger and frustration, but seemed almost pleased when they could recount instances of administrative barriers to their performance. They proclaimed that their inventive ideas were vetoed by the administrator-in-charge or bogged down in logistical difficulties or administrative inaction. Some teachers said explicitly that they had decided there was nothing they could do under this administration; they were simply putting in time until the school could be moved out of the building and receive a new administration.

Even when teachers were encouraged to take some initiative in defining and developing the program, they tended to resist doing so on the grounds that such development was primarily an administrative responsibility. One teacher expressed this view very explicitly in an interview.

'There's a lot of vagueness surrounding this whole concept of gifted and talented. There isn't much [administrative] leadership in developing just what the program is supposed to be. . . .

'One of our tasks [in team meetings of teachers who teach the academic subjects for a grade] was to be exploring that. It's as if we have been given the task of trying to define and put into words what they haven't been able to tell us. It's as if the program has been established without a clear philosophy or clear view and clear sense of what this whole thing is supposed to be about. Which is really kind of a futile thing to do. You establish a program and then try to figure out what it is. We haven't made any progress on that. There isn't enough dialogue going on between all the people that need to be involved. . . . The administrators would need to be involved.'

Such complaints from teachers would have seemed more reasonable had they been asked to develop a full program from the ground up. In fact, they were asked to consider rather small changes, such as cooperative student projects, or non-traditional instructional techniques. Further, only a few teachers were willing to participate in inservice courses or weekend and university courses in gifted and talented education about which the administration regularly informed them. Their resistance to considering steps they might take is quite striking in the context of studies of implementation of educational innovations which stress that teachers like to be given an opportunity to shape the innovative practices they are asked to implement (e.g. Deal and Nutt, 1983; Sarason, 1971; Sussmann, 1977).

In short, since the teachers' position here does not seem to make common sense from an outsider's perspective, one is alerted to look for a subcultural perspective from which it does make sense. The teachers at Mann seemed to be saying not only, 'We are good teachers, but what can you do with these students?' but also, 'We are good teachers, but what can you do with this administration?' They held to their perspective so tenaciously that it inhibited them from taking initiative to shape the program. They protected their claim to be good teachers by attempting to demonstrate that circumstances were so difficult that there was no way that they could function effectively.

Variation among the Mann faculty

Although I have spoken of the teachers as one group in the forgoing description, there were variations among them. Most strikingly, there were some new teachers, who had joined the faculty after the move to Mann, who did not share either the behavior or the attitudes of the majority. These were almost the only teachers who pursued non-traditional activities, even such small departures as classroom discussion in other than a question and answer format. These new teachers found the student body more stimulating than frustrating, and they were far less critical of the administrators than the teachers who had come from Atlantic. There were only a few such teachers, however, and they did not form a group of their own. They focused their attention and efforts on their own classrooms. (There were a few other new teachers who became assimilated to the dominant faculty culture and were some of its most expressive proponents.)

The black teachers were a separate group within the faculty, although they were a set of socially and personally very diverse people. They had some social solidarity and some common perspectives around issues of race. They were not much happier with the administrators than were the dominant group of teachers and they shared some of the same style of response to them. Their discomfiture with the student body took a different form because

189

of their much greater sympathy with black students[12] and their impatience with the self-assurance of some of the white students.

The white men and the white women who had had experience at Atlantic Avenue also differed from each other, but in more subtle ways. It was the white men who formed the dominant core group of the faculty and who most fully exemplified the faculty culture. This core was led by a group of white men who constituted one department and who all had started together at Atlantic Avenue ten years prior to the study. The white women from Atlantic Avenue also expressed negative feelings about the school. But they were more sympathetic with the administrators despite some specific criticisms of particular policies or actions.

These differences among the faculty help to uncover the sources of the dominant culture expressed by the white men from Atlantic. Most of what follows will concentrate on the development and meaning of their version of the subculture because they were the dominant voice. However, the ways in which other groups differed from and were similar to them will be discussed.

Historical sources of faculty culture at Mann

A few of the white teachers who talked about their collective past at Atlantic Avenue provided some insight into the historical roots of the faculty culture. One white woman from Atlantic Avenue described her experience there in vivid terms. She could not understand why the dominant group of teachers were so negative about their present situation because to her it seemed a vast improvement over Atlantic.

> INTERVIEWER: What was Atlantic like before the change [to a magnet program]?
> MS ROHR: That's a funny thing. This is just like you've died and gone to heaven. I don't understand why a teacher would moan and groan and complain and say that it is such hell here.
> I spent ten years at that hellhole, and there is just no describing it unless you've taught in an inner city junior high school with seventh, eighth, and ninth graders. We had ninth graders that were eighteen years old. In its real heyday, we had two and three fires a day, constant false alarms, horrible vandalism, fights. I couldn't count the number of knives and

junk that I saw in my classroom in ten years. I mean, there's
no comparison. Teacher assaults, you know, teachers
knocked in the face and the mouth, in the eyes, knifings. Two
art teachers I know were knifed. I mean just gross, gross
misconduct and horrible, horrible behavior. For a few years
there the kids were right off the walls.

This teacher's comments are consistent with the reputation of
Atlantic Avenue in the city. It was clearly a school where the
kind of opposition which can develop between poorly achieving
working-class and minority students and their teachers was in full
flower.

One of the white men from Atlantic, who was not socially close
to the other white men and did not share their degree of discontent
with Mann, articulated the feelings which the experience of
teaching the students at Atlantic engendered in him with unusual
frankness.

MR SELIG: At Atlantic I probably didn't smile at all. Maybe
until February. And you really almost had to do that for
survival. . . . Teachers didn't have as much authority. After a
while you really lost your sense of self-worth, you really did.
INTERVIEWER: Tell me some more about that.
MR SELIG: Well, I just simply felt that – I realized I had a
family and that they had to be fed. I really hadn't been
trained for anything else besides teaching. And I simply went
to work every day. Tried to do the best I could and it really
didn't bother me whether a student got this or a student got
that. It didn't bother me. I'd just go and do my job. . . .
    At Atlantic you almost think that what the kids are doing
to you is a personal affront. You know, you tend to get
extremely angry. It takes a long time to get over that, to
realize that the kids aren't really angry at you. They really
aren't striking out at you as an individual. It takes a long time.
. . . 'Cause I'm telling you a lot of times you can go home
and start questioning your own values. You start stereotyping.
It's really shameful how you lose all that self-respect and
idealism.

Another white man from Atlantic Avenue who was active in
the core group clearly still felt the anger Mr Selig said it took him

191

so long to get over. He described a similar process of withdrawal from caring how much the students learned:

> 'If kids are all the time fighting in class and calling you names and so on, when it's time for your prep period or you go home at night, you don't spend your time thinking up nice little activities for those children. It's sort of as though – well, I guess every child deserves a good education – but it's as though, "If you don't respect me and what I have done for you, why should I do this for you?" '

All of these white teachers suggest that conflict between students and teachers was high at the old Atlantic Avenue school and that teachers responded to feelings of rage and frustration with withdrawal. (Of the three teachers quoted, only Mr Selig saw that the students might have had an understandable reason for their hostility. None suggested that the teachers' withdrawal and anger might have contributed to students' aggressiveness.) The Atlantic faculty learned to support one another in seeing themselves as good teachers who could not display their abilities because the students were difficult. When they experienced new difficulties at Mann – even though they now had a situation other teachers in the city envied – they continued to see themselves as good teachers who could not display their abilities because of the students they were given.

At Atlantic, the teachers had also blamed the principal, in fact a succession of principals, for their inability to be effective. The Atlantic principal had not been transferred with the program, and the teachers now spoke of him fairly kindly, as they spoke disparagingly of their new principals. When difficulties developed at Mann, they continued to see themselves as competent persons in impossible circumstances, making new administrators the source of their inability to show their true worth.

At both Atlantic and Mann, the faculty culture assumed that the locus of control of the situation was not with teachers. As they said, 'We are good teachers, but what can you do with these students?' and, 'We are good teachers, but what can you do with this administration?' Their deepest, most tacit, assumption was that good teaching is only possible when organizational conditions are favorable. Teachers cannot control these conditions, yet they can only practice their craft effectively and demonstrate their professional capabilities when appropriate conditions are provided.

None the less, there were some interesting ways in which teachers did attempt to express themselves as actively competent professionals. These were ways in which they were not inhibited by the context. As a group they dressed extremely well. Most of the men wore ties and jackets and the women wore dresses and suits which would have been appropriate in downtown offices. Their dress proclaimed both their professionalism and their middle-class status, which their association with the old Atlantic students had called into question. Furthermore, in some situations where teachers worked with groups composed only of very able students, in a few classes and in some extra-curricular competitive teams with an academic character, teachers worked with a publicly visible energy and enthusiasm which they did not display in their regular classes.

The importance of pride in faculty culture at Mann

Cognitively, the Mann faculty were declaring that they could not control the quality of their teaching unless they were given cooperative, able students homogeneously grouped by ability and ideal facilities and problem free scheduling. But emotionally they were declaring that they were unjustly accused, that despite constant disparagement of their abilities, and so their professional and personal pride, they were in fact competent even though they could not show it. The transition to a gifted and talented magnet school, even with its apparently enviable student body, did not change their pattern of withdrawal, or at least not the men's, because the change in student body altered the source of attacks on their pride but did not eliminate them.

Faculty pride and identification as 'inner city teachers'
The initial development of the gifted and talented program did much to wound teachers' pride. In the year that the program functioned at Atlantic Avenue with seventy seventh graders, while the rest of the school served remaining neighborhood students, a small group of teachers were chosen to teach the gifted and talented students. Central office personnel and teachers from Peach Street worked intensively with the chosen teachers. Other

teachers were literally forbidden to have any contact with the gifted students. They might help a colleague set up a lab or an art room, but they were expected to leave the room when the students entered.

The teachers not chosen for the gifted and talented program took serious offense at this treatment. They made barbed jokes about 'gifted and talented teachers' in the direction of their chosen colleagues. Always unspoken was the assumption that if some teachers were 'gifted and talented' by association with their students, others were 'inner city teachers' by association with theirs. When the whole student body became gifted and talented students in the next year, these excluded teachers became part of the gifted and talented faculty, but the stigma of their former students still clung to them.

The administrator in charge of the middle school at Mann spoke of the Atlantic teachers as a category. He said he considered one of his tasks to be 'reawakening enthusiasm for teaching' in them. Some parents similarly assumed that after dealing with a population of inner city students, the teachers from Atlantic would be unprepared to work with 'gifted and talented' students unless they received considerable special retraining – and perhaps not even then.

Parents' aggressive public criticism of the teachers has already been described. The following account given by a white woman teacher from Atlantic, who appeared to be a very conscientious teacher, suggests the kinds of criticisms of individual teachers they also engaged in.

'A parent said that she was not only going to take me to the administration [because of her child's grade], she was going to take me all the way to the board and that I wasn't fit to be a teacher. And it was ironic because at the beginning of the year she complimented me and said that her child was enjoying the course and that she thought it was a well-taught course. I was just doing fine. But then as soon as her child was not performing well, she assumed that it was the teacher's fault and not the child's fault. It really shook me up as an experience more than almost anything else had. But I was just determined to stick with it. I felt that I was not being unprofessional. I was not doing it – giving that grade – out of motives of vengeance. I was on solid ground.'

In sum, the teachers from Atlantic Avenue found their pride assaulted, sometimes with brutal directness, by the arrangements of the transition process, by administrators, and by parents.

Faculty pride and the shared Mann school building
The Atlantic faculty had left their building reluctantly. They felt that their program was perched in the Mann High School building without really belonging there. They felt belittled that the principal for the building oversaw the high school, while the middle school faculty related to an assistant principal, who was under the authority of the principal, as their 'administrator in charge.' There were many small but symbolic signs of the middle school's secondary status and many little inconveniences that made its faculty feel unappreciated. When announcements for the two schools were given, those for the high school always came first, and sometimes middle school announcements were interrupted for high school ones. The middle school got a separate office only after much parental pressure was applied. The high school office remained the main office. Teachers found their mail was often delayed there and that it was often inconvenient to get supplies, which were routed to the middle school office only in small amounts. There was a single small bulletin board near the front door on which were posted 'school' events, but only those for the high school. In the spring big banners announced a 'Mann all school picnic' – which was just for the high school. The presence of the high school in the building and its symbolic priority was one more blow to the already battered pride of the Mann Middle School faculty.

Faculty pride and the transition to a middle school
Sharing the building with the high school also made vivid for the teachers the lower status of middle school teaching than high school teaching. Most of them were licensed to teach high school and many had hoped to do so before being assigned to younger students. Atlantic Avenue had at least been a junior high school with a ninth grade and departmental organization. The adoption of the districtwide middle school plan in the year of the study constituted yet another blow to the teachers' pride. It eliminated department heads and established a single schoolwide learning coordinator. It introduced grade level teams of teachers of different subjects as the primary organizational subunit instead of

departments. It emphasized the child, rather than the subject, and thus further undercut the teachers' status as bona fide secondary teachers.

When the central office and the administrator in charge reminded them further that the middle school program for the gifted and talented was intended to be an extension of the elementary one at Peach Street and should include enrichment after its model, rather than acceleration like the high school, this seemed a further infantilization of their efforts. These moves toward a more elementary style of school organization and teaching were particularly hard on the pride of the men, since elementary teaching is identified with women and with mothering. That most of the teachers engaged in highly traditional, subject-oriented teaching can be understood in part as a reassertion of their identity as secondary teachers, in the face of what they experienced as belittling pressure to become like elementary teachers.

Faculty pride and the culture developed at Mann
The Mann teachers who came from Atlantic were used to being denied any sense of pride of craft in their conflictual relations with their students there. The preceding discussion shows that when they became the faculty of a gifted and talented school they were still subjected to assaults on their pride from many directions. It was then not surprising that these teachers should together build a meaningful system centered around collective maintenance of their threatened pride. They interpreted the world through a cultural filter which allowed them to preserve their sense that they were good teachers. That they could not show their good qualities, indeed that they would not even attempt new departures which might show them, was, through the logic of meaning which they developed, demonstration of their worth as teachers. Their passivity made evident the impossible constraints under which they labored.

From an outsider's perspective their behavior was baffling and self-defeating as they made little attempt to develop enriched, accelerated, or even imaginative educational experiences with their well-behaved and generally able classes and as they entered a relationship of spiraling conflict with administrators. But their behavior can be understood if one comprehends the subculture which supported it and made it both sensible and, in a limited sense, rewarding for the teachers.

The exercise of power and school character

Of all the barbs which currently nettled the pride of the Mann Middle School teachers the unusual administrative structure of the school and the administrators' exercise of their authority over the teachers were probably the most significant, especially for the men.

The administrative structure

The Heartland School District has a policy that there may be only one principal in a building. Consequently there was a single principal for both Mann High School and Mann Middle School, Dr Joliet. An assistant principal, Mr Mueller, was designated administrator in charge of the middle school but as such was clearly subject to the final authority of the principal. He also remained an assistant principal on the high school administrative staff and occasionally had time-consuming duties in that connection. In a sense, Mr Mueller functioned as the principal of the middle school, but in another sense Dr Joliet did, with Mr Mueller as his clear subordinate. Both men must be considered in describing the use of administrative power in the school.

Mr Mueller ran middle school faculty meetings, and teachers were expected to see him concerning any issue from permission for a field trip, to problems with a student, to designing the curriculum. Mr Mueller also met with the PTO. He worked with the faculty as a group and individually, trying to encourage them to teach in a more distinctive way for the gifted and talented program. Still, if he wanted to make any policy decision of importance he had to clear it with Dr Joliet, with whom he met and consulted daily. When the middle school teachers wanted a decision or permission for some special activity, they went to Mr Mueller, but often had to wait for an answer until he could check with the principal. Sometimes Mr Mueller gave answers and then changed them, giving the appearance that he had been overruled from above. The sensitive middle school teachers felt that they had no access to the man at the top but were subject to a distant power, while the high school teachers were favored with direct access to the principal.

Horace Mann School

The principals' efforts to launch the program

Since the study took place when both administrators had been in office less than two years, neither could have had the kind of pervasive influence on the perspective of the faculty which Mrs Michaels and Mr Osten had developed over seven and eight years of contact with the core of their faculties. Further, they both had to stretch their efforts over a much larger set of tasks than did the principals and assistant principals of the other two schools. There were more than twice as many students in the building and two separate schools to run, but there were only three administrators in all. The press of immediately necessary administrative tasks left the principals at Mann with less time than the other principals had to deal with teachers or with students around substantive or personal issues.

Like Mrs Michaels at Adams, Dr Joliet and Mr Mueller had to set up the new program promised to parents by imposing it on teachers from above. At the same time, they also had to launch two new programs simultaneously in a building which was still being remodeled during the first months that they occupied it. They had to establish new routines and develop patterns of communication and cooperation among persons who, especially in the high school, arrived as strangers to one another.

Dr Joliet, who bore prime responsibility for these tasks, used the full formal powers of his office to gain cooperation, just as Mrs Michaels did in establishing IGE. He made it very clear that he was in charge and that he expected compliance. He set up routines and insisted that teachers adhere to them. Because the school was so complex and initially in short supply of everything from staff time to materials, he made routines very formal. There needed to be work orders for secretarial time and requisitions for even small amounts of materials. As he faced the demands on his own time, he asked teachers to make formal appointments if they wanted to see him, an unusual policy which was talked about beyond the borders of the school. He addressed teachers by their last names and interacted with them in a courteous but briskly task-oriented manner. In conversations with me, he spoke of 'managing' the staff, a word which reflected his emphasis upon the hierarchical character of the principal's relationship with teachers.

According to several of the women teachers in the middle school, he developed a very well-organized, dependable style.

198

Those who dealt with him frequently, because they had minor administrative tasks, found that procedures were clear and predictable; he made it possible for them to accomplish their work efficiently. In other words, in administering the school he made bureaucratic hierarchy a matter of actual practice, and he realized the benefits for which it is designed.

In the first year of the program, Dr Joliet related directly to the middle school teachers over some issues, but in the second year he tried to delegate direction of the middle school to Mr Mueller as much as possible. The new middle school office in the wing of the building which housed the middle school teachers' classrooms gave some sense of physical and social separateness to the two administrations as well. (High school teachers and students also used this wing for classes, however.) In the second year, which was the year of the study, most teachers said they had little direct contact with Dr Joliet. New teachers found him to be a shadowy figure with whom they had little acquaintance.

Mr Mueller's personal style was far more informal than Dr Joliet's. He addressed the teachers by their first names and had an outgoing, friendly style which made him appear more accessible than Dr Joliet. He did not require appointments, though it was sometimes hard for teachers to find him free.

Like Dr Joliet, however, he was under pressure to get the routines of the school established and running smoothly and to induce teachers to deliver the special education promised to parents. Thus while he was friendly to the teachers in informal contacts, he pushed them quite hard for change both collectively and individually. He told me of having selected four teachers from the old Atlantic with whom he was working especially closely. Two teachers who were new to the school told me themselves of having had evaluation conferences with him (some of them with Dr Joliet also present) in which he was very critical of them and made it clear he expected them to change classroom practices. Many teachers spoke of his having turned down projects and ideas they had had, though several said that it was never clear whether these decisions were his own or the result of his conferring with Dr Joliet. In short, despite Mr Mueller's informal and friendly social manner, he also made much use of the formal hierarchical powers of his administrative office.

Horace Mann School

Relations between the principals and the faculty

The response of the core members of the faculty culture
The white male teachers made no complaint about the hierarchical control used by the administrators. Instead, they complained of a *lack* of strong clear control over the middle school. They said the school was left to drift; they complained that Mr Mueller was the person with whom they were supposed to deal but that he could not make real decisions because he was constantly overruled by Dr Joliet. They also complained that Mr Mueller was insufficiently strict and firm with students sent for discipline. They carefully noted situations where there were frustrating snarls with supplies, facilities, and scheduling of events and talked about them in interviews with grim pleasure, as evidence of their perspective on the school and the administrators' capabilities.

Like the dissidents at Adams, the white males who formed the core of Mann's faculty culture complained that their immediate superior, who from an observer's point of view and according to other teachers was making strong new hierarchical demands, was weak and incapable of strong direction. Unable to reject their principal's use of authority by saying it was illegitimate, they instead said that the individual person wielding the authority was incompetent. The Mann teachers' complaints that Mr Mueller was weak in control of students or in yielding to Dr Joliet provided a basis for legitimately ignoring or defying Mr Mueller's directives.

These teachers did engage in some clear acts of non-compliance. Much of this was visible in their response to expectations for team activities. Two men on one team simply refused to look at students' questionnaires expressing interest in topics for exploratory classes when the curriculum coordinator brought them to a team meeting to plan exploratory offerings. The same two teachers often brought papers to grade during team meetings and even left some meetings, saying that if there were anything significant to do they could be found in the lounge. Members of another team, when Mr Mueller met with them early in the year, had insisted on discussing matters that he was not involved in or had ostentatiously graded papers. They then complained that the team's efforts were undercut because Mr Mueller would not meet with the team later in the year. This team, according to a couple of its members, spent many of its meetings discussing the shortcomings of the administration. By the spring, it simply did not meet on most days.

Other teachers' response

It is important that the teachers who responded in the way just described were almost all men. The women spoke directly of strong administrative structure and direction which they generally attributed to Dr Joliet. In interviews, they spoke of having their feelings hurt by the way they were treated by the principals and by the high school office staff and of sometimes feeling 'like stepchildren' as part of the middle school vis-à-vis the high school. They did not lay much personal blame on the administrators, however, but spoke of enduring a difficult situation. They recognized that the need to establish two programs with great speed led to the principals' strong use of authority, and that the logistical complexity of running two programs in a single building led to many arrangements which created problems for teachers.

It was women who took what initiative was taken to develop special projects through the teaching teams. A few women also attended courses and workshops on gifted and talented education on their own time. Though their teaching was generally not much different from the men's at the time of the study, these excursions may have affected it in the long run.

All but one of the black teachers were women. In addition to the problems all the teachers experienced, some spoke of feeling subject to suspicion of incompetence because of their race as they dealt with white parents and administrators. Some of them responded like the white men in angry resistance to the administration, and some responded more like many of the white women, acknowledging that this was a difficult situation but attempting to construct cooperative relationships among the adults for the sake of good teaching for the students.

The effect of the male role on the core teachers' response

The men felt at least as much belittled by the strongly directive administrative conduct of the administrators, the status of the middle school vis-à-vis the high school, and the lack of resources resulting from logistical problems, as the women did. However, as males they said little of feelings of wounded dignity. In American culture, it is considered unmanly to say one's feelings are hurt because one feels undervalued. In fact it throws doubt upon one's manhood to be undervalued in the first place, as it does not throw doubt upon one's womanhood.

When the men spoke of Mr Mueller's role in interviews, they used words which suggested not only that he was a subordinate – and thus not worthy of much attention or obedience – but that his subordination implied a lack of manliness. They called him a 'flunky,' 'underling' or 'gofur.' As an assistant principal and as administrator in charge, Mr Mueller was in a position clearly subject to Dr Joliet's hierarchical authority. The male teachers' choice of words suggested that there is something personally demeaning, and more important, unmasculine, about being a bureaucratic subordinate.

If this was true of Mr Mueller's position as assistant principal, it was also true of theirs as teachers, as the principal and Mr Mueller together fully exercised the latent powers of administrative authority over them. Furthermore, if Mr Mueller, as head of the middle school, was in a demeaningly subordinate position in relation to the high school principal, then the whole staff of the middle school was also in such a position in relation to the high school. It seems, then, that the male teachers' use of terms which suggested a lack of masculinity in Mr Mueller's subordination as an assistant principal expressed a threat they felt to their own sense of masculinity from both principals' active exercise of their formal authority and from the subordination of the middle school to the high school.

Summary and implications

The middle school for the gifted and talented felt the impact of its place in the larger system as it was used twice to fill a building which had formerly housed black children from the neighborhood, while they were scattered elsewhere. It also felt the impact – and limitations – of parental power. Parents played a large part in its founding, but then were moved without warning along with the staff, only to be once more accommodated in a variety of arrangements, some of which were inconvenient for the staff. The school felt the power of parents most directly as they vociferously complained and expressed their opinions to the principals, in public meetings, and with individual teachers. Mann felt the politics of race and class which lay behind the magnet plan, as some white middle-class 'gifted and talented parents' assumed that teachers who had worked with Atlantic's students would lack not only the specific skills, but quite possibly the mental qualities, their children needed from their teachers.

In the context of comparison with Adams and Owens, Mann's program can be taken as typical of traditional junior high school and middle school programs which stress a secondary rather than an elementary school style. Given Mann's relatively academically skilled student body who were selected by teachers for some special ability, the school is the likely cause of the lesser cordiality between students and teachers and the more difficult relations between students of different races at Mann than at the other schools. The structure of the curriculum, academic reward system, and classroom activity structure – which were of the type predominant in American schools for children this age – seem to have had much to do with these more difficult relationships. In addition, limited extra-curricular activities and in-school special events provided few opportunities in the school at large to equalize the status of students of different races or to provide opportunities for cooperative activities and so to improve inter-racial relations. Logistical patterns, encouraged by the location and size of the school and its combination with the high school, but also quite typical of urban schools for children this age, fostered impersonal, control-oriented relations between adults and students and discouraged the kind of cooperative activity which helps inter-racial relations.

Mann's faculty were far less engaged in their relationships with students than were teachers at the other two schools. Their belief that they needed ideal students to be good teachers was poles apart from the acceptance of students regardless of color, class, respectable behavior patterns, and academic skills at the other schools. As they talked about the school with each other and in the research interviews, they gave their major attention to issues of organization of the school, especially selection of the student body, and to relationships among the adults. At Atlantic Avenue, the teachers, at least most of the white teachers, had learned to despair of finding intrinsic rewards in the classroom. Assaults to their pride as teachers, which had come from students at Atlantic, seemed to continue, though from new sources, when they became the faculty of a program for the gifted and talented.

Teachers relied upon the fundamental cultural beliefs and attitudes which had defended their pride at Atlantic to defend it at Mann. This belief system prevented the majority of teachers from developing the kind of involvement with the students and with classroom teaching which characterized the majority of teachers at the other two schools. It also prevented them from developing the kinds of cooperative relationships with principals which predominated at Owens and moderated discontent with Mrs Michaels's hierarchical imposition of IGE at Adams.

If the teachers from Atlantic Avenue were predisposed to find fault with Mann's principals and to resist their efforts at directing them out of patterns developed in Atlantic's faculty culture, the principals' use of all their formal powers of direction over the faculty was very important in increasing their opposition. Like the dissident teachers at Adams, the male teachers at Mann responded angrily to the principals' use of strong hierarchical control without admitting that it existed. The anomalous position of the middle school in the building and its accompanying administrative arrangements exacerbated the conflict between administrators and teachers.

It would be a great mistake to attribute the tensions at Mann Middle School primarily to its various idiosyncratic circumstances or to the personalities of its staff, though these had some impact. Mann differed from the other two schools in this study precisely because it was more typical of schools in general. The striking fact in the contrast between Mann and the other schools lies in the fact that Adams and Owens were able to muster such positive relationships despite the lack of academic skills and the socially marginal backgrounds of many of their students. If Mann did not do as well as they did, it was because it did not have their unusual technological approaches and unusual faculty cultures. The comparison highlights the importance of the special causal conditions analyzed in discussing those schools.

Furthermore, the important sources of Mann's problems were anything but idiosyncratic. The fundamental sources of tension at Mann stemmed from practices which are traditional and nearly standard in secondary education and from the culture and structure of the larger society. The typicality of Mann's time schedule, curriculum, academic rewards and activity structure have already been noted. The conflict between students and teachers at Atlantic, while it may have been encouraged by very specific actions on both sides, reflected the despair of the poor which is based in the larger economy and in racial and social attitudes which pervade the society. As the literature discussed in Chapter 3 attests, the conflict at Atlantic was by no means atypical for schools with economically poor, poorly achieving students of a minority race.

There has been much less discussion of the pattern seen here in which the stigma which the society places on poor black students also attaches to their teachers – even when they are white and middle-class. However, there is no reason at all to think that middle-class parents and administrators in Heartland were unusual in thinking along such lines. Finley (1984) has recently noted that teachers in a comprehensive high school tended to receive levels of respect from colleagues, and even to develop occupational self-confidence, matched to the track level they taught.

Similarly, the male teachers' sense of demotion in the changes that accompanied the transition from a junior high school to a middle school organization, and their insistence on their status as secondary teachers, are easily understandable in the context of the larger culture. Working with children does not have high status in this society (Bronfenbrenner, 1970), and the younger the children, the lower one's status. Furthermore, elementary school teachers are overwhelmingly women, while secondary teachers are half male. For men to be identified with elementary teaching is to be identified with a feminine occupation in a way not implied in being a secondary teacher. For the women, identification with a feminine occupation was less problematic, though many of them certainly identified themselves as secondary teachers.

The different responses of the men and the women to the primacy of the high school and to the principals' exercise of all their powers of superordination also reflected broader societal expectations for men and for women. The words Mann's male teachers used for the administrator in charge are not often used for women. One does not speak of female administrative assistants or of secretaries as flunkies, gofurs, and underlings though they certainly act out the roles implied by these terms; subordination is culturally expected for women. These words suggest that men *should* not be subordinates, that there is something wrong with them, something unmasculine about them, if they are. At the same time, bureaucratic hierarchy, which implies the subordination of most participants to some one above them, is thoroughly culturally legitimate. The male teachers at Mann were struggling with an important paradox in American culture.

Observers from elsewhere have remarked repeatedly upon Americans' ambivalence toward authority (Spindler and Spindler, 1983). While we accept its legitimacy in principle, we are suspicious of it and often make cultural heroes of persons who ignore or defy it. Indeed such defiance is one strand in our conception of manliness. At least in the middle class, there is a cultural theme which suggests that obedience to authority compromises manhood unless the man who obeys is in full agreement with the orders being given or unless he can reasonably aspire some day to take over the position of the person who gives him orders.

While this cultural stance creates a problem in many contexts, it is clearly problematic in schools because most teachers will never be promoted. The loose coupling typical of school districts and the informal autonomy which principals normally grant to teachers in practice provides a buffer for the injury to pride which hierarchy can create. Even though principals issue hierarchical commands about some activities, if teachers have a significant zone of autonomy they can satisfy the demands of bureaucratic hierarchy while preserving a feeling of self-direction. They may be cooperative subordinates in some matters but they are not 'underlings.' When principals use all of their formally available powers of direction – as Mrs Michaels and the principals at Mann had to in order to establish their new alternative programs – they are likely to undercut the teachers' sense of self-direction. The anger and resistance which resulted at Adams and Mann can be expected at other schools in similar situations.

Chapter 7

Lessons from the Heartland schools

Both Heartland's overall design for magnet schools and life within the individual schools reflected the historical specificity of a particular time and place and the decisions and actions of important actors. At the same time, the drama of the district desegregation plan and that of the development of the individual schools took place within the larger context of American cultural attitudes toward schooling, race, and social class and within the context of typical organizational structures. Consequently, despite the fact that the district's desegregation plan and the character of each school will not be replicated exactly elsewhere, the major influences which shaped them will be found in other school systems far from Heartland.

The potentialities of magnet schools

The ironic politics of magnet schools

In the political arena, many of the lessons to be learned from Heartland's schools are shot through with ironies. At each step, what was publicly unrecognized was often what was practically most important or analytically most informative. Despite publicity to the contrary, Heartland did not desegregate a large city without mandatory reassignment by instituting magnet schools, but by closing and reducing enrollment in central city schools and busing black children to neighborhood white schools. The magnet schools played a part in desegregating Heartland's system only by effecting a small amount of reciprocal movement of whites and by distracting the city from the fact that desegregation was occurring. By relying mostly on one way busing of blacks to white neighborhood schools and by making the magnet schools implicitly superior, the school system created a situation where no one had to move 'down' in terms of the popular definitions of the quality of schools based on race and class, and so defused resistance to desegregation. The rhetoric of the school system avoided mention of race and class, as administrators touched on none of this, but spoke instead of relieving crowding in the city's center and filling empty seats on its periphery, offering diversity in educational programs, and giving parents an opportunity to choose their children's schools.

Further, there is some evidence that the introduction of magnet schools led only a few parents to make choices of schools on new criteria. Some parents I interviewed or talked with at parent meetings did speak of choosing magnet schools by making a careful assessment of several programs as matched to their children's needs.[1] However, among the middle schools, Mann quickly developed the longest waiting list even though there was little distinctive in its program, while Owens drew the majority of its students from its surrounding area despite its distinctiveness. If these schools were at all typical, it appears that Mann developed a long waiting list because many middle-class and ambitious working-class parents sought a school where their children would be with children of the highest social class and achievement level possible, while Owens drew heavily from less ambitious working-class families, who sought to keep their children near home whatever the kind of school they attended. The Heartland paper published the numbers of children turned away from magnet schools by race in the spring of 1984; they reflect the same pattern.[2] Magnet schools with a reputation for drawing many middle-class families and strong students had many more applications than they could accept from both white and black students, while other magnet schools were over-subscribed only for students of the race of the surrounding neighborhood.

The introduction of magnet schools led to a complex series of ironies. First, in order to attract volunteers away from other schools, they could not be different from but equal to other schools, as their rhetoric proclaimed. They had to be made to appear practically superior. Consequently, it was ironic to set up a desegregation plan – intended partly to create more actual equality in the quality of schooling – with a set of superior schools as its centerpiece. School system leaders were sensitive to this irony. As much as was consistent with attracting enough parents and creating a political base, they did try to make the magnet schools attractive through diversity rather than superiority. But notwithstanding those efforts, the magnet schools had a semi-formal superiority which openly violated the American ideal of equality of educational opportunity through the provision of equal education resources. They consequently generated significant political resistance in the long run.

There was a second irony in the process, however. If the magnet schools violated the norm of standardized, and so equalized, education in precept, in practice they were no more superior than many officially standard schools, and they improved the access of not only black, but poor white, students to such superior schools. Now, instead of needing a white skin and enough money to buy or rent a place to live in the city's most expensive neighborhoods to get into schools with the best reputations, parents needed only to watch for enrollment periods, to fill out an extremely simple form which could be turned in at the neighborhood school, and to be willing to send their child to a distant school. While the ability to do these things is still correlated to some extent with social class, it discriminates far less than do qualifications associated with housing. Furthermore, almost half the spaces in magnet schools were explicitly reserved for black children. Thus, while on the one hand, the majority of black children did not attend magnet schools, on the other, the children in magnet schools were nearly half black. The whites were from more diverse economic backgrounds than those in the previously elite schools.

A third irony, amply demonstrated by the discussion of the three schools in this book, lay in the fact that, while some of the magnet schools, like Mann, had more than their share of students who were middle-class or upwardly mobile and were good achievers, many magnet schools, like Adams, did in fact serve a population which reflected the demographic patterns of the city. Others, like Owens, served a population even poorer in economic standing and academic achievement than average. The educational innovations supported by the magnet plan enabled these schools to introduce innovations which made it easier to work with diverse groups of students and with those who had had academic and social difficulties in their previous school experience. In other words, the magnet schools both could and did serve the less privileged children of the city well.

In sum, while no one would present Heartland's overall desegregation plan, with its heavy reliance on one-way busing of black children to white neighborhood schools as a model of equity, it is not at all clear that the magnet schools created as much inequity as they were accused of. If one compares them to an ideal of equal schooling where all schools are alike in their share of easy and difficult students and of high and low achievers, then they were inequitable since, as an overall group, they attracted more than their share of good achievers and cooperative students. But if one compares them to traditional residence-based public school systems, even many which are desegregated, they appear exemplary in their ability to open access to good schooling for both racial minorities and poor whites. Furthermore, while parent bodies like that at Mann did get some special resources, schools like Adams and Owens used their license to innovate in ways which were supportive of children who were not high achievers and whose parents were not politically powerful. If the magnet schools' gains in equity and effectiveness of education were modest, the pressures against which they, and all schools, battle on these fronts are very strong. If magnet schools make even modest headway, they deserve further support and investigation.

Magnet schools' multiple missions – unheralded successes

Magnet schools were formally created to aid desegregation and to do so by developing diverse educational innovations. As I have already suggested, the magnet schools made their greatest contribution to desegregation in the city as a whole by making the process palatable rather than by creating very much actual movement of students. Further, parents were not attracted to them primarily for their distinctiveness. The study schools exemplified the tangential relevance of distinctiveness as Mann drew the most applicants because its gifted and talented label gave the promise that its recruits would be among diligent, ambitious, high achievers – as families expect when they move to expensive neighborhoods or suburbs for the sake of the schools there. Owens, which was the most successful in actually institutionalizing a distinctive innovation, had the most difficulty in attracting students and consequently came under pressure from the central office to become more traditional in response to the needs of the students it actually drew.

A final irony lies in the fact that it was in their unstated mission – to instruct and integrate diverse student bodies – that the schools were probably most successful. Probably the most difficult task that these schools were asked to accomplish was that of stimulating academic progress in students who came to them at widely differing starting points while creating islands of social equalitarianism in a competitive and racially and socially divided society at the same time. Adams and Owens, in particular, but to a degree Mann as well, handled diverse student bodies with notable success.[3] That handling such diversity is a task in itself was not given public recognition. It is popularly understood to be so difficult that the administrators apparently did not want to call attention to the fact that it had necessarily to be accomplished. The schools' success is the more striking since they worked with few more than the usual public school resources and with faculties which were by no means specially recruited. Though Mann had more of the kind of problems middle-class parents and teachers generally fear with diverse student bodies, all of the schools avoided being incapacitated by them.

The success of these schools indicates that it is not as insuperably difficult to educate children in racially, socially, and academically diverse groups as the conventional wisdom of our culture indicates. That the special qualities of magnet schools were helpful in giving the schools freedom to alter traditional technologies or in pushing them to do so is undeniable. Volunteerism and the positive publicity surrounding them certainly gave a boost to students', parents', and teachers' morale. Still, much of what they did could have been done without the magnet label or voluntary recruitment, and therefore shows traditional schools what is possible.

The internal lives of magnet schools – creating school character

Detailed analysis of the character of each of the study schools, and the attempt to identify the influences which led to that character, were undertaken in the hope of finding influences and patterns of influences which can be expected to be important in shaping the character of schools, both magnet schools and others. A summary of the effects on each school of each of the major influences discussed will be presented here to help the reader to remember the pattern of cause and effect at each school. It will also draw together observations on the role of each influence across schools.

The impact of the environment

Because the magnet schools were being used to reach several goals simultaneously, they often were subject to conflicting pressures and demands. Thus the goal of desegregating the system led to actions, for example moves of the magnet programs, which undercut their ability to offer distinctive educational approaches. Similarly, the system's insistence on the development of official innovations sometimes distracted parents and even teachers from recognizing that the schools also had to pursue the difficult innovative task of creating a program which met the needs of all of a racially, socially, and academically diverse student body. Since the school system was pursuing multiple goals, it is not surprising that efforts in pursuit of one goal sometimes undercut another.

There were a number of specific actions and diffuse pressures in the schools' environment which had profound effects on each one. Aside from being moved around the city, or facing the constant possibility of such a move, all were profoundly affected by the union's successful campaign to have the faculties of magnet schools inherited from programs formerly occupying their buildings. All were affected by the enhanced power of parents.

The central office established tightened linkages with all the schools which became magnets. It set down and insisted upon some policies which had pervasive effects on all programs. Responding to possible, and later actual, charges of elitism in the magnet schools, it would allow no criteria for admission, except at Mann; even there, the decentralized system of selection through nominations requested of all fifth grade teachers in the city assured breadth of access to the school. To prevent resegregation within the schools, it insisted that all schools refrain from sorting students into classes according to academic achievement. Additionally, principals and teachers were informed that they were expected to create the special programs promised by the central office from the time the schools opened.

I have attempted to show how pressures from its environment shaped each school. The program at Adams did not suffer a move, but the constant threat of one made its staff feel a certain insecurity. The continuity of its faculty with that at Williams Annex worked to the school's advantage, as the faculty culture developed at Williams supported the new program's primary distinctiveness in the faculty's approach to the students. Parents at Adams were demanding and, in the first years, sometimes critical. The teachers resented this, but channeled most of their resentment toward the principal who served as a lightning rod for both groups. Parents also used their power to get resources for the school and to prevent its being moved. In doing so they expressed some faith in the school and supported the teachers, thus collectively reassuring them and earning some good will from them.

The demand to create a functioning IGE school on a month's notice created considerable anger in the faculty and tension between them and the principal, who used all her powers of office to realize this expectation. Still, some teachers came to see some virtue in IGE. And even when teachers were not aware of it, several of its elements seemed to support their positive relationships with students. It facilitated their work with the academically diverse classes mandated by the central office.

Owens, as the only pre-existing alternative program, found its inclusion in the overall magnet plan a mixed blessing. The school board's decision to move it to Rodgers and double its size created a blow to its capacity to be distinctive, especially in combination with the necessity to include faculty from Rodgers, who did not necessarily have an interest in, or sympathy with, open education. Owens had enjoyed the support of active parents from its inception; however, competition with other citywide programs drew away some of its support.

The central office mandate to be distinctive came as long-sought support at Owens. The magnet program for the city as a whole legitimated its status and made it easier for its principal to ask for exceptions to standardized practices. However, as attention in the district began to move toward test scores rather than desegregation, and as a result of the politically motivated decision not to let the school require fourth grade reading skills for entrance, it began to come under increasing pressure from the central office to conform to more traditional patterns. It began to experience some of the pains of tightened coupling which the other schools felt at the inception of the magnet plan.

For the gifted and talented program, the sudden move from Atlantic to Mann was traumatic and its situation as the second school in the Mann High School building difficult. The Atlantic Avenue School, from which the magnet program inherited its faculty, had been the scene of chronic conflict; the move and its aftermath irritated the faculty's still open wounds and left them preoccupied with maintaining their professional dignity. Parents who were also insulted by the move took their anger out on the school level staff.

In this context, the majority of the faculty were not inclined to search for inventive ways of reconciling the tension between the central office's imperative to offer a distinctive program for the gifted and talented and the fairly broad range of skills produced by the system's broadbased, non-elite method of identifying students for the program. Further, most teachers did not even think of seeking alternatives to standard secondary methods of teaching, although these are not well-suited to the academically diverse classes which the central office required. The presence of the high school, along with both administrators' and teachers' acceptance of traditional secondary school scheduling as a given, prevented flexible use of time and space.

There are two lessons to be learned from this set of causes and effects. First, if change is planned at the level of a school system and imposed upon all schools, it is likely to have quite varied effects. The mixture of influences within a school which are crucial to its character are a filter through which externally imposed changes must pass.

Second, there are some discernible patterns in the interaction of district level pressures and school level policy. While one cannot say how increasing parents' power or keeping an existing faculty will affect a school without knowing something of the substance of the perspectives of either group, one can say that both of these actions will have an impact on a school and that the perspectives of the groups will shape the kind of impact. Similarly, it is predictable that when district level actors are pursuing district level goals which affect individual schools, those district level goals will take priority, and their side effects in individual schools will be overlooked. While one cannot say what unintended difficulties may arise from the pursuit of a given district level policy without looking at its impact on individual schools, one is alerted to look for such difficulties. In other words, while one cannot set out generalizations that certain acts will have certain consequences, one can point to a list of important factors and to the kind of variation in those factors which will determine their impact. This kind of analysis allows a person looking at a new situation to go quickly to the factors which make a difference.

The importance of technology

The schools' technological arrangements seemed to have had an important impact on relationships between students and teachers and among students of different races. These effects were similar in Adams Avenue's IGE program and Owens's open education program. Both schools expected students in the same grade to have different levels of skills and both gave them the opportunity to work on material at the level of skill appropriate to them. Further, both gave academic rewards based on students' individual progress, not based on comparison with others in the group. Finally, both used an activity structure which provided the student some privacy in performance, while allowing the teacher discretely to check on the progress of students having difficulty and to offer extra assistance where needed without calling undue attention to the student. This activity structure also isolated student–teacher conflict and allowed the teacher to respond at length in ways tailored to the individual student's situation or needs. These technological arrangements dissolved or muted most of the sources of poorly achieving students' conflicts with teachers which were discussed in Chapter 3.

These arrangements also moderated the visibility of differences in academic achievement between the black and white students, although because of the composition of the student bodies these differences were not dramatic. Both schools further offered a variety of extra-curricular activities and activities during the school day which required skills other than those displayed in basic academic work and thus allowed students to relate to one another in contexts where the hierarchy of their skill levels varied. These activities provided some opportunities for cooperation among students, which also furthered positive inter-racial relations. Cooperation was also encouraged as students worked around tables in the classroom, especially at Adams where students were assigned tablemates of different races who were generally working on the same task.

These technological arrangements had effects on the lives of the schools. Adams and Owens had fewer incidents of student–teacher conflict than most studies of schools with similar student bodies report. At both, students spoke of teachers in generally positive tones. There was also very little evidence of inter-racial tension and evidence of more inter-racial mixing in voluntary situations than is described in many other studies of desegregated schools.

At Mann, with few exceptions, all students were taught the same curriculum together, starting at the same place and covering the same material with the same assignments. Academic rewards compared individual performance to a group standard. The activity structure involved primarily whole class recitation and seatwork. Because most teachers remained at the front of the room during both recitation and seatwork, academic performance, requests for assistance, and discipline were public acts. Mann's technology – which is the one taken for granted in most secondary schools – did not offer low achievers the chance to catch up, to be rewarded for progress from their individual starting points, and to receive the shelter of privacy afforded by the technological approaches at the other two schools. Publicity constrained discipline to be standardized and interactions around it to be brief.

Mann's technology did not equalize the status of students of different races as did that of the other schools. Even though poor achievers were rarely called on in class everyone knew who they were, and that most of them were black. Moreover, there were not as many special activities as at the other schools and the most visible extra-curricular activities emphasized individual performance using academic skills; they thus provided neither an opportunity to equalize status nor one in which to experience inter-racial cooperation. The use of chairs in rows rather than tables in the classrooms did not encourage inter-racial cooperation during seatwork.

Though Mann did not have the technological arrangements which seem to have inhibited conflict between students and teachers at the other schools, it also did not have many of the poorly achieving and low income students most likely to engage in such conflict. Since its students had been nominated by teachers as gifted or as talented, they presumably knew how to please teachers. It is not surprising, then, that the school did not have much overt conflict in the classroom, but it is some sign of the effects of technological arrangements at both schools that Mann had more than twice as many yellow cards per student as Adams. Further, Mann had more graffiti expressing racial hostility than either Adams or Owens; students spoke of more racial anger and avoidance, and, at least among interviewees, the longer students had been in the school, the fewer friends of another race they reported.

On the whole, then, evidence from the three schools together suggests that the kinds of curricular structure, academic rewards, and activity structure used at Adams and Owens are more conducive to positive student–teacher relationships when students are low achievers than are the dominant kinds used at Mann. Evidence from the three schools also supports generalizations from social psychological experiments (Cohen, 1980; Slavin, 1980) and from some ethnographic observation (Schofield, 1982) that positive inter-racial interaction among peers is encouraged by efforts to equalize the status of the races and to establish cooperative activities.

The importance of faculty culture

There were important common themes in the faculty cultures at Adams and Owens, despite their different visions of the content of education. At both schools, teachers assumed that students who were treated with personal respect would return that respect. At both, teachers considered it an important part of their role to make an effort to know the students as individuals; Owens teachers pursued that knowledge in greater depth in both cognitive and emotional matters. The majority of both faculties felt that they were able to establish generally positive relations with most of their students, and, when unable to do so, they felt a responsibility to continue in the attempt.

In interaction with a technological approach, which gave both student and teacher evidence of accomplishment if the student progressed during a year, these faculty cultures allowed the teachers and the students to experience considerable feelings of success, and as a result, positive student–teacher relationships. In turn, these good relationships re-enforced the faith in human nature implicit in both faculty cultures.

The interaction of the faculty cultures with the technology at these schools qualifies the importance of the technology alone in affecting students' experiences and their resulting behavior toward teachers. The effects of the technological arrangements depend upon their meaning. While arrangements such as those at Adams and Owens allow low achievers to experience a sense of progress (if they make an effort), to be rewarded for it, and to maintain their dignity before other students, all those benefits can be undermined by a few publicly disparaging words from a teacher.

At Mann, the faculty were much less involved in their relations with students. They emphasized the academic aspects of teaching. They encouraged classroom cooperation and academic diligence but did not concern themselves with students' broader personal or social development – even as a means to academic ends – unless students were engaging in behavior which disrupted classroom routines. When students failed or rebelled, teachers simply handed out successive low grades or referred the student to a staff expert. The students interviewed returned their teachers' impersonal attitude and considered the subject, rather than the teacher, important in making an interesting class.

The Mann teachers had withdrawn their psychic engagement from the classroom as a result of the conflict they experienced in classes at Atlantic Avenue. At Mann, the faculty found that it was difficult to teach the fastest and slowest children in heterogeneously grouped classes with traditional technology. This difficulty simply confirmed their cultural belief in their lack of control over the effects of their efforts, and justified their continued psychic withdrawal from involvement with the students. This withdrawal inhibited reflection on the sources of their difficulties which might have led them to experiment to find more efficacious technical methods. As at the other schools, the relations between technology and faculty culture were circular.

Technology is itself a cultural product. The adults at Mann reflected a broad consensus in American secondary education when they used the methods they did. When I asked some of the administrators and teachers about their methods, they said simply that Mann was expected to offer a standard curriculum with enrichment, taking it for granted that a standard curriculum included traditional technological methods.

At each of the schools, the faculty developed a subculture with premises and values which differ noticeably from those of the larger society. At Adams and Owens, it could be said that the teachers displayed a faith in human nature which would seem naive in the culture at large. At least in their activities in the school, they also laid less stress on class and race differences than is common in this society and than is described in most studies of other schools. Their beliefs played a part in creating a response from the students which confirmed those beliefs. The meaning system had consequences for their interaction with students and played a part in creating a school character which is not common among schools with similar student bodies described in the literature.

At Mann, the teachers departed from culturally common views in seeing teachers as having no control over their work unless they have homogeneously able students and administrators who clear all external obstacles from their paths. This view had the effect of preventing them from designing more effective ways of dealing with students' learning needs. It also created a great deal more tension among the adults, and somewhat more tension among the students, than was present in the apparently more difficult circumstances encountered by the teachers working with less select student bodies in the other schools.

The importance of principal–teacher relationships

The principals at each of the schools were charged with the formal responsibility for seeing that the faculty offered the kind of innovative education the district advertised for the school. Their relations with teachers, as they went about this task, were profoundly shaped by the history of each school, particularly by the source of the innovation and by the teachers' collective experience before the school became a magnet.

In this context, Adams and Mann were generally similar, while Owens differed, though Adams was in part a hybrid. At Adams and at Mann, innovation came down from above, though Mrs Michaels had chosen IGE as the *kind* of innovation which would be introduced at Adams. At Owens, by contrast, the principal, curriculum coordinator, teachers, and parents all fought for the right to offer a special open education program and to have the freedom to engage in a variety of special practices they thought important to it.

Because change was imposed at Adams and Mann, the principals adopted a hierarchial, directive, and even peremptory approach to the faculty in order to implement the innovations. At both schools, while the faculties acknowledged the principals' formal right to behave in this manner and the formal legitimacy of their commands, the teachers experienced their relationship with the principals as insulting to their professional pride and demeaning to them as individuals. At both schools, a portion of the faculty sought to evade the obligation to obey the principals' demands by suggesting that the individuals occupying the office were not competent, and that therefore their commands did not adequately enact the overall purposes upon which the powers of the office rest.

By contrast, at Owens, where the principal actually supervised the teachers more closely than the other principals supervised theirs, most of the teachers responded with admiration for Mr Osten's dedication to the school rather than with resentment of his close involvement with their work. Mr Osten was able to exert this close supervision and control because faculty and administrators shared a sense of collective purpose. They considered him a first among peers, united with them in a common mission, rather than a representative of the district hierarchy imposing its agenda within the school.

The teachers' response to the principals' superordination was entwined with the meaning with which they endowed their own participation in the school; it was affected by the principals' relationship to their shared values. At one extreme, the Mann faculty culture, carried over from Atlantic Avenue, defended the teachers' sense of themselves as good teachers by pointing to each of a series of allegedly incompetent principals as the source of their inability actively to exercise their talents. At the other extreme, Owens teachers had forged a bond of solidarity with the principal as a result of having worked together to define the special mission of the school and to win district support for variations from standard practice. At Adams, the majority were offended by the hierarchical tone Mrs Michaels took in imposing IGE. Still, despite anger at her hierarchical manner, which they thought demeaned them, the majority felt in accord with her over the central meanings of their common effort, and so were generally cooperative with her. The situation at all three schools suggests that while teachers tend to resent the full use of formally legitimate hierarchical authority by a principal, their response to the use of hierarchy is very much qualified by their whole relationship with the principal and by his or her contribution to purposes which are significant in the teachers' meaning system.

The interdependence of influences shaping the schools

This summary of the influences which impinged upon these three schools and their effects should make clear the complexity of the causal interactions at work in shaping the daily and yearly life of the schools. Influences from outside each school set conditions which interacted with internal processes to form the context of the school's life. The influences which operated within the school generally had their effects in a highly interactive way, so that circles of causation were more common than chains of causation.

Still, as this summary of the effects of technological approaches, faculty cultures, and relationships between the principals and teachers suggests, while all were important, the development of meaning in the faculty subcultures was pivotal in determining the final effects of all three. The teachers' common meaning systems became shared by most of each faculty and took on the tacit and deep-set qualities of a subculture. Such a subculture has roots in the larger culture of the society and that of the occupation of teaching on the one hand, and in conditions which shape teachers' experience in a particular school on the other. But once formed, it also shapes later experiences, especially interactions with students and other adults; these tend to confirm whatever perspective is initially developed. Such a subculture will color the way that teachers understand and respond to initiatives from the district and directives from the principal. It will determine their actions toward students in the thousands of verbal and non-verbal classroom interchanges which can clearly convey a teacher's feelings toward and expectations for students, and change the significance and impact of their technologically shaped activities.

This analysis has important implications for persons interested in creating change in schools. It implies that the teachers, and specifically their subculture, are crucial in determining the experience of students. We have heard much recently about the importance of principals in schools. But they must have their effects through influencing the teachers who have most of the actual contact with students both in classes and in extra-curricular activities.

It is important that the principals at Adams and Owens, who seemed to have an influence in shaping their faculties' subcultures, started at Williams Annex and Rodgers Annex with mostly inexperienced teachers and with groups which were newly gathered, without a common history and perspective. The task is far more difficult for principals in a situation like Mann where they must work with an established faculty who have already formed their culture. If it is the principal's purpose to change that culture, he or she cannot work in accord with its values. But simply to issue commands violating its precepts is likely to generate opposition, sabotage, and personal animosity; teachers will seek to delegitimate the principal by proving him or her incompetent. A principal who wants to change a faculty culture must try to understand it and its sources, and then try to find a way to change the circumstances which gave rise to it, to give currency to alternative interpretations of common events, and to offer other, more constructive, ways of meeting the needs it serves.

The importance of pride in the life of city schools

The teachers' pride

To say that faculty cultures are crucial to the character of schools, and so to what happens within them, is not, however, to say that we can know little about any school without a study of it in depth. Faculty cultures are not random in their patterns or inscrutably idiosyncratic. They tend to grow up in response to a limited set of problems presented to teachers by themes in the larger culture and by the structures of schools.

If one considers the themes of the faculty cultures in the schools studied here, the issue of pride of craft runs through them as a red thread.[4] At Adams, the majority of teachers had a sense that they were effective, which was confirmed in daily constructive relations and the slow but steady academic progress of at least the majority of students. This sense of efficacy made them able to cope with the pressures of instituting IGE and with the principal's hierarchical style, even though these undercut their pride as professionals. At Owens, the teachers' sense that they had discovered a superior kind of education gave them both an individual pride of craft and a collective *esprit de corps*. They felt their efficacy confirmed by their relationships with students; though they were also moved by the students' low skills and low test scores to make some changes. At Mann, the teachers' lack of pride of craft was critical in instigating their protective belief that they could only exercise their talents in ideal conditions.

In Heartland, if teachers were able to feel some sense of satisfaction with the quality of their efforts, they developed generally positive relations with those around them. If they felt that they could not take pride in their work, they developed angry or distant relations with other adults and with students. Based on the evidence from these schools, it is clear that teachers' shared sense that they are working effectively is a necessary element of a culture which induces them to be engaged with the school's tasks and which supports their constructive relationships with students and other adults.

Pride, then, creates a starting place for administrators interested in change. For example, at Mann, if a principal could construct social conditions in such a way as to encourage teachers to risk their pride, their energies might be released. Indeed the active efforts of some of the members of the core group at Mann with academically selected classes and with academically oriented extra-curricular groups provide a glimpse of what might become possible.

Since teachers' pride of craft is intimately interwoven with their students' achievement, they are immediately at risk in a school where most students enter achieving below the median. Such students' frequent withdrawal or hostility further threaten both teachers' occupational pride and their personal dignity. Since persons outside teaching tend to judge teachers by their students, teachers in schools where students achieve poorly, or come from racial and economic backgrounds which lead others to expect them to achieve poorly, suffer public opprobrium along with their students. The faculty who moved from Atlantic to Mann exemplify the devastating effects such a set of experiences can have on the teachers. Schools which serve large numbers of low achievers, then, can be expected to have characters deeply affected by the faculty's attempts to deal with their own hurt pride, as well as that of the students.

The students' pride

The schools in this study were not only magnet schools; they were city schools, and as such served large proportions of poor and minority race children. For these children, a complex web of cultural differences, lack of skills useful in school which are fostered in middle-class homes, and teachers' low expectations leads to high rates of low achievement. Damage already done to such students' pride creates a major dynamic in their relations with secondary schools.

Pride would be less of an issue if students found school achievement of as little importance as many pretend. But it is the rare student who does not know in some way, that school achievement is symbolic of legitimate status as a participant in public life, and a necessity for rewards in interesting work, money, power, and respect. The topic would still not be so emotionally charged if competence in learning were enough. But mastery of the essential skills is not enough, because most schools are competitive settings. Honor comes only with competitive success, with knowing more and being more skilled than others are.

According to the ideology of equality of opportunity, since schools provide standardized offerings and an open competition, learning depends on individual characteristics. Poor achievement is a reflection of lack of talent or lack of effort. This ideology together with the competitive activities offered by traditional schools generates constant assaults on the self-confidence and pride of students who achieve poorly. The constant comparisons made possible by traditional recitation in classes and traditional grading systems, and the difficulty of catching up, once one falls behind a class proceeding at a single pace, separate students into clearly distinct categories by achievement. In repeated competitive contexts, schools show those who achieve poorly that they deserve fewer later opportunities and rewards than do those who achieve well. Texts with grade levels and standardized tests with scores reported in grade level equivalents or percentile rank drive home the lesson in schools where there are few high achievers present to provide a comparative standard.

It is therefore not solely the culture of an *individual* school which leads poor achievers to create conflicts with their teachers, to cease to work very hard, and to engage in hijinks to avoid public performance. Rather such behavior is repeated in many schools because it is a response to the larger society's values and its method of allocating new generations to its adult positions.

All schools which include significant numbers of low achievers must recognize and deal with the issue of injury to pride in some way, a task which is not easy in a competitive society. The tone of interaction in classes where students and teachers both feel their pride most degraded almost has to be experienced to be believed.[5] Both teachers and students may be angrily belligerent, or may expressively ignore each other. While occasional physical violence gets headline attention, direct and indirect mutual verbal assault is much more common; its messages of fundamental disrespect are insidious for all parties. Experienced over several years, as it often is by both students and teachers, it must inflict on both a lasting harm.

If one wishes to avoid such conflict, it may be necessary to stop asking students to participate in competition in which they know they will not succeed. It may be necessary to set up greater rewards for competence, as opposed to excellence, and for progress in comparison to one's own former accomplishments, as Adams and Owens did.

Some readers will doubtless feel uneasy with such a suggestion. Indeed some persons to whom I have described the schools, have suggested that Adams and Owens were creating 'happy failures,'[6] with the accent on failures. Schools clearly should not hide students' true comparative standing from them, but not to stress it may be healthy. In a competitive society, half of the students necessarily fall in the lower half of any ranking. To improve the overall level of competence, or to shift individuals' standing in the ranking, does not affect this fact. Children who do less well than others, children in the bottom half – or third or quarter – of academic rankings, will be labeled failures. As long as failure is comparatively defined, there will always be children who are failures and teachers who teach failures. Consequently, it is a mistake to place the accent on failure in the phrase 'happy failure.'

Children learn many things in school. To learn that they are worthy of respect and that they can expect to be treated civilly if they act respectfully toward others, is an important lesson, all too often not taught as low achievers and their teachers defend their pride from one another. To learn that peers of other races are not very different, and that some might even be candidates for friendship, is an important lesson in a multi-racial society, and one made harder to learn by fierce competition which scorns the loser. While few students who fall low in the academic rank order in the early years of secondary school will become successes in a competitive context, most have the capability to make steady, modest academic progress and to be productive adult members of the society. They are more likely to do so if their schools enable them to engage in mutually respectful relationships with their teachers and with a broad range of peers.

Appendix A

Time line of events in the Heartland district and middle schools

Time	District	Adams – IGE	Owens – Open Ed	Mann – G and T
Fall 1970			Rodgers Annex opens with overflow of seventh graders from Rodgers Junior High.	
Fall 1972		Williams Annex opens with overflow of seventh graders from Williams Junior High. Multi-unit approach used.	Jesse Owens Open Education School opens in Rodgers Annex buildings.	
Summer 1975	Dr Stewart becomes superintendent.			
January 1976	Federal judge rules for the plaintiffs in desegregation case.			
Spring 1976	Central Office develops desegregation plan to offer to court. School board appeals federal court decision.			

Time	District	Adams – IGE	Owens – Open Ed	Mann – G and T
	Citizens' Committee is formed, constituted of elected parent/citizen representatives of each high school 'cluster' of feeder schools.			
Summer 1976	Plans for first year are completed.	William Annex is identified as a magnet and renamed Adams Avenue.	Jesse Owens is moved into the Rodgers Jr High building in August.	Peach St Elementary school for gifted and talented is announced.
	Administration–union conflict over staffing of first year magnet schools is settled by the court with a small number of 'superintendent's choices' for staffing. Other slots are filled by incumbents who wish to remain in their buildings, in order of seniority. Those who remain must take an inservice course in the educational approach.	Mrs Michaels requests IGE approach. Teachers have one week of inservice in late August.	The student body is doubled. Some Rodgers staff with seniority stay to join the program. Some Owens staff 'bumped.'	
Fall 1976	Slightly more than one-third of city schools are desegregated. Voluntary plan is a success so far.	Adams Avenue opens as sixth to eighth grade school offering IGE/ Multi-Unit approach. Students enroll as volunteers from throughout the city within racial quotas.	Jesse Owens moves to the former Rodgers Jr High. Two open education elementary schools open.	Peach Street opens for grades four to six.

Time	District	Adams – IGE	Owens – Open Ed	Mann – G and T
Spring 1977	Teachers strike for several weeks. Staffing for magnet schools is main issue. Most black teachers and some staffs of elementary magnet schools do not strike. Strikers win staffing of magnets by seniority, though inservice training will be required in the first year. All students wishing to attend Heartland public schools in the fall must list three school choices for 1977–8.			Parents from Peach Street and central administrators seek a site for a gifted and talented middle school. Atlantic Avenue Jr High School is chosen and approved by the board for a two-year trial.
Fall 1977	Two-thirds of city schools are desegregated. In late September appeals court sends the case back to Heartland court for reconsideration of citywide remedy. The superintendent allows students bused elsewhere to return to neighborhood schools if they wish and if seats are available.	Federal money buys released time for teachers to write IGE curriculum. More materials for IGE are also bought.	Several Rodgers teachers unwilling to be certified as elementary teachers are replaced by new teachers with elementary backgrounds.	Atlantic Avenue Middle School for Gifted and Talented opens with seventy seventh graders. A small class of continuing eighth graders from the neighborhood are also in the building.

229

Time	District	Adams – IGE	Owens – Open Ed	Mann – G and T
Spring 1978				Students recruited for full sixth to eighth grade gifted and talented program. Half are from schools other than Peach Street.
August 1978				The school board closes the Atlantic Ave. School and transfers the gifted and talented program to the Horace Mann High School on August 1. Parents obtain a court restraining order which bans activity toward the move for two weeks. In mid-August, the board reaffirms its action after proper announcement of the agenda item.
Fall 1978	Schools open in an uncertain legal climate. The superintendent aims for and succeeds in maintaining previous levels of desegregation in the system as a whole.	Closing of Adams is proposed to the board by the administration, but is not acted upon.		The gifted and talented middle school starts its first year of operation as Mann Middle School for the gifted and talented. Books and supplies from Atlantic are transferred through mid-October.

Time	District	Adams – IGE	Owens – Open Ed	Mann – G and T
January–June 1979	An out of court settlement of the desegregation case is accepted in March.	The study takes place at Adams.		Study at Mann starts with attendance at several meetings of the parent group.
Fall 1979	The new middle school plan goes into effect for the city. High schools pick up ninth grades. Former junior high schools serve grades seven and eight and are called middle schools. Citywide middle schools continue to serve grades six to eight.	Administration lists Adams for possible closing in fall 1981.	The study takes place at Owens September–March.	The study takes place in the Mann 6th grade and at faculty meetings. Mann institutes the new middle school curriculum and the team structure of staffing. Mann middle school parents are asked to form a committee to name criteria for a new site. Board takes no action toward moving the school.
Spring 1980				The study continues in the seventh and eighth grades.

231

Appendix B

The methodological approach

This Appendix describes the procedures used for gathering data in more detail than is presented in the text. Since research necessarily involves subjective elements, it also gives the reader some idea of how my qualities as a person may have affected the collection of the data and the conclusions I drew from it.

Data collection

The field work in the three schools took place between January 1979 and June 1980. In the spring semester of 1979, I spent two to three days a week at Adams Avenue, though I did not always stay all day. The study at Adams Avenue was completed in June 1979. In the spring of 1979, I also began the study at Mann with attendance at some parent meetings. In the fall of 1979, I started attending faculty meetings as well as parent meetings at Mann. I attended these throughout the year 1979–80, and maintained contact with the Mann administrators all year. However, in the fall I spent only one full day a week at Mann; on those days I observed sixth grade students, as they were getting oriented to the school, and interviewed their teachers. Most of my time in the fall of 1980 was spent at Jesse Owens; I was there up to three days a week. I worked at Owens from September 1979 to March 1980. From March through June of 1980, I concentrated solely on Mann, and especially on the seventh and eighth grade students and teachers.

At Adams and at Mann, where students changed teachers and

rooms for different subjects, I started the research by following students through class days. This strategy allowed me to get acquainted with the building, the teachers, and the style of classes at the outset of the study. At Adams, I followed three students, one in each grade, and then asked teachers, starting with those who seemed most cordial, if I might observe another one or two of their classes and interview them. I interviewed nearly all the teachers at this small school.

At Mann, the sixth graders moved from class to class in constant groups. I followed two of the five groups for all of a day, and the remaining three, who had several different subjects with the same teacher, for part of a day. I then interviewed their teachers, except one who was a long-term substitute. In the seventh and eighth grades, I followed five students, then interviewed teachers. The teachers in the seventh and eighth grades at Mann were by far the least comfortable with observation of any in the study. I therefore was reluctant to ask them for further observation lest I make them too uneasy to establish rapport. Since I followed more students than at Adams, I saw almost all of the school's teachers, some of them two or three times, as the chance of students' schedules brought me to them. However, I did miss seeing three teachers, whom I later learned it would have been informative to observe because they had a reputation for distinctive teaching.

I interviewed twenty-two of the thirty teachers at Mann, at least one teacher of every subject except wood shop. Most of the teachers omitted were in specialized roles, such as a reading laboratory teacher, or in non-academic subjects. As at Adams, I started by interviewing those who seemed most friendly and at ease during my observations. I eventually interviewed everyone I had observed and some others whom I had reason to think might have a special point of view. (One black teacher I had observed greeted me at our appointed time for an interview by saying that she did not want to be interviewed. We sat down and talked, without the tape recorder; although I did not ask my usual list of questions, I did learn a good deal about her perspective on the school.)

At both schools, I sat in on two or three meetings of each team of academic teachers. At both I observed faculty meetings, at Mann regularly for a year, but at Adams mostly at special meetings. (Regular ones were held at the time at which I taught a college class.) At both schools, I attended informational and social gatherings for parents and performances by students. At Adams I spent two days following Mrs Michaels through her activities, and at Mann I spent a day following Mr Mueller. I interviewed the assistant principal and principal at Adams and the counselor, curriculum coordinator, and administrator in charge at Mann.

At Jesse Owens, where students did not move about in the regular patterns used at the other schools, I observed in a different pattern. I started by attending orientation sessions every afternoon for the first two weeks of school in two different self-contained centers, each staffed by a team of teachers for this special event. I later spent half a day in every self-contained classroom and also observed classes in music, art, shop, and home economics. I interviewed all the teachers whose classes I had seen and also the counselor, curriculum coordinator, assistant principal, and principal. I attended weekly meetings of support groups, groups of teachers who shared the same preparation time, and spent a full day with Mr Osten. I also attended parent meetings which were composed of parents from Owens and the two feeder elementary schools. The combined parent group called itself 'Parents for Open Education.'

My observations and interviews were affected by the logistics at each school. The long distances and short times between classes at Mann meant that when I followed students to their classes I had little time to explain myself to teachers (though I had already explained the research at a faculty meeting and they knew that I would be following students). Furthermore, the whole class form of instruction gave little chance for even brief explanations to teachers or students during classes. Observations were less comfortable there than at the other schools – though it was also important that this faculty was under the most critical pressure from outside and above at the time of the study. At Adams, if I arrived at a class with little time to explain myself, the teacher could circulate to me and receive a fuller explanation during the class. Students also could come over to me and ask me who I was without disturbing the class as a whole. At Owens, I arrived before the self-contained classes started work in the morning; there was time to talk with the teachers or students as needed before, during, or after the class.

I interviewed teachers during preparation periods. Since it was awkward to come back a second day, I tried to fit the interviews into one period. This meant they had to be completed in forty-eight minutes at Mann and in approximately that in the periods of slightly varied length at Adams. At Owens they could run a leisurely eighty minutes. The interviews at Mann and Adams thus were more formal and hurried than those at Owens.

At all three schools, I interviewed students toward the end of the field work. I tried to construct comparable samples of students and to ask each group similar questions; however, Jesse Owens's special structure made that task difficult. At each school, I chose a purposive stratified sample. I chose it to represent boys and girls and blacks and whites in equal numbers. I attempted to get equal numbers from each grade; sixth graders were less numerous in the sample at Adams, and especially at Owens, because there were fewer of them in the schools. Within categories of race, gender, and grade level, I tried to find children who represented all levels of academic ability. Where I had noticed children in classes who seemed to be articulate or to lead in either a cooperative or uncooperative direction, I often chose them to interview. But I relied in part upon teams of teachers to name children who would fit my categories of race, gender, and grade level, and would provide variation in academic ability. I also asked for variation in cooperativeness or enthusiasm toward the school.

At Owens, the procedure in getting teachers to identify students differed. I asked each self-contained teacher to describe several children who were fast or slow and positive or negative in attitude who might be willing to talk to me. I then constructed the total sample by using two children from each self-contained center, creating as much balance as possible in race, gender, achievement, and cooperativeness.

After drawing the sample, I wrote to students' parents for permission to interview them and followed up with telephone calls if they did not send in the attached permission slip. This process proved difficult in a few cases where parents did not have telephones or the numbers on the school's information cards were not current. The final sample of students was short one student at Adams and three, all black, at Owens.

The researcher's influence on the research

The data which I obtained were necessarily influenced by the role I developed for myself in the school and by the general social roles which I brought along by virtue of my person. It must have made a difference to my informants that I was visibly white, a woman, and in the middle years of adulthood. I attempted through my demeanor and actions to take a learner's role. Though my explanation of the research included the fact that I had a doctorate and was doing further research funded by the National Institute of Education, teachers, but not principals, tended to forget this explanation and to ask me how my 'dissertation' was coming along. Apparently, they perceived me more as a student than an expert. Principals were far more concerned than teachers about the possible effects of the research on the reputation of the schools, and so paid more attention to details about my biography and my procedure. When I asked them for permission for the research I was teaching at a local private women's college. In the second year of the field work I commuted to a new position at a university in a distant city, but since I was only absent from the school on Fridays, most teachers, at least, were not aware of my institutional affiliation.

The development of the analysis proceeded dialectically and worked more from the stories of the schools to the categories than the reverse. I immersed myself in the lives of the schools and spent a great deal of energy in attempting to bring out of the flow of events a coherent characterization of each school as a whole. This proved to be a difficult and a time-consuming task. Simultaneously, I was trying to identify the causal patterns shaping that character and to identify common causal patterns at the schools. For a long time, however, the whole reality of each school – or my attempts to grasp it – was more salient than the causal influences in the generalized form they are presented here.

That the analytic categories with which I emerged are ones with histories in the sociological study of organizations indicates that I did not develop an explanation completely inductively, solely on the basis of what I saw, nor would such an explanation have been possible. Despite my immersion in the colorful stuff of daily life in the schools, I arrived with the intellectual perspective of a sociologist trained in the study of organizations and I saw events through that perspective. Still, some of the literature which I cite in Chapter 3, especially with regard to the effects of technology in schools, was published after the field work and after I was far into my analysis. In this matter many scholars are apparently thinking along parallel lines. Though some of the social psychological literature on racial relations is older, I discovered much of it after the outlines of the analysis given here began to be clear to me. It confirmed rather than suggested my analysis.

Researchers bring more than a disciplinary perspective to a study, however; they bring a whole intellectual autobiography. I proposed this research shortly after finishing the manuscript of another book, *Classrooms and Corridors*, which had been undertaken as a study of classroom authority and had evolved to include an analysis of the linkages between classrooms and schools and of the development of different atmospheres in schools with similar students. I intended this study to follow that one by starting at the level of the whole school and looking at the linkage between it and the school system. Since the schools in the other study were 'traditional' public schools, though desegregated, I chose magnet schools because I was curious what would happen when the conditions of a traditional school were altered.

That previous study and another smaller study affected this one in ways I did not plan. I would not have been so struck with the positive relationships at Adams had I only read the literature on the negative relationships which can develop between low achievers and teachers and never myself watched and listened to teachers and students in conflict. Had I not systematically analyzed classroom authority and the precise acts which lead students to rebel, I might not have analyzed the meanings of the altered technology at Adams and Owens in the same way.

Participant observation generates data through *participation*, that is, through the researcher's subjective experience. It provides access to an important kind of information, but since it is necessarily filtered through one person's perspective, it requires close scrutiny. It is partly because of the force of the experience of participation that I have stressed the importance of constructive social relationships at Adams and Owens. For a while, I was suspicious that my concern with the quality of relationships reflected a personal bias. Gradually, however, I came to see that it was not primarily a reflection of my individual values – I had not started research in schools with a concern about the emotional quality of relationships and I had not expected to be much concerned with student–teacher relations in this study. Rather, my experience in the schools allowed me to understand that the quality of relationships has an enormous impact on the participants and shapes their instrumental activities. If each individual is different from others, she is also like others; I was experiencing feelings which the students and teachers were also experiencing. The quality of relationships in schools might be given more attention if most adults who write about schools, or even make policy for them, were not years away from the kind of daily participation in a school which allows it to affect the quality of their own lives.

Researchers of any kind participate in a private life at the same time that they pursue a research project. Their experiences and reflections in that private life will inevitably affect how they understand the data from their research, whether those data are ethnographic field notes or the neatest of computer-generated tables. In my private life, I participated in the city of Heartland as a citizen and in its elementary schools as a parent. When I started the field work, I had lived on the South Side of Heartland for almost four years, on a block with twenty children. In the years of the study, seventeen of those children, two of them mine, were in elementary school. As I talked with parents on the block and at my own children's soccer games and elementary school picnics, I learned a good deal about how parents, but especially South Side and Anderson Springs parents, viewed the elementary schools of the system. I also, of course, saw the school system from a South Sider's perspective in my private life.

In the summer before the study started, before I heard whether the project would be funded, the magnet school where my older son had just finished the first grade was abruptly closed and the program combined with another in an unfinished new building. The board took this action at the same time that it moved the gifted and talented program from Atlantic to Mann. I had reluctantly agreed the previous spring to chair the struggling parent group at the school. There were not enough other parents to lead a protest to the school board without me, so I joined in the combined steering committee of the two schools' parents. The protest failed, but the experience gave me a three-week-long intensive course in Heartland's school politics from the perspective of a full participant, not an observer. I came away understanding why feelings run so high in school protests, as I never could have by simply listening to others. As I participated in groups which met and talked with several board members on both sides of the issue, I heard their views on the internal politics of the Heartland school board. I also became acquainted with many of the parents who were later activists at Mann.

239

It took some time to separate myself from the intensity of that experience and to look at the pressures which led to moving the magnet programs around the city with reasonable dispassion. The experience also had some slight effect on my relations with persons at Mann. It facilitated conversations with parents as I encountered individuals I knew at parent meetings – even though my acquaintances joined opposed factions supporting and criticizing the school administration. I told all of the principals that I had had this experience, as a part of a full and frank introduction; Mr Mueller, at Mann, was occasionally cautious in talking about issues related to parents, thinking I had more personal ties to these parents than I did.

This political involvement in a district I was studying mixed my personal and professional life more than is desirable; I never would have planned such a double role, but was overtaken by unforeseeable circumstance. After that summer's protest, I withdrew from personal participation in school politics, and even from an active role in parent groups at the elementary schools, in order to separate my roles as much as possible.

None the less, as I reflected on this experience, it seemed that it simply made me consciously aware of a subjectivity in my perspective which is universal to all researchers who study aspects of the society in which they live, not special to ethnographers or to researchers whose children attend school in school districts they study. I have a bias in favor of the viability of urban schools because I lived in Heartland in a house in which my husband and I had invested most of our capital and because we entrusted our children to Heartland's public schools. If we had lived in a suburb, I would not have been a different, more objective person. More important, I would not have stood outside the competitive politics of schooling, for these include the whole of each urban area. I would simply have had a different set of life choices to justify and support, and a different set of neighbors to shape my perspectives on the city schools.

Notes

Chapter 1 Introduction

1 Magnet schools are used in many cities in the United States in quite a variety of patterns (Blank, Dentler, Baltzell, and Chabotar 1983; Royster, Baltzell, and Simmons, 1979). Some cities use only one or only a few magnet schools while others, like the one studied here, have developed large networks of them offering a systematic set of alternatives to the children of the city as a whole. Some magnet schools are frankly elite institutions for children with special talents while others are open to all comers who have an interest in their special approach.

2 Rutter, Maughan, Mortimore, and Ouston (1979) speak of a school 'ethos' which has important consequences for students' behavior and academic progress. It does not consist of specific school practices, but of an indirect message which is expressed in clusters of practices. It appears to affect students' levels of achievement and of cooperation in school. Brookover, Beady, Flood, Schweitzer, and Wisenbaker (1979) summarize aggregated measures of teachers' attitudes toward students as 'school climate.'

3 The practically oriented literature on 'school effectiveness' has used the term 'school climate' to refer to the general ambience of a school, using practitioners' common-sense understandings of that ambience and the influences which shape it. A circular from the Heartland School District sent to parents in the spring of 1983 summarizes the thrust of the effective schools literature as it describes how that literature typifies a 'positive school climate' in this way.

> An effective school has a climate (atmosphere) that is orderly without being rigid, quiet without being oppressive, and is favorable to accomplishing the instructional business at hand. The school's teachers believe that all students can learn. They have high standards and expectations for personal and academic excellence. They also assume responsibility for the learning of their students. Admin-

241

istrators, teachers, and other school staff members have positive working relationships among themselves and with students and parents.

4 The following description, including the table and the map, are true to the essence of Heartland's character but changed in minor details to make the city more difficult to recognize.

5 The state reorganized the Heartland board in a plan phased in during the early 1980s. The numbers have been cut from fifteen to nine and all but one member is elected from a geographic district.

6 The higher percentage of blacks in the schools than in the general population reflects primarily differential birth rates, but also a flourishing system of parochial schools in this heavily Catholic city.

7 Some also travel to the suburbs. A state-funded plan places small numbers of black children in suburban communities and pays the suburban system more than the cost of educating an average child for each one. Some suburban white children come to city magnet schools in exchange.

Chapter 2   The school system's influence on the magnet schools

1 The best evidence available is probably from the voucher experiment in Alum Rock. According to Cohen and Farrar (1977), parents there were hardly quick to embrace diverse education at a distance over known patterns close to home. A true test of the issue would have to create genuinely equal though diverse schools, a nearly impossible task, since there are so many conditions which can make schools unequal. It would also be very difficult to create genuine equality within the practical politics of any diverse large district as the argument below suggests.

2 As Meyer and Rowan point out (1978), parents in traditional settings often judge a school on such visible criteria as a new or elegant building, special programs more advanced than those usually offered to children at a given age, or extra staff.

3 Murray Edelman (1977) has argued that our political life is shot through with such contradictory beliefs, which virtually all of us hold side by side. We pull forth now one, now the other, as it suits our ideological and political purposes. Both as individuals and as a polity, we use both points of view according to convenience without a sense of contradiction.

4 I spent an hour in the outer office of Pupil Personnel at the central office in mid-August of 1978, just before the beginning of the third year of desegregation. Though I had not come to observe the workings of that office, I soon began to notice a pattern in the transactions at the counter beside me. Black parents were coming in to seek fall placements for their children. It was not clear whether they were new to the community, had moved, or had simply failed to receive notification of fall assignments. The clerks behind the counter followed a repetitive routine. They assumed that the child would be

bused to an outlying white school, and then discussed with the parent the best corner for the child to catch the bus. With patience and courtesy, they search computerized lists of bus pickup points near the child's home and studied maps to see whether the child would be required to cross a major street to reach them. If the parent expressed any reservations about their final suggestion, they would look for an alternative. They named the school the child would attend if the parent chose a particular pickup point, and they might give its address or general location. But neither the clerks nor the parents initiated any discussion of the nature of the school.

This process of choice was far removed from the high considerations of matching the educational style of student and school which the superintendent stressed in promoting the plan of voluntary desegregation. In 1981, when I asked a high administration official about the scene I had witnessed, he said that early attempts to have counselors and clerks discuss available schools with parents were met with a single-minded parental interest in how children would get there. So the clerks were instructed to 'go with the flow' and address transportation issues.

5 Another, smaller, city followed what one of its administrators called the Fat Cat–Little Cat theory in setting up a series of magnet schools. This theory held that if magnets could be designed to draw the prosperous and community leaders, then ordinary working people would follow their lead and enroll as well. Experience bore out the theory in that city. (Alex Sergienko, private communication.)

6 This competitiveness among the magnet schools prevented their principals or staffs from coalescing as a group around their very genuine common interests. Though parents from alternative schools formed a group within the city advisory committee, as best I could discover there were no formal or informal coalitions among principals or staffs of magnet schools.

7 There was some difference between persons involved with secondary and elementary education in this matter. Elementary curriculum supervisors had been the inventors, and remained protectors, of some of the elementary school magnet programs.

Chapter 3 Organizational processes and life within the schools

1 Loose coupling in organizations is also common where there is little interdependence in the work of subunits and they must respond to quite disparate localized environments (Metcalfe, 1981). This condition applies to schools within a school system.

2 Several studies describe subcultures within schools, without emphasizing the concept (e.g. Cusick, 1973, 1983; Lightfoot, 1983; McPherson, 1972; Swidler, 1979). Some recent studies are beginning to treat the issue more explicitly (Lesko, 1983; McNeil, forthcoming; Page, 1984). Some studies have looked systematically at the way in which students develop subcultures in response to adults' structuring

of their school experience but with a primary interest in the school as a site for the reproduction of the broader societal culture (Everhart, 1983; Willis, 1977).

3 Anthropologists are not in agreement on the nature of culture (Geertz, 1973; Sanday, 1979; Smircich, 1983). I use a meaning which has wide, though not universal, currency.

Chapter 4 Adams Avenue School for Individually Guided Education

1 The IGE plan was developed at the Center for Cognitive Learning at the University of Wisconsin and had by this time been widely disseminated by an efficient national network. (See Popkewitz, Tabachnick, and Wehlage, 1982.) The plan as it was originally developed for elementary schools is described in several places by Klausmeier and his colleagues (e.g. Klausmeier, Quilling, Sorenson, Way and Glasrud, 1971 and Klausmeier, Rossmiller, and Saily, 1977).

2 Popkewitz, Tabachnick and Wehlage (1982) describe a set of six IGE schools which were nominated for their study as models of the approach. They exhibited three very different educational styles.

3 Relations at Adams seemed to be better than those described by Collins (1978), Hanna (1982), Rosenbaum and Presser (1978), Scherer and Slawski (1979), or Sullivan (1979). Though exact comparisons are difficult to make, they seem to have been nearer the levels described by Schofield and Sagar (1979) and Schofield (1982). Those described by Clement and Harding (1978) and by Clement, Eisenhart, and Harding (1979) appear to have been less intimate than Adams's, though less polarized than those described by the first list of authors. Both the schools described by the latter two sets of authors shared some of Adams's technological arrangements.

4 No one analyzed its logic in abstract terms, noting that it takes learning to be linearly cumulative and to consist in the acquisition of small, specifiable skills, though some teachers suggested this idea in questioning the appropriateness for their subjects of discrete, testable objectives and clearly demarcated levels of skill by which to place students in groups. One teacher, who had come from Jesse Owens, discussed in the next chapter, where assumptions about the nature of knowledge and learning were radically different, did criticize the effects of IGE on students' approach to learning. She argued that the Adams students became more passive than the Owens students, and observed that they lacked initiative and independence of mind. However, she said this in a conversation with me which occurred early in the research and soon afterwards resigned to stay home with a young child. I did not hear the questions she raised discussed again.

5 While the teachers spoke of the fit of their subjects to the IGE approach, the relative fit of different subjects is open to debate. If one believes in the efficacy of its underlying logic of learning, more subjects will fit than if one questions the validity of that logic.

6 Since this study did not gather detailed data on students' achievement,

it is difficult to know whether this was true or whether years of experience with competitive grading systems made teachers expect it to be true. There is an inherent tension between systems which rank everyone on a single standard and those which reward for effort and progress from varied starting points. A single standard of accomplishment gives cumulative advantage to the winners in the competition, which strengthens their confidence and induces them to compete more sharply with each other for relative advantage, but it may drive the least successful to quit the competition in which they no longer have a chance, and therefore a stake. Recognition based on effort and progress gives all players a chance to keep receiving rewards, but makes those given to the winners less a mark of distinction.

7 The proportion of black teachers was high for Heartland schools. It was a legacy of the district's earlier tendency to concentrate its few black teachers in schools with black children. Under the terms of the desegregation order, the proportion of black teachers at Adams was falling from a higher level at Williams Annex. In the year following the study, all schools' faculties were to reflect the district-wide percentage of black teachers, between 11 and 21 percent black. Adams's black teachers knew some of them would have to be exchanged for white teachers from other schools.

8 Several studies have noted that a norm for avoidance of mention of race, a kind of artificial color-blindness, can grow up in desegregated schools as a way of managing discomfort and the possibility of conflict around racial differences (Clement, Eisenhart, and Harding, 1979; Schofield, 1982).

9 This teacher was one of those most likely to treat black children differentially. Clement, Eisenhart and Harding (1979) in a study of a southern desegregated school point out that one of the points of tension between blacks and whites was actions which had a symbolically offensive meaning for blacks which whites did not see, at least not consciously. This led to anger on the part of blacks and puzzlement at the anger on the part of whites, which led to even greater anger by blacks at what seemed to them must be feigned surprise and disingenuous accusations of over-sensitivity.

10 Like other visitors, I initially found the building cramped and thought it looked shabby. But as I passed a semester in the building, I, like the staff with whom I was mingling, grew fond of the building. If it was worn, it was also lived in and comfortable. It was built to human scale; the halls and cafeteria did not make one feel overwhelmed. It was a good setting for friendly face-to-face interaction in groups of manageable size.

11 In a school described by Rosenbaum and Presser (1978), faculty values and assumptions undercut structures which were much like Adams's and so created different outcomes for students – except in one section of the school where a small group of faculty shared values which led them to work hard to make the most of opportunities given by its technological arrangements.

12 The smallest school I had previously studied was the most hostile,

even though it was approximately the same size as Adams (Metz, 1978a, 1978c). Further we know that the intimacy of family life can breed anger to the point of homicide, as well as loving care and support.

13 Howell (1973) makes a distinction between 'hard-living' and 'settled-living' lifestyles among the poor. It is only the former, as they drink too much, are promiscuous, or engage in various dishonest dealings, who are 'disreputable,' but a few students from such families can give all the poor students in a school a negative reputation and cause the teachers to withdraw from the social infection of association with them.

14 The part-time assistant principal, who in his interview consistently compared Adams to the racially isolated black middle school where he spent the other part of his time and to a middle school in a poor white neighborhood where he had previously been assistant principal, spoke of Adams's allowing students to put aside their early sophistication and to act like children. He noted that they played games during recreation while students at the other schools would lounge about trying to impress one another. In a similar vein, the National Institute of Education's Safe School Study (1978) found that when schools in poor neighborhoods with high crime rates *are* safe, they are often perceived by the students as islands of refuge in a dangerous world.

15 In matters of faculty relationships, at least, some teachers were more self-conscious. One of the informal faculty leaders was articulately aware that interaction in the faculty lounge over lunch and card games had a healing effect on rifts of race and of attitudes toward the union among the faculty. He not only talked about this in his research interview but, apparently, advised a new teacher to participate in conversation and card games because it would help her to become integrated in the faculty and would help the group as a whole. She mentioned this advice in her research interview and, not yet socialized, she exclaimed upon its oddity; she dismissed it saying she had no time for such social niceties.

16 Mrs Michaels told me that, in the first year at Williams Annex, she told the faculty they were either not to say anything negative about the students, or to couple their remark with a suggested plan for improvement. She said that she had taken such an extreme stance because she had found the faculty at Williams constantly encouraging one another in a critical attitude toward the students. She was supported in her efforts by some of the teachers who had volunteered to move from Williams because they did not like the negative atmosphere there. Also helpful in the process was the fact that most of the faculty were very young and so did not have well-established individual beliefs and attitudes about teaching and students.

17 Other authors have commented upon the deep wounds to their professional pride which teachers experience when parents are allowed to give them unsolicited advice on how to do their jobs better,

a situation which is not limited to magnet schools, but to which they are particularly vulnerable (Biklen, 1982; Lightfoot, 1978; Rist, 1978).

18 All of the principals made light of the role parental pressures played in shaping their decisions or behavior even in their research interviews, though they might talk about parental pressures as a time-consuming problem to be managed. They also said little publicly to the teachers about pleasing parents. For a principal to acknowledge that parental desires had shaped decisions or policy would be to acknowledge his or her loss of organizational control and claim to professional expertise. Hence this area was as sensitive for principals as for teachers. Cohen and Farrar found a similar reaction to parental power among principals involved in the voucher plan at Alum Rock (1977).

19 Mrs Michaels's race and her gender doubtless had an impact on her relations of authority with all the teachers and certainly with these dissidents who were all white, and the two leaders of whom were male. Although it is clear in this statement that Mr Haupt's resentment was bolstered by his subjection as a white man to a black woman, in most cases, it was hard to get any clear evidence of the effects of these factors. The processes I discuss in the text which led to resentment of her authority by all the faculty were probably intensified by her race or her gender at least for those who did not share both. I wondered whether the faculty would have given her more credit for initiating their own 'caring about the kids' if she had been a white man. But then, in working to develop or change attitudes she often used a stereotypically feminine indirection.

20 They were not the teachers discussed earlier who had hostile interactions with the students. These three had specially defined positions so that they worked only with small groups; I did not see them interact with students, except fleetingly.

21 Mr Haupt seemed to be engaged with the principal in a struggle for power. He was ambitious. He was active in the union and had already gained some visibility in the system as a whole for his activities on its behalf concerning systemwide issues. There was some evidence he hoped to be instrumental in having the principal removed from her position; successful opposition to a principal would have made him a figure to be reckoned with by both union members and administrators.

He used his testimony at the hearing on the union grievance of the transferred teacher, from his own account, to question the principal's competence and good faith in a public forum. However, the ruling issued the next fall supported the principal. Mr Haupt resigned soon after it was announced and moved to another city. Mr Haupt's activities illustrate the way in which the ambitions and desires of individuals and groups intertwine with the more task-oriented aspects of organizational life, creating a dimension of internal politics in that life.

Chapter 5   Jesse Owens Open Education School

1 Junior high schools in Heartland are generally named for inventors and elementary schools for the street on which they are located. The

real name chosen by the school's students and staff was that of a well-known black person who was not an inventor.

2 The Jesse Owens staff felt they never received recognition for pioneering many patterns which later became widely used innovations that were a source of pride to the district. They were annoyed that though they started changes which were later hailed as improvements at other schools, Owens continued to be perceived as an oddball or fringe effort.

3 The workshops which the teachers and administrators had first attended had presented an approach developed by Virgil Howes, who had also written several books on open methods (Howes, 1970, 1974). The Owens staff used his ideas most, but also drew from other national figures in open education. Professor Howes's visits to the school and approval of it gave a significant boost to the staff's morale, and were especially important for the principal in validating the program's design.

4 In order to check my own perceptions of the students' interviews which were conducted at the close of the fieldwork at each school, after I had formed impressions of the school as a whole, I gave transcripts of the student interviews at all the schools to an independent rater who knew nothing about the schools except their announced special approaches. I asked him to describe the schools based on the students' interviews. He remarked upon the great variability of Owens students' comments and styles in comparison to those of the students at the other two schools where more of a common style emerged. I am grateful to Gregory Gossetti for performing this work.

5 Some children came to Owens from the two elementary schools which offered open education, but their numbers were small because many families from these schools chose more traditional approaches for middle school.

6 The school did have something of a working-class ambience. Students dressed casually, not with the casual elegance of expensive leisure clothes, but in plain, well-worn shirts and jeans. One of the staff at Mann had his son transferred from Jesse Owens to Mann during the year of the study. He spoke of his relief and pleasure when after a few weeks at Mann he began to dress up more for school and to talk about different subjects on the telephone with friends. He was being trained in middle-class behavior as well as being drilled in traditional subjects and skills.

7 It was not incidental to this difference between Mr Osten's approach and that of the other principals that he had no desire or expectation of advancing in the system hierarchy – though he did sometimes toy with the idea of taking early retirement and starting a second career in education. The other principals, including the administrator in charge at Mann, were all young enough to consider advancing in the system hierarchy; three years after the field work all in some sense had done so. Such an explicit identification with the school as Mr Osten's and such willingness to argue with the rulings of superiors are

not usually the stuff of which mobile careers in administration are made.

8 This was more practicable at Owens than at a school using whole class instruction where a conference with a teacher during class time meant interruption of the students' learning.

Chapter 6   Horace Mann School for the Gifted and Talented

1 After the controversy over Atlantic Avenue and an elementary school which was transferred in a parallel way the board developed a regular process and schedule for considering school closings. Decisions had to be made by early January before parents chose schools for the following year.

2 Biklen (1982), Lightfoot (1978), and Rist (1978) have all observed upper-middle-class parents' readiness to question teachers' methods and judge them according to their own criteria; however, all of them were writing about elementary schools. The introduction of subject specializations at the middle school level did not reduce parental claims of this sort at Mann.

3 Interviews with parents at all the schools suggested important differences in parents' attitudes toward the magnet program. Parents with less education, with jobs lower in hierarchies, and with less experience in community leadership responded with deep gratitude to the school system. They found the magnet schools a great improvement over their children's previous schools, and they were pleased and appreciative as a result. Parents with more education and experience of exerting control tended to judge their children's experience not against their previous schools but against an ideal. They often eventually found the magnet schools wanting.

4 There was some evidence that some people at the central office had fostered the suggestion to move the program from Atlantic to Mann, in the belief that if the school were closed the Atlantic staff would lose their claim to staff it and new teachers could be hired. But because the board's language closed the Atlantic school building, but 'transferred' the program, the Atlantic teachers had the right, under the union contract, to transfer with the program.

5 When my project assistant, Greg Gossetti, read all the student interviews from the three schools without knowing anything else about the schools, he described the Mann students as competitive and highstrung. He found these qualities the most strikingly evident pattern in any of the three sets of student interviews.

6 Attendance rates are probably more affected by parents than other measures of school behavior. Poorer families are more likely to keep students out of school for family needs, while more affluent families are more likely to have parental supervision to ensure that the child at least leaves for school on time.

7 I interviewed a middle-class black mother with daughters at both Adams and Mann. The daughter at Adams had joined a group of

friends mixed in race and sex. The daughter at Mann was friends only with black girls who called others 'Oreo' if they made friends with whites. (An Oreo is a chocolate cookie with a vanilla center, 'black on the outside, white on the inside.')

8 Other studies have also found that girls are less likely than boys to form inter-racial friendships (Schofield, 1982). This pattern did not hold at Owens, however.

9 The teachers in Rosenbaum and Presser's (1978) magnet school for the gifted and talented also forgot that desegregation was the school's reason for existence.

10 This teacher was one of only two or three in the school who pushed the chairs together in groups of four or six so their arms formed tables.

11 Black students at Mann judged one another more harshly than did black students at the other schools. Several black students when asked why they would prefer a mixed race high school said that black students alone in a school are too rowdy or are given to fighting and not working. More complained about black students at the present school who like 'to act tough.' These statements could have reflected the larger number of middle-class blacks at Mann who may have been taught by their families to beware the rough ways of peers of a lower social class. But there were fewer rowdy or 'tough' kids at the school than at the other two; the 'respectable' black children at Mann may have taken more negative notice of the few that there were as they had to work harder to differentiate themselves from them in the eyes of white students and teachers in the school.

12 It is possible to see a racial meaning in the white teachers' complaints about the lack of giftedness in the student body. In making these complaints white teachers never spoke of race, while the black teachers often mentioned the presence of a few black students who were totally unqualified for the school and a dearth of really strong black students. If black teachers found the association of race and academic skill obvious, presumably white teachers noticed it too, but did not mention it for fear of seeming prejudiced. Their complaints about a lack of giftedness in the student body may in fact have been a coded way of saying that desegregation kept the school from being genuinely one for the gifted and talented.

Chapter 7 Lessons from the Heartland schools

1 Some parents with large families had placed children in several different schools to meet varied styles and needs. These were usually middle-class families, however, and they often chose among the schools with middle-class reputations. In several cases, middle-class families consulted with others and together moved a group of friends to a school they had mutually agreed upon.

2 These figures appeared in Heartland's leading paper on Sunday, February 3 1985 as parents were about to make choices for the

following fall. The judgment about patterns in the numbers turned away by race are my own, based upon popular images of the schools I had heard voiced in discussions in the community and on annual reports of test scores for each school. The article giving the figures was headlined 'Do alternative programs drain other schools of leaders?' It spoke mostly of principals' complaints over what I have called 'creaming' and of the difficulty of entering the alternative programs if a child is turned away in the entry grade. The debate over elitism in the magnet schools was thus still lively in the ninth year of desegregation as I was making the final revisions in this manuscript.

3 In exploring the schools' lives, I have said very little about the schools' effects on academic achievement. Observation did not give me good data on which to judge how much students were learning, and the teachers had cultural beliefs likely to inflate or deflate their estimates. Standardized test scores provide only a rough estimate, since they cover only a narrow part of what is learned, but they do tell something. The school system gave standardized tests to the students at the end of the seventh grade, that is, after two years in middle school, for those students who started a citywide middle school in the sixth grade. I compared the scores of the cohort of students who were seventh graders during the study at each school to those of the same cohort as fifth graders. The absence of almost one in ten students at each wave of testing requires one to treat this data with caution, however, since the presence or absence of a few high or low achievers would significantly change the pattern of the data. The school system would not give me data which allowed comparison of individuals' scores at the two times; it is only possible to say what proportion of the cohort scored above or below given points.

At Mann the test scores for the high end of the cohort were higher in the seventh than in the fifth grade, while the scores at the low end held steady between fifth and seventh grade. At Adams, the pattern was more mixed for both reading and math, as one looks at the proportion of students scoring at or below the 90th, 75th, 50th, 25th, and 10th percentiles. The strongest students improved slightly and so did the very weakest, while those in the middle held steady or lost slightly.

There was some corroborating evidence from Adams's internal evaluation processes that the students were at least holding their own and perhaps improving relative to their age cohort. At Mann, there was some evidence of improvement in the strongest students and deterioration among the weakest. In math, where the strongest students were put in separate classes at the seventh grade, and the very strongest received special coaching as members of the 'math track team,' the improvement of the stronger students on seventh grade standardized test scores was dramatic. At the other end, ten of Mann's eighth graders failed two or more academic courses and were required to take them and pass in summer school in order to go on to high school.

At Owens, standardized test scores yielded less encouraging results, especially in math, but this finding does not tell us a great deal about the academic effects of the school because of the absence of testing in the regular life of the school, the low emphasis on standardized tests up to the time of the study, and the tendency of low achievers, who were predominant among the students entering Owens, on a national basis to fall further behind on standardized tests with each passing year.

The importance of the practices relative to testing at Owens was underscored by contrasting practices at Mann. I was in a seventh grade math class two weeks before the tests were given. The teacher explained to the class that they would have the test a week later than announced by the central office so that they could finish the unit they were currently working on. He then explained that they would have the tests in their own classroom, not the big room where they had formerly been held, starting Tuesday not Monday, and on three days not two, because each of these changes could be expected to improve their performance. He demonstrated how carefully the staff thought about ways to improve students' scores. In giving the students this information, most of which they did not need, he gave them the indirect message that the staff were working hard to improve their scores and they should therefore put forth their very best effort. If such arrangements and messages to students make any difference in students' scores, the difference in improvement between Mann and Owens tells us as much about the emphasis the school staffs put upon tests as it does about the overall academic learning of the students.

4 This finding is consistent with research on teachers as individuals which suggests that, because teaching is an occupation with few extrinsic rewards, a sense of competence, most easily measured by the response of clients, becomes especially important to a teacher's sense of worth and self-respect (Jackson, 1968, Lortie, 1975).

5 I am drawing here on my earlier research in other schools with low achievers where conflict was more common than in Heartland's schools (Metz, 1978a, 1978b, 1978c). In the most conflictual of these schools (Metz, 1978a, 1978c), the teachers who stood out as really capable were those who simply treated students with ordinary civility and elicited courtesy in return. As an observer, one does not experience the full impact of these exchanges, but the tone still has an effect upon one's feelings.

6 I am grateful to Diana Slaughter for this provocative phrase.

Bibliography

Apple, M. (1983), 'Curricular form and the logic of technical control,' in M. W. Apple and L. Weis, (eds.), *Ideology and Practice in Schooling*, Philadelphia, Temple University Press, pp. 143–65.

Ball, S. J. (1981), *Beachside Comprehensive: A Case-Study of Secondary Schooling*, Cambridge, England, Cambridge University Press.

Barnard, C. I. (1939), *The Functions of the Executive*, Cambridge, Massachusetts, Harvard University Press. (First published 1938.)

Barry, B. (1974), 'Review Article: Exit, voice and loyalty,' *British Journal of Political Science*, vol. 4, no. 1, January, pp. 79–107.

Bell, D. (1980), *Shades of Brown: New Perspectives on School Desegregation*, New York, Teachers College Press.

Bellaby, P. (1974), 'The distribution of deviance among 13–14 year old students,' in J. Eggleston (ed.), *The Scales of Justice*, London, Methuen, pp. 167–84.

Berman, P. and McLaughlin, M. (1976), 'Implementation of educational innovation,' *Educational Forum*, vol. 40, no. 3, March, pp. 347–70.

Bidwell, C. (1965), 'The school as a formal organization,' in J. G. March (ed.), *Handbook of Organizations*, Chicago, Rand McNally, pp. 972–1022.

Biklen, S. K. (1982), 'Autonomy in the Lives of Women Elementary Schoolteachers,' Paper presented to the annual meeting of the American Educational Research Association.

Blank, R. K., Dentler, R. A., Baltzell, D. C., and Chabotar, K. (1983), *Survey of Magnet Schools: Analyzing a Model for Quality Integrated Education*, Final Report of a National Study of the U.S. Department of Education, Office of Planning, Budget, and Evaluation, Contract No. 300-81-0420. Washington, D.C., James H. Lowry and Associates.

Blauner, R. (1964), *Alienation and Freedom*, Chicago, University of Chicago Press.

Bossert, S. T. (1979), *Tasks and Social Relationships in Classrooms: A Study of Instructional Organization and its Consequences*, New York, Cambridge University Press.

253

Bibliography

Braverman, H. (1974), *Labor and Monopoly Capital: The Degradation of Work in the Twentieth Century*, New York, Monthly Review Press.

Bronfenbrenner, A. (1970), *Two Worlds of Childhood*, New York, Russell Sage Foundation.

Brookover, W., Beady, C., Flood, P., Schweitzer, J., and Wisenbaker, J. (1979), *School Social Systems and Student Achievement: Schools Can Make a Difference*, New York, Praeger.

Burlingame, M. (1981), 'Superintendent power retention,' in S. B. Bacharach (ed.), *Organizational Behavior in Schools and School Districts*, New York, Praeger, pp. 429–64.

Clark, B. R. (1970), *The Distinctive College*, Chicago, Aldine.

Clark, B. R. (1972), 'The organizational saga in higher education,' *Administrative Science Quarterly*, vol. 17, no. 2, June, pp. 178–84.

Clement, D. C. and Harding, J. R. (1978), 'Social distinctions and emergent student groups in a desegregated school,' *Anthropology and Education Quarterly*, vol. 9, no. 4, December, pp. 272–82.

Clement, D. C., Eisenhart, M., and Harding, J. R. (1979), 'The veneer of harmony: social-race relations in a southern desegregated school,' in R. Rist (ed.), *Desegregated Schools: Appraisals of an American Experiment*, New York, Academic Press, pp. 15–64.

Cohen, D. K. and Farrar, E. (1977), 'Power to the parents? – the story of education vouchers,' *The Public Interest*, vol. 48, Summer, pp. 72–97.

Cohen, E. (1980), 'Design and redesign of the desegregated school: problems of status, power and conflict,' in W. Stephan and J. R. Feagin (eds.), *School Desegregation: Past, Present, and Future*, New York, Plenum Press.

Collins, T. W. (1978), 'Reconstructing a high school society after court-ordered desegregation,' *Anthropology and Education Quarterly*, vol. 9, no. 4, Winter, pp. 248–57.

Connell, R. W., Ashenden, D. J., Kessler, S. and Dowsett, G. W. (1982), *Making the Difference: Schools, Families, and Social Division*, Sydney, George Allen and Unwin.

Corwin, R. G. (1974), 'Models of educational organizations,' in F. N. Kerlinger and J. B. Carroll (eds.), *Review of Research in Education*, vol. 2, 1974. Itasca, Illinois, F. E. Peacock Publishers.

Corwin, R. G. (1981), 'Patterns of organizational control and teacher militancy: theoretical continuities in the idea of "loose coupling",' in R. Corwin (ed.), *Research in Sociology of Education and Socialization*, vol. 2 of A. Kerckhoff, (ed.) *Research on Educational Organizations*, Greenwich, CT, JAI Press, pp. 261–91.

Cusick, P. (1973), *Inside High School: The Student's World*, New York, Holt, Rinehart and Winston.

Cusick, P. (1983), *The Equalitarian Ideal and the American High School*, New York, Longman.

Deal, T. E. (1975), 'Alternative schools: an alternative postmortem,' in J. V. Baldridge and T. E. Deal (eds.), *Managing Change in Educational Organizations: Sociological Perspectives, Strategies, and Case Studies*, Berkeley, CA, McCutchan.

Deal, T. and Kennedy, A. A. (1982), *Corporate Culture*, Reading, Massachusetts, Addison-Wesley.

Deal, T. and Nutt, S. (1983), 'Planned change in rural school districts,' in J. V. Baldridge and T. Deal (eds.), *The Dynamics of Organizational Control*, Berkeley, McCutchan, pp. 137–66.

Dreeben, R. (1973), 'The school as a workplace,' in R. M. W. Travers (ed.), *Second Handbook of Research of Teaching*, Chicago, Rand McNally, pp. 450–73.

Edelman, M. (1977), *Political Language: Words That Succeed and Policies That Fail*, New York, Academic Press.

Everhart, R. B. (1983), *Reading, Writing, and Resistance: Adolescence and Labor in a Junior High School*, Boston, Routledge and Kegan Paul.

Farrar, E., DeSanctis, J., and Cohen, D. K. (1980), 'Views from below: implementation research in education', vol. 82, no. 1, Fall, *Teachers College Record*, pp. 77–116.

Felix, J. L. and Jacobs, J. N. (1977), 'Issues in implementing and evaluating alternative programs in Cincinnati,' in D. U. Levine and R. J. Havighurst (eds.), *The Future of Big City Schools: Desegregation Policies and Magnet Alternatives*, Berkeley, CA, McCutchan, pp. 105–15.

Finley, M. (1984), 'Teachers and tracking in a comprehensive high school,' *Sociology of Education*, vol. 57, no. 4, October, pp. 233–43.

Firestone, W. (1980a), *Great Expectations for Small Schools: The Limitations of Federal Projects*, New York, Praeger.

Firestone, W. (1980b), 'Images of schools and patterns of change,' *American Journal of Education*, vol. 88, August, pp. 459–87.

Furlong, V. (1977), 'Anancy goes to school: a case study of pupils' knowledge of their teachers,' in P. Woods and M. Hammersley (eds.), *School Experience: Explorations in the Sociology of Education*, London, Croom Helm, pp. 162–85.

Geertz, C. (1973), *The Interpretation of Cultures*, New York, Basic Books.

Gregory, K. L. (1983), 'Native-view paradigms: multiple cultures and culture conflicts in organizations,' *Administrative Science Quarterly*, vol. 28, no. 3, September, pp. 359–76.

Gross, N., Giacquinta, J., and Bernstein, M. (1971), *Implementing Organizational Innovations*, New York, Basic Books.

Hanna, J. L. (1982), 'Public social policy and the children's world: implications of ethnographic research for desegregated schooling,' in G. W. Spindler (ed.), *Doing the Ethnography of Schooling: Educational Ethnography in Action*, New York, Holt, pp. 317–55.

Hanson, E. M. (1981), 'Organizational control in educational systems: a case study of governance in schools,' in S. B. Bacharach (ed.), *Organizational Behavior in Schools and School Districts*, New York, Praeger, pp. 245–76.

Hargreaves, D. H. (1967), *Social Relations in a Secondary School*, London, Routledge and Kegan Paul.

Hargreaves, D. H., Hester, S. K., and Mellor, F. J. (1975), *Deviance in Classrooms*, London, Routledge and Kegan Paul.

255

Herndon, J. (1969), *The Way it Spozed to Be*, New York, Bantam Books.
Herriott, R. and Gross, N. (1979), *The Dynamics of Planned Educational Change*, Berkeley, CA, McCutchan.
Hirschman, A. O. (1972), *Exit, Voice, and Loyalty*, Cambridge, MA, Harvard University Press.
Howell, J. T. (1973), *Hard Living on Clay Street*, Garden City, N.Y., Anchor Books.
Howes, V. M. (1970), *Individualization of Instruction: A Teaching Strategy*, New York, Macmillan.
Howes, V. M. (1974), *Informal Teaching in the Urban Classroom*, New York, Macmillan.
Jackson, P. (1968), *Life in Classrooms*, New York, Holt.
Kanter, R. M. (1983), *The Change Masters: Innovation and Entrepreneurship in the American Corporation*, New York, Simon and Schuster.
Keddie, N. (1971), 'Classroom knowledge,' in M. Young (ed.), *Knowledge and Control*, London, Collier Macmillan, pp. 133–59.
Kemnitzer, L. S. (1977), 'Another view of time and the railroader,' *Administrative Science Quarterly*, vol. 50, no. 1, March, pp. 25–9.
Klausmeier, H. J., Quilling, M. R., Sorenson, J. S., Way R. S., and Glasrud, G. R. (1971), *Individually Guided Education and the Multiunit School*, Madison, WI, Wisconsin Research and Development Center for Cognitive Learning, The University of Wisconsin-Madison.
Klausmeier, H. J., Rossmiller, R. A., and Saily, M. (1977), (eds.), *Individually Guided Elementary Education: Concepts and Practices*, New York, Academic Press.
Kozol, J. (1972), *Free Schools*, Boston, Houghton Mifflin.
Lacey, C. (1970), *Hightown Grammar: The School as a Social System*, Manchester, England, The University Press.
Leacock, E. B. (1969), *Teaching and Learning in City Schools*, New York, Basic Books.
Lesko, N. (1983), *The Moral Order of a Parochial High School and the Nature of Student Peer Groups*. Unpublished dissertation, University of Wisconsin-Madison.
Levine, D. U. and Havighurst, R. (eds.) (1977), *The Future of Big City Schools: Desegregation Policies and Magnet Alternatives*, Berkeley, McCutchan.
Lightfoot, S. L. (1978), *Worlds Apart: Relationships Between Families and Schools*, New York, Basic Books.
Lightfoot, S. L. (1983), *The Good High School: Portraits of Character and Culture*, New York, Basic Books.
Lipsitz, J. (1984), *Successful Schools for Young Adolescents*, New Brunswick, New Jersey, Transaction Books.
Lodahl, T. M. and Mitchell, S. M. (1980), 'Drift in the development of innovative organizations,' in J. R. Kimberly and R. H. Miles (eds.), *The Organizational Life Cycle: Issues in the Creation, Transformation and Decline of Organizations*, San Francisco, Jossey-Bass, pp. 184–207.
Lortie, D. C. (1975), *Schoolteacher: A Sociological Study*, Chicago, University of Chicago Press.

Marshall, H. M. and Weinstein, R. S. (1984), 'Classroom factors affecting students' self-evaluations: an interactional model,' *Review of Educational Research*, vol. 54, no. 3, Fall, pp. 301–25.

McDermott, R. R. (1974), 'Achieving school failure: an anthropological approach to illiteracy and social stratification,' in G. Spindler (ed.), *Education and Cultural Process: Toward an Anthropology of Education*, New York, Holt, pp. 82–118.

McNeil, L. (forthcoming), *Contradictions of Control*, Boston, Routledge and Kegan Paul.

McPherson, G. (1972), *Small Town Teacher*, Cambridge, MA, Harvard University Press.

Metcalfe, L. (1981), 'Designing precarious partnerships,' in P. C. Nystrom and W. H. Starbuck (eds.), *Handbook of Organizational Design*, vol. 1, New York, Oxford University Press, pp. 503–30.

Metz, D. L. (1981), *Running Hot: Structure and Stress in Ambulance Work*, Cambridge, MA, Abt Books.

Metz, M. H. (1978a), 'Clashes in the classroom: the importance of norms for authority', *Education and Urban Society*, vol. 11, no. 1, November, pp. 13–47.

Metz, M. H. (1978b), *Classrooms and Corridors: The Crisis of Authority in Desegregated Secondary Schools*, Berkeley, CA, University of California Press.

Metz, M. H. (1978c), 'Order in the secondary school: some strategies for control and their consequences,' *Sociological Inquiry*, vol. 48, no. 1, pp. 56–69.

Metz, M. H. (1982a), *Magnet Schools in Their Organizational Environment*, Final Report to the National Institute of Education, Project no. 8-0640, Washington, D.C., Department of Education.

Metz, M. H. (1982b), 'The principal's role in the establishment of a magnet school,' in G. W. Noblit and B. Johnston (eds.), *The School Principal and School Desegregation: An Anthology of Interpretive Studies*, Springfield, IL, pp. 61–95.

Meyer, J. W. and Rowan, B. (1978), 'The structure of educational organizations,' in M. W. Meyer and Associates, *Environments and Organizations*, San Francisco, Jossey-Bass, pp. 78–109.

National Institute of Education (1978), *Violent Schools–Safe Schools: The Safe School Study Report to the Congress*, vol. 1, Washington, D.C., Department of Health, Education and Welfare.

Ogbu, J. (1974), *The Next Generation: An Ethnography of Education in an Urban Neighborhood*, New York, Academic Press.

Page, R. (1984), *Perspectives and Processes: The Negotiation of Educational Meanings in High School Classes for Academically Unsuccessful Students*. Unpublished doctoral dissertation, University of Wisconsin, Madison.

Pascale, R. T. and Athos, A. G. (1981), *The Art of Japanese Management: Applications for American Executives*, New York, Simon and Schuster.

Perrow, C. (1967), 'A Framework for the comparative analysis of organizations,' *American Sociological Review*, vol. 32, April, pp. 194–208.

Perrow, C. (1979), *Complex Organizations: A Critical Essay*, 2d edn, Glenview, Illinois, Scott, Foresman and Company.

Peters, T. J. and Waterman, R. H. (1982), *In Search of Excellence: Lessons from America's Best Run Companies*, New York, Harper and Row.

Peterson, K. D. (1984), 'Mechanisms of administrative control over managers in educational organizations,' *Administrative Science Quarterly*, vol. 29, no. 4, pp. 573–97.

Pettigrew, A. M. (1973), *The Politics of Organizational Decisionmaking*, London, Tavistock.

Pettigrew, A. M. (1979), 'On studying organizational cultures,' *Administrative Science Quarterly*, vol. 23, no. 4, December, pp. 570–81.

Pfeffer, J. (1981), 'Management as symbolic action: the creation and maintenance of symbolic paradigms,' in L. Cummings and B. Staw (eds.), *Research in Organizational Behavior*, vol. 3, Greenwich, Connecticut, JAI Press.

Popkewitz, T., Tabachnik, B. R., and Wehlage, G. (1982), *The Myth of Educational Reform: A Study of School Responses to a Program of Change*, Madison, WI, University of Wisconsin Press.

Rist, R. C. (1973), *The Urban School: A Factory for Failure*, Cambridge, MA, The MIT Press.

Rist, R. C. (1978), *The Invisible Children: School Integration in American Society*, Cambridge, MA, Harvard University Press.

Roethlisberger, F. J. and Dickson, William J. (1947), *Management and the Worker*, Cambridge, MA, Harvard University Press.

Rosenbaum, J. and Presser, S. (1978), 'Voluntary racial integration in a magnet school,' *School Review*, vol. 86, no. 2, February, pp. 156–86.

Royster, E. C., Baltzell, D. C., and Simmons, F. C. (1979), *Study of the Emergency School Aid Act Magnet School Program* (Contract No. OE-300-77-0393), Washington, D.C., Office of Education.

Rutter, M., Maughan, B., Mortimore, P., and Ouston, J. (1979), *Fifteen Thousand Hours: Secondary Schools and Their Effects on Children*, Cambridge, MA, Harvard University Press.

Sanday, P. (1979), 'The ethnographic paradigm,' *Administrative Science Quarterly*, vol. 24, no. 4, pp. 527–38.

Sarason, S. B. (1971), *The Culture of the School and the Problem of Change*, Boston, Allyn and Bacon.

Scherer, J. and Slawski, E. (1979), 'Color, class, and social control in an urban desegregated school,' in R. Rist (ed.), *Desegregated Schools: Appraisals of an American Experiment*, New York, Academic Press.

Schofield, J. W. (1982), *Black and White in School: Trust, Tension, or Tolerance?*, New York, Praeger.

Schofield, J. and Sagar, H. A. (1979), 'The social context of learning in an interracial school,' in R. C. Rist (ed.), *Desegregated Schools: Appraisals of an American Experiment*, New York, Academic Press, pp. 155–99.

Schwartz, F. (1981), 'Supporting or subverting learning: peer group patterns in four tracked schools,' *Education and Anthropology Quarterly*, vol. 12, no. 2, Summer, pp. 99–121.

Selznick, P. (1957), *Leadership in Administration*, New York, Harper and Row.

Sharp, R. and Green, A. (1975), *Education and Social Control: A Study in Progressive Primary Education*, London, Routledge and Kegan Paul.

Slavin, R. E. (1980), 'Cooperative learning,' *Review of Educational Research*, vol. 50, no. 2, Summer, pp. 315–42.

Smircich, L. (1983), 'Concepts of culture and organizational analysis,' *Administrative Science Quarterly*, vol. 28, no. 3, September, pp. 339–58.

Spindler, G. and Spindler, L. (1983), 'Anthropologists view American culture,' *Annual Review of Anthropology*, vol. 12, pp. 49–78.

Spradley, J. P. and Mann, B. (1975), *The Cocktail Waitress: Woman's Work in a Man's World*, New York, Wiley.

Sproull, L. S. (1981), 'Beliefs in organizations,' in P. C. Nystrom and W. H. Starbuck (eds.), *Handbook of Organizational Design*, vol. 2, *Remodeling Organizations and Their Environments*, New York, Oxford University Press, pp. 203–24.

Stinchcombe, A. (1964), *Rebellion in a High School*, Chicago, Quadrangle Books.

Sullivan, M. L. (1979), 'Contacts among cultures: School desegregation in a polyethnic New York City high school' in R. C. Rist (ed.), *Desegregated Schools: Appraisals of an American Experiment*, New York, Academic Press, pp. 201–40.

Sussmann, L. (1977), *Tales Out of School: Implementing Organizational Change in the Elementary Grades*, Philadelphia, Temple University Press.

Swidler, A. (1979), *Organization Without Authority*, Cambridge, MA, Harvard University Press.

Waller, W. (1965), *The Sociology of Teaching*, New York, John Wiley. (First published 1932.)

Wax, M., Wax, R., and Dumont, R. V., Jr. (1964), 'Formal education in an American Indian community,' an SSSP Monograph, supplement to *Social Problems*, vol. 11, no. 4, Spring.

Werthman, C. (1963), 'Delinquents in schools: a test for the legitimacy of authority,' *Berkeley Journal of Sociology*, vol. 8, pp. 39–60.

Wilcox, K. (1982), 'Differential socialization in the classroom: implications for equal opportunity,' in G. Spindler (ed.), *Doing the Ethnography of Schooling: Educational Anthropology in Action*, New York, Holt, pp. 269–309.

Willis, P. (1977), *Learning to Labour: How Working Class Kids Get Working Class Jobs*, Westmead, England, Gower.

Wolcott, H. F. (1974), 'The teacher as enemy,' in G. W. Spindler (ed.), *Education and Cultural Process: Toward an Anthropology of Education*, New York, Holt, Rinehart and Winston, pp. 411–25.

Wolcott, H. F. (1977), *Teachers Versus Technocrats: An Educational Innovation in Anthropological Perspective*, Eugene, Oregon, Center for Educational Policy and Management, University of Oregon.

Index

Index

Brookover, Wilbur, 42, 241
buildings, *see* logistical influences, moves of programs
bureaucratic organization, 45–50; and principal-teacher relations, 96–100, 145–8, 198–202, 204; *see also* hierarchy
Burlingame, Martin, 47
busing, 11, 21, 110, 158, 184, 207–8; *see also* desegregation plan

central office: decisions of, 58, 105–7, 151, 158, 174–5, 184, 212–14, 249; expectations of schools, 33–4, 46–8, 108–9, 162–3, 193, 212–14, 243; interaction with principals, 97, 102, 143–51; racial composition of, 8
Chabotar, K., 241
character, *see* school character
Clark, Burton R., 54, 118
class, *see* social class
classroom activity structure, 74–6, 126–8, 150–1, 173–4, 175–7, 179, 204, 215–17
Clement, Dorothy, 182, 244, 245
Cohen, David, 2, 35, 242, 247
Cohen, Elizabeth, 44, 77, 217
Collins, Thomas W., 244
cooperation, 44, 77–8, 100, 130, 179, 203, 216, 217
competition, 44, 74, 174, 177, 224–5, 244–5
conflict in the classroom, *see* discipline, student-teacher relations, students' peer relations
Connell, R. W., 41
Corwin, Ronald G., 46
court decisions, 9, 10
creaming and dumping, 36–7, 113–14, 152, 159–62, 251; *see also* recruitment of students
culture, 217–19, 221–2, 225; at Adams, 63–4, 82–9, 100–2, 198, 246; defined, 54–5; dissidents from, 86, 88–9, 137;

maintenance of 87–8; managing, 53–4, 90–2, 98–9, 101, 246; at Mann, 184–96; in organisations, 53–4, 243; at Owens, 135–43, 151
curriculum, 62–3, 72–3, 115–17, 121–5, 134, 148–50, 173–5, 204, 215–17
Cusick, Philip, 243

Deal, Terrence E., 2, 54, 118, 189
Dentler, R. A., 241
DeSanctis, John, 2
desegregation, *see* desegregation plan, integration, inter-racial relations, race
desegregation plan: black community and, 16, 21–2; development of, 9–11, 15–18, 20–1, 242–3; magnet schools' role in, 9, 11, 16–18, 27–8, 207–8; parental involvement in, 16–17; politics of, 15–24, 207–10; *see also* moves of school programs
Dickson, William J., 34
discipline, 64, 118–19, 166–70, 176–8; in classroom, 50–1, 65–7, 75–7, 167–70; and graffiti, 119, 170, 177; and logistics, 80, 183–4; and technology, 50–1, 75–6, 126–8, 215–17; yellow cards, 67, 167–8, 217; *see also* student-teacher relations
distinctiveness of schools, 12, 17–18, 28–9, 108–9, 165, 209–11
diversity of student bodies, 29–30, 211; *see also* standardization; student recruitment
documents, 14
Dowsett, G. W., 41
Dreeben, Robert, 46, 48
Dumont, Robert, 41

Edelman, Murray, 242
educational innovation, *see* innovation
Eisenhart, Margaret, 182, 244, 245
equality of status, *see* status

265